Poor
Man's
University

75 years of Technical Education in Footscray

Carolyn
Rasmussen

FOOTPRINT
The Press of the
Footscray Institute of Technology
1989

First published 1989

Footprint
The Press of the Footscray Institute of Technology
Footscray, Melbourne, Victoria 3011

© Footscray Institute of Technology, 1989

Photographs published with acknowledgement to:
the late Miss Doreen O'Reilly, by permission of
Miss Deborah O'Reilly
Barry M. Sutton, A.I.P.P.
Information and Public Relations Office, F.I.T.
Student Representative Council, F.I.T.
Tom Loncaric, F.I.T.

Maps drawn by Patrick Miller.

Endpapers: aerial views of F.I.T. 1965 and 1987

Cover photographs: Yarraville skyline, 1988;
Footscray Technical School, Buckley and Nicholson
Streets, early 1930's; Student with single-cylinder
steam engine.

National Library of Australia
Cataloguing-in-Publication Data

Rasmussen, Carolyn.
Poor man's university: 75 years of technical education
in Footscray.

Bibliography.
Includes index.
ISBN 1 86297 000 9.

1. Footscray Institute of Technology — History. 2. Technical
education — Victoria — Footscray — History. I. Title.

378.945'1

Designed by Vane Lindesay
Typeset by Bookset, North Melbourne, Victoria

Printed in Australia by
The Book Printer, Maryborough, Victoria

To the memory of my mother Jean Robertson, 1928–1970

To Western Oregon State
College
in friendship.
Carolyn Rasmussen.

and expressing to its
President, Dr. Richard
Meyers.
with regards.

Jim Henry
20.3.89

Contents

vi

Preface

It takes a confident institution to commission its written history. When the F.I.T. council agreed to 'take the plunge' two years ago, that action reflected a sense of institutional maturity and an understanding of the value of history.

As an erstwhile historian and as convener of the committee supporting the project, I judge we were fortunate to engage as institute historian an individual with a fine reputation and with the ability to produce an authoritative, yet interestingly readable work. We did not entirely realise at the beginning that Carolyn Rasmussen possessed the kind of personality and empathy which quickly made her one of us. This contributed to the success of the project which now yields the first major work to be published by the institute's newly established press, *Footprint*.

Footscray Institute of Technology (F.I.T.) is now firmly into its eighth decade of existence since its founding as a junior technical school. The institute has just completed a remarkable period of development, with student numbers doubling over six years, its academic programs broadened and its campus transformed in the process.

As F.I.T. looks to the future, as one of the nation's eight major metropolitan technological institutions with multi-cultural, and indeed, international commitments at a time of great change in Australian higher education, its surest guide is its history. The problems, indeed, the paradoxes unveiled in this history will have a familiar contemporary ring.

A most pertinent example is the debate within successive councils over whether the institution should serve the people of the western metropolitan region exclusively, or be something more in addition.

Good leadership from the outset eschewed narrow vocationalism to foster a multi-discipline institution. Hoadley stands out amongst his contemporaries as promoting education for women, and he and his successors reached constantly to provide higher studies. We are conscious of this legacy as we enrol our first Ph.D student this year. The commitment of staff and council stands out as well, and the willingness of many to take risks in furthering development of the institution. *Plus ça change, plus la meme chose.*

We look forward to our deepening commitment to the people and institutions of the western metropolitan region. We may well view as prophetic those words quoted in the text from the *Footscray Advertiser*, 26 August, 1916, pointing to the institution becoming the seat of scientific investigation into all the great manufactures around it.

Dr. Rasmussen's work is more than a source of nostalgia for those who played roles big and small, and more than an interesting account (albeit important) of Victorian technical education. For those of us who are committed to seeing that the next decade of the F.I.T. experience is at least equal to the seven previous decades, 'A Poor Man's University' will constitute an inspirational and instructive guide.

Irwin Herrman
Director, FIT.
October, 1988

Acknowledgements

Writing a commissioned history involves special pleasures, not the least of which is the opportunity to become, for a time at least, part of the institution about which you are writing. FIT made me welcome at all levels and I shall vacate my office with real regret. My deepest debt of gratitude is to the 'Committee' that first made the writing of the history possible, and then nurtured me along the way. Irwin Herrman, Rob Pascoe, Gwen Dow, Sheila Byard, Doreen Parker and for shorter periods, Lea Giles Peters, Chris McConville and Clem Macintyre all patiently read rather messy draft chapters, often at short notice. Their comments were constructive and instructive and our meetings stimulating. They mitigated the inherent loneliness of writing and curbed my worst excesses. There was never, however, any pressure to present an official 'line', a privilege which leaves me entirely responsible for all the emphases and interpretations in this history. Amanda Whiting provided intelligent research assistance and service beyond the call of duty in even taking the bus to the Public Records Office at Laverton during a heatwave. Vern Jones and Ken Burbridge were always ready with help; Robert Taylor unravelled a host of mysteries in the course of numerous conversations. Mary Joy Gleeson and June Webb cheerfully attended to my smallest needs, as did Elise Downs, Margaret Prawduit and Jan Hec Murto and Philomena Pastore, in particular, aided my search for records. All the staff of the Directorate and central administration went out of their way to help as did numerous others throughout the whole Institute. Pam Barnes made a special contribution in transferring the text to 'Spelbinder'. A number of people kindly donated historical records that will become part of a permanent archive. The staff of the Education History Unit, in the Ministry of Education were especially helpful. I appreciated the enthusiasm of Bill Jamieson and Ted Walker (senior). Dick Armitage's 'Last Tech Bemoan' provided rare insights and much amusement in a beautiful setting. The following were only too willing to be interviewed, or casually discuss the latest question that was puzzling me: S. Abeyesekere, D. Allen, L. Armour, David Beanland, Graham Beanland, Howard Beanland, Rex Boschen, Alf Bradshaw, J. Bristow, Harry Carlin Smith, John Chadwick, J. Docherty, Lyndsay Davies, J. Dooley, D. Ell, D. English, O. Ford, R. Fordham, Fred Giles, N. Gillespie, O. Gimesy, M. J. Gleeson, E. Green, P. Green, E. Haire, Tom Hall, J. Hoadley, M. Hoyne, Margaret Hughes, J. Lack, K. Lansley, P. Lipshut, K. Luke, Jim McDonald, J. McLaren, D. McTiernan, W. Maxwell, E. Mollard, Stephen Murray-Smith, I. Pellizzer, J. Pitt, R. Rankin, P. Rumpff, J. Sargeant, J. Sillitoe, J. Sinclair, J. Stearne, R. Toomey, B. Thomson, J. Thompson, K. Thornton, H. Tribe, E. K. Walker, G. Wills, Stanley Willcox, B. Wise. I regret that time did not allow for more interviews. Sadly, Doug Mills died before this project was much advanced, but his warm interest was clear, as was his well-founded confidence that the story was worth telling.

Sources of Illustrations:

FIT SRC

FIT Information office and EDD & Tom Loncaric

FTAFE

R Dunstan Photographic
22 Drummond Street,
Carlton.

Ritter-Jeppesen Studios
107-111 Lonsdale Street,
Melbourne.

Royal Australian Air Force.

D. O'Reilly
50 Peel St,
Newport.

Allan Studios
318 Smith St,
Collingwood.

Barry M Sutton
50 Ferguson Street,
Williamstown.

Squire Photographs
633 Rathdowne St.
Carlton North 3054

Significant Dates

1910   Education Act extending Government funding to some forms of secondary education in Victoria
First discussion in Footscray City Council of a technical school for Footscray
1916   Footscray Technical School opened
1917   Preparatory classes for evening school commenced
1918   Turning and Fitting workshops and additional classrooms completed
School declared a Soldiers' Training Centre
1919   School converted to a public hospital to help with Spanish Flu epidemic for part of the year
Junior Technical Certificate course extended from two to three years
Work commenced on workshops for Commonwealth Retraining Scheme
1920   Footscray becomes first Education Departmental School to offer full diploma courses
1925   First Footscray diplomas awarded
1927   Abolition of fees for junior technical school courses
1928   Apprenticeship Commission established
1931   Board of Enquiry into Certain Matters Concerning the Education Department, Victoria set up under C S McPherson
1938   Two storey extensions along Nicholson Street completed
1939   Fourth year of part-time evening study added to diploma course
1943   First building on Ballarat Road site (Building A) occupied
1945   Junior technical school course extended to four years
1946   Engineering diploma extended to four years full-time study
1948   Full day training for apprentices introduced

1950   New Boilermaking and Steel Construction Workshops at Ballarat Road occupied (Officially opened 1952)
Block exemptions in the first two years of an engineering degree at Melbourne University became available

1952   Entrance exam abolished

1958   Footscray designated a Technical College, the senior technical institution in the Western Region

1961   State Advisory Council on Technical Education set up

1964   Leaving Certificate (form 5) introduced in secondary school
New building for forms 1–5 at Ballarat Road and new office and administration block completed
Martin Report *Tertiary Education in Australia*

1965   Victoria Institute of Colleges Act
Footscray Technical College among the first affiliates
Junior Technical Certificate abolished
New four year Diploma courses in Engineering and Applied Chemistry introduced to follow Leaving Technical Certificate
C H Beanland Sports Centre opened

1967   Abolition of tuition fees for Diploma students resident in Victoria

1968   Footscray Technical College becomes Footscray Institute of Technology under revised VIC Act
Intermediate Certificate abolished

1971   Opening Building D
The three departments of Engineering grouped to form a School of Engineering

1972   First degree courses (Civil and Electrical Engineering)
Footscray secondary technical school separated from FIT

1973   Trade section changed its name to Footscray Technical College (A Division of the Footscray Institute of Technology)

1974   First conferring of degrees under the VIC
Campus Plan approved by Planning Appeals Tribunal
Kangan Report on Technical and Further Education

1975   School of General Studies established with Departments of Business Studies, Humanities and Physical Education and Recreation
Footscray secondary technical school council established

1976   Work commenced on Berry St. Annexe

1977   Building E completed

1978   Partridge Report on post-secondary education in Victoria

1979   School of General Studies split into Schools of Business of General Studies
Newport Technical College opened
Wiliams Committee Report *Education Training and Employment*

1980	Footscray Technical School transferred to new site
	Footscray Boat Club Complex completed
	Victorian TAFE Board established
1981	Refurbishment of Building C completed
	First degrees awarded in name of Council of FIT rather than VIC
1982	TAFE College separated from the Institute
1984	FIT entitled to accredit its own courses to degree level
1986	Completion of Building K
	Building G commenced

Abbreviations

ACPPIV	Association of Councils of Post-Primary Institutions in Victoria
CTEC	Commonwealth Tertiary Education Commission
FIT	Footscray Institute of Technology
FTC	Footscray Technical College
FTS	Footscray Technical School
RMIT	Royal Melbourne Institute of Technology
SRC	Student Representative Council
TAFE	Technical and Further Education
TSAV	Technical Schools Association of Victoria
TTAV	Technical Teachers' Association of Victoria
VIC	Victoria Institute of Colleges
VPSEC	Victorian Post Secondary Education Commission
VTU	Victorian Teachers' Union

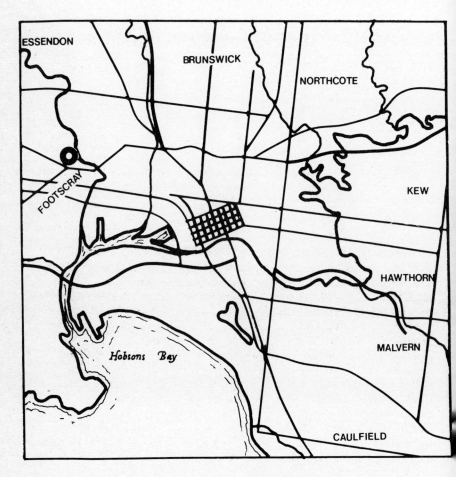

Footscray in relation to Melbourne

CHAPTER ONE "To make Footscray the Birmingham of Australia"[1]

> Footscray is, of course, an industrial centre, and it is, there-
> fore of the utmost importance to the rising generation, and
> the local manufacturers, that facilities for imparting technical
> knowledge should be available and easily accessible.[2]

So declared the *Footscray Advertiser* in May 1910 in response to
Cr Shillabeer's "Important and Momentous Proposal" that the
Footscray Council arrange a public meeting to gauge support for
a technical school in the district. The reasons why Shillabeer
raised the subject at this time are fairly clear. The recent opening
of the Eastern Suburbs Technical School, supported by a £2000
donation from the Hon. George Swinburne and his wife, had
wounded Footscray's civic pride. As one writer put it, Footscray
needed such an institution more than the eastern suburbs did
because "fully 80%" of its young men were workers and 300 to
400 of them were already attending the Working Men's College
in Melbourne.[3] At the same time, rumours were circulating that
the proprietor of Sunshine Harvester, H. V. McKay had offered
£2000 and five acres of land following an appeal by the Director
of Education, Frank Tate, to Victorian industrialists to follow the
example of their American counterparts in endowing schools.[4]

Footscray's civic leaders were at this time engaged in a campaign to strengthen both the image and the reality of Footscray
as an industrial centre, and the model to which they looked was
Birmingham, the great manufacturing city of England. Birmingham's economy consisted of a large number of small-scale establishments employing highly skilled artisans to manufacture a
great variety of finished products. The result was a community

1

characterised by mutuality and interdependence between 'masters' and 'men', and the development of what became known as a "civic gospel". Birmingham was as renowned for the special quality of the responsibility it took for the welfare of all its inhabitants as it was for its industrial output.[5] From the *Footscray Advertiser*'s viewpoint, a technical school was the centrepiece of its vision for Footscray.

Birmingham was proud of the absence of large and crowded factories and the hostile relations between capital and labour that seemed their inevitable accompaniment, whereas Footscray's industrial development tended in precisely the opposite direction. During Victoria's boom years in the nineteenth century, Footscray and adjacent suburbs west of the Maribyrnong became the location of a great many noxious and offensive industries. In 1888 the Footscray/Flemington/Kensington area alone contained almost half of Melbourne's abattoirs, fellmongers, fertiliser plants and tanneries. By the turn of the century, Footscray was "synonymous with stinks in the public mind".[6] Such aspersions had "stimulated the growth of a perverse local pride" in these industries as "the identifying badge of an industrial working class community".[7]

By 1910, however, Footscray's developing role as a more complex manufacturing centre allowed a fierce localism and an abiding appreciation of the qualities of simple working men and women to blossom into a less perversely based civic pride. The story of Footscray was not characterised by "tense situations and stirring emotions", but by

> the romance of honest work — the romance which is making the barrens bloom — the romance which is blowing the forge and beating the iron into plow shares so that the earth may be made to yield her increase and the tribes of man to prosper.[8]

H. Michel, author of *Footscray's First Fifty Years*, cherished no "delusions".

> Nature has lent us no adventitious aid in the way of picturesqueness and physical charm. All she has given us is some very good bluestone. Whatever we are our work has made us. And our destiny is to go on working. With this we have no fault to find because in the first place we will not be required to work for nothing, and in the second place we can take pride in work that will help Australia. The gift of making things has been granted us. We make plows for Australia's fields,

manures for her crops and some day we hope to make her ships. Our prosperity will indicate hers — the foundations of her palaces will be hewn from our quarries.

Our position then in the scheme of things is defined and, while some may not account it high, at any rate it can never be deemed dishonourable. We enter upon our heritage of toil without regret and without misgiving. We desire no undue aggrandizement, but we have sufficient self respect to know that we can carry out in a workmanlike manner our appointed task. [9]

By 1909, when this was written, the appointed task was being recast in terms of skill as well as sheer hard work, and other forces, quite independent of those inspired by the image of Birmingham, were shaping the local desire for a technical school as the emblem of the new direction that was being proposed for the district. The first of these was what might be called the 'spirit of the age'. The "romance" which was "blowing the forge" was the romance of engineering. Men standing in front of a steam hammer in Mephan Ferguson's Engineering Works "methodically banging a block of white hot metal into shape", could be moved to think

instinctively of Herbert Spencer's great generalisation in the domain of science that 'force persists'. The hammer does its work with inexorable, untiring, insistent pertinacity. It is like fate beating out human destiny. [10]

The frontispiece of the Footscray history — a train steaming toward the reader, surrounded by decorative Edwardian scrolls — was designed to invoke pride in industrial development. The establishment of railways — the romantic symbol of progress — electricity, and great drainage works such as those Ferguson's were constructing the pipes for, all required engineers, and this was indeed the age of the engineer. Over the preceding 50 years, they had transformed the relationship between man and his physical environment. Railroads now linked cities and towns. Bridges spanned rivers and canyons. Sewers drained disease and filth from cities, while water was available wherever it was needed. Engines provided transport and power and men were at last able to fly. Machinery turned out vast quantities of everyday necessities at a fraction of the price of hand-made items, and increased food production many times over. As a later Director of Education, J. M. McCrae, observed:

The modern world is essentially a world of machines. In it the human mind and hand have been busy turning Nature's bounties to good use and overcoming her oppositions. One potent instrument in attaining these ends has been man's mechanical inventiveness. This has found expression in thousands of processes and appliances that minister to our needs and add to our enjoyment and comfort.[11]

Technology and progress were inextricably bound and there seemed no limit in 1910 to what man, his ingenuity and his machines could do. Technology held the promise of 'paradise regained', and the faster people acquired the skills needed to design and run the new technology, the better for everyone.

Engineers were a self-consciously proud elite who believed that their expertise should be more widely dispersed, and advocates of technical education agreed that all industry would benefit from a more technically literate workforce. Engineers were also a proudly 'practical' group. They were not scientists or researchers, but builders. As men of action, engineers believed that a thorough knowledge of technology could only be gained through practical experience, and when people in Footscray talked about a technical school, it was with the training of practical engineers in mind. The "Song of the Engineer", in the *Footscray Technical School Song Book* of 1922, captures much of the spirit in which the school was conceived:

> Let doctors hunt for festive germs,
> And lawyers talk and reason;
> But iron and steel are the stuff for me,
> And concrete made of one to three,
> And timber cut from the ironbark tree
> At proper time and season.

> Chorus

> *For second to none is the engineer,*
> *To Kaiser, King or Sirdar —*
> *He makes a trestle, a dam, a pier,*
> *A toasting fork or a cask of beer;*
> *A roof, or a plate-web girder.*

> For others may talk of the modest maid,
> And the charms of Jean and Nellie;
> But the cold grey engine is our delight,

With its shining crank and cylinder bright,
With its genial smile and its jovial might,
As it squashes a man to a jelly.

Chorus . . .

For nought to us are letters, and art,
And music and soulful blisses;
But give us plenty of sweat and toil,
When the clothes are covered with grime and soil,
And the hair is dripping with grease and oil,
And the steam valve kicks and hisses.

Chorus . . .[12]

That man had first to dream of flying, to imagine flying, before he could build a machine to fly in was of little concern. Spurred on by engineering's promise, Footscray saw its future in the production of a skilled workforce which could design, maintain and build machines and devise systems linking them to the productive process.

Footscray's desire for a technical school was, however, also associated with Victoria-wide events. The year 1910 was a watershed in the history of technical education in Victoria, for it was then that local initiative was replaced by state responsibility for the establishment of new institutions. Although Footscray people continued to look to the past for guidance, the fortunes of any school in Footscray were now firmly tied to a new system. The Victorian Education Act of 1910, which marked the entry of the state into secondary education, was the product of widespread community concern at the inadequacies of the existing educational arrangements and the unwillingness or inability of the private sector to take up the challenge. As a consequence, while local players and details are of immense significance, the struggle to establish and develop technical education in Footscray cannot be separated from the wider context of the politics of education in Victoria.

Throughout Australian history there has been a persistent shortage of skilled labour, but it was not until well into the nineteenth century that education came to be seriously regarded as a possible solution. Prior to the 1880s the provision of education resulted more often from charitable impulses and moral concerns than from practical utility (except perhaps in agriculture where special conditions were seen to apply)[13] and employers preferred to rely on immigration for additional skilled workers. In Victoria, the technologically-hungry mining industry prompted the first significant development in technical education — the establishment of Schools of Mines, notably at Ballarat in 1870 and Bendigo in 1873. The fortunes of these Schools, however, were tied closely to those of the gold industry and the "vigorous provincial cultural and economic life" it fostered, all of which were waning by the 1880s.[14]

It is unlikely that a great deal of higher technical education went on in these schools, for most enrolling students lacked basic mathematics and literacy skills. The institutions' major significance "probably lay in their pragmatism and opportunism which allowed them to develop as 'poor men's grammar schools'",[15] responding to an evident demand in the community for a more broadly based post-primary education. Unfortunately, many of the subjects that proved most popular, for example 'commercial' subjects such as accounting and short-hand writing, generally did not fall within the official definition of 'technical'. Under the Technological Commission, established in 1869, these subjects were excluded from government funding.

The experience of the technical schools that sprang up throughout Victoria in the period 1870 to 1910 did little to ease the struggle of those few enthusiasts who sought to establish in the public mind a relationship between scientific instruction, useful knowledge and industrial efficiency. The Mechanics Institutes which had appeared all over Victoria in the mid nineteenth century were strongly imbued with these concepts, which they wedded to a notion of personal 'improvement' through the pursuit of knowledge and skills. Although this movement had little success in achieving its specific goals, it was important in giving force to the idea that education for working people was both a right and a necessity.

Towards the end of the the nineteenth century a growing demand for access to education and training was boosted by a deepening understanding of the relationship between the level of technical skill in a community and its overall economic strength. Liberalism, perhaps at the height of its influence in Victorian politics in the two decades before World War I, embraced technical education as essential to the continued development of Victoria's infant industrial economy. Historian of technical education, Stephen Murray-Smith, goes so far as to suggest that technical education became "the dominant intellectual fixation of the period",[16] incorporating both the call for democratisation of education and the utilitarian demands of national progress.

> Educational thinkers, drawing on overseas precedent, discovered new pedagogic values in practical studies and found these especially useful in devising schemes for post-primary education which would satisfy newly felt aspirations and needs without interfering with the functions of the traditional middle class colleges. . . . It reflected a mating of real or imagined technological demands with the philosophy of liberalism and came to be seen as a specific treatment for a wide variety of social ills.[17]

In an era of optimism and enthusiasm for the dignity of labour and the working man, progressive liberals saw education as a key to establishing an harmonious social order of the type symbolised by Birmingham's 'civic gospel'. The boom conditions of the 1880s encouraged the impression that labour and capital could establish a mutually beneficial partnership that would advance the prosperity of the state without radically disturbing traditional social and economic divisions.

Almost all the strands of thought that provided the rationale for technical education were embodied in the philosophy of Francis Ormond. He recognized the importance of scientific and technical training for the working classes and the role this could play in alleviating Victoria's "urgent necessity of arming herself for the great industrial fight" that was looming.[18] He also brought together the moral and utilitarian arguments that had been central to the earlier Mechanics Institute movement, arguing that education would "make men more God-fearing, and better members of society", able "to perform their parts more intelligently in the world and in business life".[19] As a consequence of this view, Ormond not only generously endowed the university college named after him but contributed significantly to the establishment of the Working Men's College, believing them both of crucial importance to the future development of Victoria.[20] Although, especially impressed with the potential of education to break "down the lines of demarcation between rich and poor",[21] the nature of his philanthropy in establishing two different kinds of institutions reveals the limits to his desire to alter the established social order.

Perhaps the spirit that moved Ormond might have developed

to the point where privately endowed technical institutions would have become the norm had the depression of the 1890s not intervened, but the evidence seems to suggest that Ormond was rare in his willingness to exercise his philanthropy in Victoria, let alone in the cause of education for the working man.[22] Significantly, it appears that only the "national self interest" arguments were persuasive in drawing wider support for the Working Men's College from "leading citizens".[23] The dream of endless progress and social harmony based on it was severely damaged by the economic and industrial crises of the 1890s. Clearly, the financial and administrative resources necessary to create a viable and sophisticated technical education system could now only be expected to come from the state, to which the bulk of the population looked for its provision. Given that the state already fully financed compulsory elementary education and substantially funded the University and many of the activities of the existing technical schools, it was not unrealistic to expect that within a short time it would also accept responsibility for secondary and junior technical education.

In the 1890s men such as Alfred Deakin, and David Syme of the *Age*, combined with the Chamber of Manufactures, the Trades Hall Council, the Royal Agricultural Society and the Workingmen's College to rouse the government of the day to greater interest in technical education.[24] The result was the appointment of the Fink Royal Commission on Technical Education, the report of which combined a scathing attack on the existing system of education with rational and progressive recommendations designed to raise the standard of work in primary schools and bridge the gap between elementary and higher technical schools. Assuming that only children of relatively wealthy parents were suited to higher education, the new schools were to be vocational, designed to fit boys and girls better into the existing system.

> The class of students for whom provision would be made by continuation schools would be largely the children of the working classes, who will ultimately have to support themselves by manual work; and the instruction would differ distinctly from secondary education which has for its main objective the training of young men destined for the professions.[25]

In the short term, very few of the recommendations were acted upon and "the public mind lapsed into its accustomed apathy toward education",[26] but in the long term they set the parameters of education planning until well into the 1920s.

The extension of the Victorian government's role in educational provision as embodied in the 1910 Education Act was justified principally on the grounds that the "continuation schools" would concern themselves with imparting useful knowledge and their products would, therefore, contribute to the national welfare. The climate of opinion was generally favourable to technical education but the motives of its supporters were mixed. It is in this sometimes odd mixture that part of the explanation of the chequered history of technical education in Victoria can be found. In the first decade of the twentieth century it became increasingly common to link technical education not only with the development of Victoria, but also with the very survival of the British Empire. As Germany and the United States drew level with Britain in industrial progress, and the success of Japan in defeating Russia in 1905 demonstrated the significant industrial strength of a non-European nation, public attention was fixed on what was assumed to be the superior education system of Germany, which placed heavy stress on broad participation and the teaching of technical skills. Australians were fully aware of the relationship between industrial and military strength, and the proposition that "the coming struggle" would be "an industrial one",[27] proved one of the most persuasive arguments for the creation of a technical education system.[28]

This argument was boosted by an expansion in Victoria's industrial base, as the number of factories in Victoria increased from 3,249 in 1901 to 5,126 in 1911, and employment in them from 66,000 to 112,000.[29] While neither the importance nor the size of the manufacturing sector should be over emphasised (in 1914 only 28% of the workforce was employed in factories),[30] there was a widespread perception that there was a critical shortage of skilled labour. In Footscray, the issue surfaced in mid-1911 in a letter headed "What shall we do with our boys". The writer feared that Australia was in danger of becoming a "nation of labourers and sports, importing its trained workers from Britain". He pointed with alarm to the fact that

> during the recent implement makers strike there were any number of labourers ready to risk reputation and face bodily danger in order to obtain work; . . . that when census clerks were advertised for and temporary billets were offered, over

1000 applications were forthcoming, [and worse still] engineering work has to be sent out of the country because artisans are not available.

Victorians were compared unfavourably with Britons for their failure to give their sons the opportunity to become skilled artisans, either through apprenticeships or technical schools.[31] Yet in the main, it was simpler, and from the employers' viewpoint, cheaper, to call for increased immigration of skilled workers. This proposal, however, greatly agitated the trade union movement, which feared consequent unemployment and a loss of the bargaining power associated with the scarce supply of skilled labour.

Although schools designed to produce technically-competent workers for newly-developing industries ought to have enlisted enthusiastic support and financial backing from the manufacturing sector, with a few rare exceptions this was not the case. Rather, what interest there was among manufacturers resulted from more diffuse economic and social concerns. Between 1890 and 1910 the social and economic divisions between the middle and working classes had widened. The formation of the Labor Party, the rise of 'New Unionism' and changes in work processes and organisation had altered the nature of relations in the work place. Many employers were alarmed at the increasing regulation of the labour market, first through Wages Boards and later by the Conciliation and Arbitration Commission. Older paternalistic factory owners, who had long demanded the unswerving loyalty of their employees, were hurt, puzzled, alienated and often frightened by the new, tougher, style of unionism that emphasised solidarity across worker ranks rather than within particular workplaces.

The assumption that education, and especially technical education, would promote social harmony and good citizenship remained widespread. The Governor of Victoria unselfconsciously declared at the opening of Sunshine Technical School in 1911 that, "the most unsuccessful man in life was the unskilled labourer". Moreover,

> it was a preponderance of unskilled labourers that did most to bring about unemployment troubles. . . . they wanted to rid themselves of the class who created the dreadful trouble of unemployment and they could do that by giving the youth coming forward some education . . . [32]

Those industrialists who supported technical education were susceptible to the national-interest argument, keen to engage in the export market and capable of making an explicit connection between skill, productivity and competitiveness. However, they generally expressed their support in terms that revealed a more fundamental concern about the breakdown of consensus and the new trends in industrial relations. In mid-1912 a member of the McKay family returned from a tour of Java with the message that, if Sunshine Harvester was to "compete with the products of cheap labour in other countries, the workers must make themselves efficient, [and] turn out good work and more of it".[33] Towards this end the older H. V. McKay was making a substantial contribution. Not only had he provided the land on which to build Sunshine Technical School, but he gave his apprentices time to attend classes and a bonus for good results. H. V. McKay was of the view that legislative enactments to raise wages were "right enough in their way" but the best way for workers to get higher wages was to earn them "through knowledge, ability and energy",[34] and "above all . . . beware of agitators".[35]

The implication that there was some essential link between political and industrial radicalism and a preponderance of unskilled workers was commonplace and by no means confined to the middle classes. S. Hampson, an organiser with the Amalgamated Society of Engineers, suggested in 1916 that turners, fitters and other mechanics were a "very desirable class of tradesman and well known as good citizens, the artisan being the best asset the state could have".[36] Later, while a teacher at Footscray Technical School, he declared that technical education would "fail in its objective if insufficient attention [was] given to formation of character; and this present industrial riot throughout Australia may be attributed to the lack of technical education in the past".[37] The moral and utilitarian arguments in favour of technical education remained almost inextricably tangled.

Notwithstanding the activity at Sunshine Harvester, the early twentieth century saw a noticeable decline in the apprenticeship system, indicating an increasing reluctance on the part of employers to contribute to the development of a skilled workforce by this means. By 1910 technical education had become an attractive proposition to employers aware of problems beyond their own immediate concerns. It promised a higher level of skill in the workforce and, by implication, a reduced tendency to social disruption or radical union activities. It would strengthen international competitiveness, and if the state took responsibility, the financial burden would be carried by the whole community rather than by employers alone.

It was not enough, however, for middle-class progressives, philanthropists or manufacturers to argue that technical education would benefit the working or lower classes unless there was a correspondingly strong sense amongst significant numbers of working people themselves that they would profit by such an education. Until 1910, technical education had generally been available only after working hours and had involved the payment of fees. The majority of working people able to participate in this form of 'self improvement' had, by and large, already been trained and until the 1890s they had been more successful in improving their conditions and wages through trade union activity than by upgrading their skills. After 1890, however, their position changed and technical education became far more important for a significant section of the Labour Movement.

Overall, the trade union movement was no more consistent in its support of technical education than manufacturers. A careful examination of the behaviour of Labor advocates of technical education in the period 1890 to 1930 reveals a narrow, defensive position based more on economic self-interest than any concern for education *per se* or working class children in general. The power of craft unions rested on their monopoly of certain skills achieved through a relatively closed apprenticeship system that reduced competition for jobs by relating the number who could be indentured to the number already qualified, thereby increasing the bargaining power of those currently skilled. "Historically it is clear that the ability to get a form of training enshrined in an indentured agreement is only possible where labour is in short supply and where unions are effective".[38]

This was the position in Victoria in the 1880s. However, if the supply of unskilled labour becomes substantial, or the wage gains appear to squeeze profits too heavily, employers can successfully erode this strategic power of skilled workers in a number of ways. Firstly, they can employ unskilled, female or junior labour in preference to skilled adult males. Secondly, they can employ outworkers who are less easy to organise into unions. Thirdly, they can decline to indenture apprentices. Fourthly, they can introduce new processes and equipment into their factories that do not require as much skill and generally reduce the total numbers of workers required. All of these practices were evident in the period 1890 to 1910 and had considerable bearing on the Labour Movement's attitude to technical education.

The Trades Hall Council, itself dominated by craft unions, in turn dominated the early Victorian Labor Party. In so far as the Labor members of parliament had a policy on education independent of that of the Trades Hall Council, it lent heavily on the ideas and assumptions of the radical Liberals, rather than developing any specifically working class point of view.[39] Arguments about economic efficiency and the national interest were persuasive, while the notion that secondary schools and universities were inappropriate for working class children was as prevalent among the poorer classes as among the upper classes.[40]

To the extent that there was an alternative working class view of education in the union movement, it was located in the 'New Unions' of unskilled or semi-skilled workers. It was derived from the concept of an *independent* working class education that rendered involvement in state-developed schemes irrelevant. Not only did this group have no skills to protect, they

> did not have the close relationship with their employer which was often a characteristic of the craft unionist working in a small shop. They were much more conscious of their class, and more hostile to their employers who were remote and antagonistic. . . . In such a situation it was not the furtherance of their skills by technical education which concerned them, but rather the changing of society by the organisation and education of their members . . . in the ideals of mateship, co-operation and socialism.[41]

From such a perspective, 'useful knowledge' was embodied in subjects like political economy which would enable the worker to understand capitalist society and how to change it. Quite clearly, people with such ideas were not interested in advocating a system of education designed to fit children better to their existing destiny. In their view, the capitalist education system had nothing to offer the worker.[42]

Advocates of independent education were, however, very much in the minority, and such Labor education policy as was developed in the period prior to 1914 was adopted in the

> face of the apathy of the great majority of Labor's supporters, which did not see education as their vital concern. It was generally left to the Party to formulate the details of Labor's policy, and this was done in a sporadic, day to day, fashion.[43]

In the final analysis, technical education as an institutionalised, state-run system, was largely "a compromise between those seeking full freedom of employment policy" and those trade union forces "who sought compulsory apprenticeship, the appointment of a supervisory body and the stringent regulation of apprenticeship training."[44] This then was the highly self-interested nature of support for technical education in 1910 when attempts were first made to build a technical school in the self-consciously industrial suburb of Footscray.

Above all, however, the major force shaping plans for a technical school in Footscray was the maturing of civic pride.

> It is admitted that self-interest was the first reason actuating our pioneers. They did not come here to found a city but to make a living. Had it been otherwise there would have been no Footscray. But with personal prosperity came the attachment to the locality, the desire that the community should hold her head high among her neighbours, the ambition to direct her affairs and the intention that her affairs should be worth directing.[45]

Many of Footscray's councillors, and most of the business leaders who consistently supported the idea of a school, were self-made men with a strong sense of civic duty. Their support was consistent with that detected elsewhere in the state. Murray-Smith, in contemplating the view of the first Chief Inspector of Technical Schools, Donald Clark, that "in practically every centre where technical schools were wanted or where they were established . . . many of their strongest advocates were professional men who had wide sympathies and a liberal education", was impressed by

> the significance of the self-made background of many nineteenth century men of wealth, which was often linked with a strong sense of social responsibility, and which expressed itself in a concern for the moral and material improvement of the working classes.[46]

This concern for the moral and material improvement of the working classes in Footscray was expressed in terms that explicitly linked the welfare of the manufacturers, their workers and the district as a whole in the style of Birmingham. A technical school would ultimately benefit the rising generation by training them to become artisans instead of labourers; the employers by providing trained men to do their work, and the district which, having a supply of trained artisans available would attract manufacturers.[47]

These men were impressed with skill and its supposed material and moral benefits to both the nation and the individual. They felt they were in tune with the spirit of the times. But Footscray and Birmingham were very different places, and the difficulties they encountered in seeing their school built demonstrate the shallowness of much of the rhetoric about education that was current at the time.

1. *Footscray Advertiser*, 11 January 1913.
2. *Ibid.*, 21 May 1910.
3. *Ibid.*, 3 September 1910.
4. *Ibid.*, 11 October 1913.
5. For an illuminating study of Birmingham and the influence of ideas emanating from it on the rest of the world see A. Briggs, "Birmingham: The Making of a Civic Gospel", in *Victorian Cities*, Penguin, London, 1968, pp 184–240.
6. J. Lack, ' "Worst Smelbourne": Melbourne's noxious trades', in G. Davison, D. Dunstan & C. McConville (eds), *The Outcasts of Melbourne Essays in Social History*, Allen & Unwin, Sydney, 1985, p 190.
7. *Ibid.*
8. H. Michel, *Footscray's First Fifty Years*, Footscray Advertiser, 1909, [No page numbers].
9. *Ibid.*
10. 'A Great Engineering Workshop', *Argus*, 4 January 1894.
11. Education Department Pamphlet, *Technical Education in Victoria*, Centenary Exhibition booklet, 1934, Forward.
12. Words by H. E. Whitfield and Arnold R. Mote, *Footscray Technical School Song Book*, 1922.
13. S. Murray-Smith, 'Technical Education: The Lines of Development', in C. Sanders (ed.), *Technical Education for Development*, UWA Press, Perth, 1966, p 5.
14. *Ibid.*, p 13.
15. *Ibid.*
16. *Ibid.*, p 15.
17. *Ibid.*
18. J. Davidson, 'Francis Ormond Patron', in S. Macintyre (ed.), *Ormond College Centenary Essays*, MUP, Melbourne, 1984, p 11.
19. *Ibid.*, p 6.

20. *Ibid.*, p 10.
21. *Ibid.*, p 6.
22. *Ibid.*, p 19.
23. *Ibid.*, p 11.
24. J. Docherty, 'The Technical Division', in L. J. Blake (ed.), *Vision and Realisation A Centenary History of State Education in Victoria*, Vol. 1, Victorian Government Printer, Melbourne, 1973, p 629.
25. From the Final Report of the Fink Commission, quoted in R. Bessant, 'Education and Politics in the Development of the Education Systems of New South Wales and Victoria 1900-1940, with particular reference to Post-primary Education', Ph.D, Monash University 1971, p 58.
26. Frank Tate, quoted in Docherty, *op. cit.*, p 633.
27. Tutton, Melbourne High School, speaking at Sunshine Mechanics Institute, *Footscray Advertiser*, February 1, 1913.
28. A long article on 'Technical Education' in the *Footscray Advertiser*, 24 September 1910, laid much stress on these arguments.
29. Figures quoted in A. G. L. Shaw, *The Economic Development of Australia*, Melbourne, 1965, p 132.
30. *Ibid.*
31. *Footscray Advertiser*, 24 June 1911.
32. *Ibid.*, 11 October 1913.
33. *Ibid.*, 11 June 1912.
34. *Ibid.*, 8 March 1913.
35. *Ibid.*
36. *Ibid.*, 22 January 1916. Hampson was organizer for Victoria and Tasmania at this stage and was speaking at the inaugural meeting of the Amalgamated Society of Engineers, Sunshine branch.
37. S. Hampson, 'Character and Occupation', *Brown and Red*, 1919.
38. C. O'Donnell, 'The Relationship Between Social Class, Labour Market Segregation and Educational Credentials,' *Melbourne Studies in Education*, 1985, MUP, Melbourne, p 142.
39. Bessant, *op. cit.*, p 30.
40. *Ibid.*, p 58.
41. *Ibid.*, p 35.
42. For a discussion of independent working class education in more detail see A. Turner, 'Independent Working Class Education in Australia 1917–1929, with an Introductory Account of the United Kingdom Background', M. Ed., University of Melbourne, 1981.
43. Bessant, *op. cit.*, p 60.
44. S. Murray-Smith, 'Technical Education in Australia: A Historical Sketch', in E. L. Wheelwright (ed.), *Higher Education in Australia*, Melbourne, 1965 p 185.
45. *Ibid.*
46. *Ibid.*, p 181.
47. *Footscray Advertiser*, 30 September 1911.

CHAPTER TWO **"A district foolish in the extreme"?**[1]
1910–1914

All attempts to persuade H. V. McKay to apply his offered endowment to a school in Footscray fell on deaf ears. He remained adamant that any school supported by his donation must be located in Sunshine,[2] and Sunshine Technical School opened its doors in 1913 while Footscray's plans languished for five years. Late in 1914, the *Footscray Advertiser* lamented that

> The history of Footscray's attempt to secure a technical college for the benefit of the youth of the district would provide humorous reading were it not that the bungling which took place in the early stages of negotiations deprived scores of boys and girls of a chance to gain knowledge which, through life, would have stood them in good stead.[3]

There was some truth in this view, but Footscray's difficulties reflected far wider problems with the attempt to broaden educational opportunities for working class children; local enthusiasm was simply not enough to overcome these without significant financial input from the state government.

The framers of the 1910 Education Act did not intend to establish senior technical schools or even a comprehensive system of secondary education. Their aim was a scheme for 'continuation' education, one of the major purposes of which was to provide the existing senior technical schools with boys who had reached a suitable educational standard to embark on higher technical work. This did not imply a new-found willingness on the part of the government to spend public money generously, however great the supposed national benefits were to be. The Act had been passed in the face of some opposition[4] by a parliament

17

which was niggardly in its expenditure on education. In 1902, for example, it spent only 10s per head of population at a time when NSW was spending 30s.[5] The Act was framed at least partly on the assumption that employers who stood to benefit would enter into a financial partnership with the state to provide facilities, and that they would also readily fall in with schemes to improve apprenticeship training by allowing day release. As the Minister for Public Instruction explained at the opening of Sunshine Technical School, the "Government could not provide for all needs without assistance". Men such as George Swinburne and H. V. McKay were held up as reminders that employers had a "public duty" to provide this assistance, but Footscray's experience reveals just how vain was the hope of large endowments.[6] Even supportive employers were not willing to provide financial support in amounts much in excess of £100. By the mid 1920s it was clear that only legislation would ensure that apprentices were given time to attend school during the day.

Sunshine's success made Footscray's claim for a technical school no less valid, but it did have the effect the *Advertiser* feared of splitting the resources so that neither district was as well served as it might have been.[7] Both the Chief Inspector of Technical Schools, Donald Clark, and the Member for Williamstown, Jack Lemmon, favoured Footscray's proposal, and the government offered £5000 for the construction of a school, provided suitable land was made available.[8] To that end Shillabeer and a small group of supporters set out to raise £2000. Shillabeer, a building contractor, was convinced that the benefits of a technical school to manufacturers of the district were so obvious that raising £2000 would present no difficulties at all.

> Footscray and Yarraville had never been behind when money was needed for a worthy cause and nothing more worthy than the technical college could be named. As Mr Tate told them other districts were ready and anxious to seize the chance that had been given this district and they would be foolish in the extreme if through any lack of enthusiasm they allowed the opportunity to pass.[9]

Shillabeer started the fund with £100. J. H. Hooper, a local department store proprietor, followed suit with £250. The district, it seems, however was "foolish in the extreme",[10] for no further donations eventuated, much less a "big donor". The

unfortunate result was several years of unseemly public brawling about a site for the proposed school culminating in the with-
drawal of the offer of £5000.

When the first meeting to discuss a site was held in September
1911, the seeds of bitter disputation were already present. Essentially the choice was between Footscray and Yarraville. The
Footscray councillors and Lemmon were enthusiastic about
Footscray's centrality but, in Lemmon's view, the available land
was insufficient. The supporters of a Yarraville site included the
Rev A. R. Byers, the Works Manager of the Mt Lyell Mining Co,
E. W. Trend, and the Williamstown councillors, who believed
the school was to serve both areas and therefore Yarraville or
Spotswood was more central. Moreover, it was argued that
"most of the large factories were in Yarraville".[11] A small committee was appointed to investigate sites[12] and, to the horror of
the Footscray Council, it recommended a Yarraville site. From
the tone of the Council's discussion, a modern reader might be
excused for thinking that Yarraville was a foreign country. One
councillor went so far as to suggest that if the school was in
Yarraville, the Footscray boys may as well go to Melbourne.[13]

It had been intended that this Committee would prepare a
definite proposal to put to the Education Department and thus
secure the promised £5000. However, the Footscray site supporters, who were in the minority, went to the next public meeting, attended by Clark, and the Director of Education, Frank
Tate, with a plan to forestall any such recommendation. The
Committee had considered five sites[14] but just as discussion on
these was about to begin, Shillabeer pointedly interrupted with
a sixth suggestion. If the Footscray Mechanics Institute Reserve
were combined with the land across the road on the corner of
Buckley and Nicholson streets owned by the Railway Commissioners it would constitute the two acres which Lemmon and
Tate considered the minimum necessary size. When the Yarra-
ville-site supporters sought to have the meeting continue
discussing the Committee's recommendation, they were side-
stepped by the Mayor who later claimed weakly that the Committee had only taken "a sort of preferential vote but no one
seemed able to decide on the result."[15]

The Footscray councillors and the *Advertiser* wanted the
school in the heart of Footscray, yet the evidence that the
strongest support for the school was coupled with a commitment to a Yarraville site is strong. Even Shillabeer admitted
ruefully at one stage that

The proposal has been hanging on week after week and no one seems to be interesting themselves in the matter in the way they should do, except a few who want to have the college in Yarraville. They have been writing letters and are likely to ruin the movement altogether.[16]

The Council's determined view that it represented "the whole of the ratepayers of the city", and therefore that it should be for the councillors, and not an "irresponsible committee to advise as to the best site",[17] obviously alienated much of the broader community. It also underlines the extent to which the project was an exercise in civic promotion and just how narrowly civic responsibility could be defined. Cr Jenkins was not entirely unjustified in his taunt that "some councillors would rather lose site and money than have a site anywhere else than in north or middle wards".[18]

The high-handed assumption that the Mechanics Institute would immediately acquiesce in Shillabeer's plan alienated another body of natural support. When the Institute objected to the idea that a new technical school should be built on its ashes,[19] they were subject to a campaign of public vilification:

I think the administration of the Mechanics Institute is a monument of incompetence. Their land has been a reproach to a progressive city for many years and has never been put to any good use. . . . It is an ideal site for a technical college and I think some steps should be taken to point out to the government that the land is not being used in the best interests of the people it was intended to benefit.[20]

When this failed to force the hand of the Mechanics Institute trustees, unsuccessful attempts were made to have the government force them to hand over the land. This activity only served to reveal the extent of support for the Mechanics Institute that still existed in the area.[21] Meanwhile, the matter dragged on and on and enthusiasm for the whole project drained away. After some attempt to promote a Yarraville site to the government independently, the Yarraville supporters simply stood aloof. The offer of £5000 lapsed in mid-1912 as the government confronted a bad harvest and instituted wide-ranging expenditure cuts. Ironically, when a school was finally built it was members of the Yarraville group and the Mechanics Institute who proved among its most solid supporters.

By the time of the municipal elections of August 1912, the issue appears to have lost all political significance. Shillabeer was strangely silent on the subject. The outcome of these elections was a Labor Party majority for the first time, but Labor councillors were just as divided on the question of a suitable site as any other group. The Railway Commissioners agreed to hand over the Nicholson Street site and lower the price by £900, but the Labor councillors exhibited little enthusiasm for what must have appeared a lost cause. The *Advertiser*, enraged by the loss of impetus towards a technical school, sought to make political capital out of this:

> If they [the councillors] prefer the youth of the city to grow up to swell the already overcrowded ranks of unskilled labourers, in preference to being artisans, with greatly increased earning capacity and a chance in life, let them say so . . . and then the citizens themselves will take a hand.[22]

However, to which citizens the *Advertiser* might have been referring is a little hard to fathom in the circumstances. Ironically, it was the Mechanics Institute, so recently the subject of the *Advertiser*'s scorn, which kept alive the little flame of interest in technical education during the next two years. In September 1912, a series of lectures on educational and scientific subjects was instituted[23] and plans to build a new hall were announced.[24] By January 1913, the Mechanics Institute members were bemoaning the "apathy of local authorities" and considering advancing the scheme themselves. They were even prepared to entertain the idea of a joint venture, provided the rights of the Institute were respected.[25]

The outcome of the 1913 Victorian state elections seemed to dampen further the district's prospects, because the political complexion of the district and the government was now clearly polarised.[26] Indeed, the *Advertiser* took the view that the Council was deliberately thwarting the school proposal because of its opposition to the state government.[27] As a consequence, Footscray had "Miss[ed] the Bus" and lost what the *Advertiser* claimed was the preferential position it had once held and was now, at best, only equal with other districts which were clamouring for a technical school.[28] By 1914 it appeared that the government had indeed withdrawn the offer to build a school, but the forces in favour of providing technical schools in areas such as Brunswick and Coburg, irrespective of local financial input, were gaining strength. By 1915, the building of at least a junior technical school on the Nicholson Street site was a foregone conclusion.

The principal reason for the long delay in establishing the school was not so much the lack of a suitable site as the lack of resources to purchase one. The Footscray Council did not have the money to purchase the land itself; in fact it was in grave financial difficulty[29] and in 1912 was forced to lower the wages of municipal employees.[30] No-one else in the district was willing to purchase or donate land. Indeed, there is some evidence that industries were withholding their support until a site was chosen.[31] Under these circumstances, the only option was to select land already owned by the government which might be granted to the Education Department, or at least handed over at minimum cost — hence the focus on the Railway Reserve and the Mechanics Institute. Matters reached an impasse because neither the trustees of the Mechanics Institute nor the Railway Commissioners were keen to hand over their land.

The conclusion that there was little depth of support for a technical school in the years 1910 to 1916, apart from that of a few individuals, is hard to dispute. Why had civic leaders and industrialists apparently failed to grasp the chance to make "Footscray the Birmingham of Australia",[32] and why was the local Labor Party so half-hearted in its support of expanded educational opportunities? There is no doubt that parochialism and petty rivalries played a large part in preventing early agreement on such sites as were available. Underneath this public brawling, however, there were deeper problems with the attempt to establish a school through local initiative in the manner of the older technical colleges.

For all Shillabeer's and the *Advertiser*'s enthusiasm for technical education, theirs was a minority position. The rhetoric of technical education was rarely matched with cash or a rush of public enthusiasm anywhere in Victoria. The situation is best summed up in the words of the Director of Education, Frank Tate, who observed a

Lack of genuine interest in the work of the technical schools on the part of the general public and in many centres an absence of desire on the part of lads and young men to make use of them . . . The technical schools are managed by local councils, the value of the work should appeal to the public more fully than ordinary educational work, and yet the measure of support as shown by subscription lists is very small, while employers and parents seem indifferent to the attendance of their lads.[33]

Shillabeer's hopes that Footscray was somehow different were misplaced. All his drum beating about Footscray's civic reputation must be balanced against other views which condemned the Council for its attitude of "doleful indifference" and a "prevailing lethargy" that left the people of Footscray "accustomed" to "the doing of things by halves".[34] Indeed, a degree of dissatisfaction with the Council is borne out by the rapid turnover of councillors in the ensuing five years. None of this, however, should detract from the reality that the resources of a council only reflect the relative wealth and power of the area it governs. While Footscray may have been home to some profitable industries, very little of this wealth translated into public services and amenities for the district.

The employers of Footscray and Yarraville did not fall over themselves to support technical education in the district. Many of those manufacturers listed as members of the 1910 Committee never again took any recorded interest in the school. Very few manufacturers or employers were prepared to support technical education financially in any district and, as has been argued previously, the appeal to economic self-interest *per se* seems to have been misplaced. Such support as did emerge can be more properly attributed to other factors such as disinterested philanthropy and concern for social harmony.[35] There is ample evidence that in Footscray the strongest supporters of technical education were those with a reputation for paternalistic employment practices and concern for the welfare of their workers.

At the first meeting in 1910, one councillor had stressed that "many local employers fairly worshipped their employes [sic] and made a point of fraternising with them in good fellowship at least once a year", as if this in itself were enough to guarantee donations to a school fund.[36] There was indeed an historical alliance between labour and capital in Footscray that dated back to its early development as a centre of noxious trades. The historian of Footscray, John Lack, suggests that the working class were predisposed to support the views and practices of their employers in Footscray, especially in the noxious trades, because of their economic dependence. They were slow to realise the extent to which their interests were being discounted in pursuit of profits gained from unregulated and heavily polluting practices which were often very inefficient:

> Ignored during the mid-century debates on the noxious trades, the workers were manipulated in the 1880s to come to the defence of these trades. Proprietors skilfully presented critics of unregulated industry as meddlers proposing expulsion of factories and the destruction of prosperity.

As elsewhere in the state, this alliance was breaking down by 1910. Lack argues that, as absentee ownership and management became more common, "entrepreneurs were not able to so easily mobilize worker support for their untrammeled operations".[37] Nevertheless, the sentiments of social and economic consensus still had strong currency in the district. Nowhere were they more obvious than in the History of Footscray, published by the *Footscray Advertiser* in 1909, and in its regular reporting of industrial affairs, but the signs of strain were unmistakable. During 1910 and 1911 there were several serious industrial disputes and protracted strikes which Shillabeer sensed keenly were threatening his plans. A technical school, he believed, "needed the support of both sides" to be a "success".[38]

While the extent to which labour and capital might be persuaded that a technical school was in their mutual interest remains hard to measure from such a distance, what is clear is that those employers and managers who supported the school in some material way were almost all noted for their progressive industrial and commercial practices. To the extent that they appear to have been concerned to maximise profits through innovation and good management rather than by depressing wages and worker's conditions, their support for a technical school seems to have been an extension of these practices rather than the result of any desire to forestall an incipient breakdown of social harmony. These employers do appear to have been convinced that skills and profits were closely associated, and that they had a role in developing of those skills, but not necessarily to the extent of large capital endowments. Michaelis Hallenstein & Company, Leather Tanners, for example, was characterised as an establishment where

> every new invention in the shape of machinery, or for the more expeditious and effective treatment of the raw material,

has their instant attention, and no expense is spared to install all that is latest and best at their magnificently equipped works.[39]

In 1909, the company employed 200 to 300 workers at what the *Advertiser* considered "satisfactory wages", and had a reputation for good relations between workers and management.[40] J. H. Hooper & Company was also singled out for praise, for its enterprise and good management practices. Hooper manufactured much of his own merchandise and had the largest mail-order drapery business in Victoria. His success was attributed to "close attention to the requirements of customers on the part of the principals, with the whole-hearted co-operation of well-treated and satisfied employes [sic]".[41] Companies such as CSR and the Mt Lyell Mining Company were also noted for encouragement of worker organisation and support systems. Surprisingly, very few of the newer, more strictly engineering-based companies in the district played any public role in the school's early history. The one notable exception was Richardson Gears Pty Ltd, a progressive and most public-spirited enterprise.

The financial contribution of the supporters of the school was not great, but the commitment in time and energy of individuals far exceeded any possibility of personal gain underlying that support. In most respects business proprietors, like E. S. Hallenstein, E. W. Cuming, J. H. Hooper and the Richardson brothers became involved with the school out of individual interest and philanthropic inclination in the tradition of Ormond and Swinburne. They liked to think of themselves as both public-spirited and progressive thinkers and they sat comfortably alongside the successful skilled-artisans-turned-businessmen like Shillabeer and Tasman Smith. Perhaps what most linked the early supporters was the extent to which they had benefited from the opportunities a young country had offered them. They were almost to a man 'self made', and in the tradition of the Mechanics Institutes, believed that the key to success lay in self-improvement. At best, they were attracted to technical education because it seemed to offer a chance for another generation to share in the success which they enjoyed. In this regard, there seems to be little to distinguish the nature of the support for technical education in Footscray from that demonstrated elsewhere, despite the early financial difficulties.

The very assumption, however, that there were large sums of

money available to be donated is open to challenge. There were some quite good reasons why large donations were not possible, even when employers were strongly sympathetic. Many of Footscray's manufacturing enterprises were newly established, and it is likely, therefore, that their capital was fully, if not in some cases, over committed. While there is no doubt that some of the local firms were successful and profitable, it seems reasonable to assume that in the economic climate of the times, most of this profit needed to be reinvested in order to maintain growth. This is in marked contrast to the established pastoral wealth of men such as Ormond. Furthermore, much of the capital sustaining enterprises in Footscray and Yarraville was not 'local'. Subsidiaries of interstate or foreign-owned companies were managed by men with little freedom to direct resources to local projects. In a dependent economy, such as Victoria's, the capital resources, especially in the area of manufacturing, were simply not very extensive. The history of Australian economic development had already clearly demonstrated the need for substantial government involvement wherever large capital outlays were required. Finally, it seems that industrialists had adopted a rather different view of their role in the provision of education than that assumed by the framers of the 1910 Act. To the extent that they accepted the arguments about economic growth and education, manufacturers seem to have seen their primary role as the provision of opportunities for skilled employment for the graduates of a state-supported education system to which they offered only advice and peripheral financial support.

Any assessment of the attitudes of the largely silent 'working class' of the district to the idea of a technical school must, of necessity, be highly speculative. What is clear is that the most enthusiastic promoters of technical education inside the Labour Movement were those already skilled, and it is reasonable to assume that skilled artisans in Footscray would have been similarly inclined. They would have been susceptible to the rhetoric and influenced by the high profile of a small, flourishing sector based on engineering as a symbol of progress in Footscray coupled with a widespread sense of crisis about a skilled labour shortage. Yet the extent of the demand for highly skilled artisans in the district was probably exaggerated. Of the 16 principal industrial establishments listed in the 1909 history of Footscray, excluding food, clothing and drink, only five directly required engineering skills. Yet, it was still assumed that engineering was the backbone of industrial development in Footscray.

The reality of Footscray's industrial situation was that it still required large numbers of unskilled or semi-skilled workers for its noxious and unpleasant industries such as fertiliser and other chemical manufacture, meat and carcass processing, tyre manufacture and rope making. To the extent that we know anything about the educational preferences of unskilled workers, some would have been attracted by the idea of an independent working class education, but many would have been too ground down by the insecurities of their existence to raise their aspirations to the heights of keeping their children at school until well into their teens. In any case, they still faced a challenge in getting their younger offspring a satisfactory primary education in the area. The Footscray branches of the Labor Party appear to have been generally conservative and not noticeably interested in education in any form.[42] Those who were especially keen for a technical education could always attend the Working Men's College or Sunshine Technical School. Nevertheless, it has to be assumed that Footscray workers were no more or less excited by the issue than those elsewhere in the state whom one historian of Victorian education policy, Bessant, has characterised as apathetic.[43]

There remains one final issue to be considered in assessing the difficulties in getting the school built and that is the changing nature of the district. Footscray in 1909 was not a working class suburb in the sense we understand the term today — that is, composed almost entirely of people working for wages in the lower paid occupations — though it was in a process of transformation. Rather, it was an economically and socially complex community where many employers still lived close to their business premises. The suburb had its share of fine houses as well as ramshackle workers cottages; of paternalistic, resident employers as well as devoted company employees who could 'take round the hat' to buy a farewell gift for their 'boss' about to leave on an overseas trip. In this sense, Footscray bore some resemblance to Birmingham and the potential for a technical school to consolidate the mutuality of industrialist and employee was not entirely fanciful.

However, the alliance between capital and labour in Footscray, as elsewhere in the state, was coming under stress during the period, and the fortunes of the technical school proposal cannot be separated from the shifts in that relationship. Deakinite Liberalism, which placed a very high value on technical education, was on the wane in Victoria as many of its leading personalities left for the federal arena and the anti-Labor alliance consolidated. Greater polarisation was evident right down to the municipal level where, as we have seen, in 1912 a Labor majority was elected for the first time. The old rhetoric about social consensus that had underpinned the initial push for a school had ceased to fit the current situation, though individuals from both sides of politics could still easily agree on the value of technical education. In the long run, Footscray was to become a more homogeneous working class suburb and for better or ill, the technical school, when it was built, would substantially improve the opportunity for the upward social mobility of the clever and motivated sons of Footscray. In the short run, as the local member for Footscray, Eddie Warde, put it, the district had principally "to thank the local Council and certain parliamentary members of their district" rather than any enthusiasm of local manufacturers, for the school.[44]

1. Cr Shillabeer, *Footscray Advertiser*, 30 September 1911.
2. *Footscray Advertiser*, 8 July, 12 & 26 August 1911.
3. *Ibid.*, 26 December 1914.
4. D. I. Robson, 'The Development of Junior Technical Education in Victoria', M. Ed., University of Melbourne, 1967, p 141.
5. *Ibid.*, p 111.
6. *Footscray Advertiser*, 11 October 1913.
7. *Ibid.*, 12 August 1911.
8. *Ibid.*, 26 August 1911.
9. *Footscray Advertiser*, 30 September 1911.
10. *Ibid.*
11. *Footscray Advertiser*, 16 September 1911.
12. The Committee consisted of Cr Shillabeer, Cr McNeilage, J. H. Hooper, W. L. Flewellen, E. W. Trend, Rev. A. R. Byers, G. B. Bennet, W. H. Cuming, Dr J. Webb (District Health Inspector.)
13. *Footscray Advertiser*, 9 September 1911.
14. Corner Buckley and Nicholson Sts; Near Seddon Station running from Pole St along Bell St; Corner Stephenson and Somerville Rd, Yarraville; York St, Yarraville; Spotswood — 5 acres attached to Spotswood Primary School site.
15. *Footscray Advertiser*, 9 September 1911.
16. *Ibid.*, 25 November 1911.
17. *Ibid.*

18. *Ibid.*, 20 January 1912.
19. *Ibid.*, 25 May 1912.
20. *Ibid.*, 25 November 1911.
21. *Ibid.*, 27 January 1912. See also 25 May, 1 June and 27 July 1912.
22. *Ibid.*, 7 September 1912. See also editorial, 12 October 1912.
23. *Ibid.*, 21 September 1912.
24. *Ibid.*, 26 October 1912.
25. *Ibid.*, 18 January 1913.
26. Edgar MLC, who had been Minister for Lands, was defeated by a Labor candidate.
27. *Footscray Advertiser*, 5 July 1913.
28. *Ibid.*, 29 November 1913.
29. There are continual references to the near bankruptcy of the Council throughout 1912 in the *Footscray Advertiser*.
30. *Footscray Advertiser*, 9 March 1912.
31. The representative of CSR, for example, stated that 'before subscriptions were called for something definite should be done as to the site of the proposed college. He would require more information on that point before recommending his company to subscribe'. *Footscray Advertiser*, 30 September 1911.
32. *Ibid.*, 11 January 1913.
33. Quoted in B. Simm 'Bendigo School of Mines,' unpublished MS, Victorian Ministry of Education, History of Education Unit.
34. *Footscray Advertiser*, 6 January 1912. Letter to the Editor dated 15 December 1911.
35. See Chapter One
36. *Footscray Advertiser*, 21 May 1910.
37. J. Lack, *op. cit.*, p 199.
38. *Footscray Advertiser*, 25 February 1911.
39. *Ibid.*, 14 February 1914.
40. *Ibid.*
41. H. Michel, *op. cit.*
42. For example the Worker's Educational Association set up by the Political Labor Council in 1913 received little support. *Footscray Advertiser*, 1 November 1913.
43. Bessant, *op cit.*, p 60.
44. *Footscray Advertiser*, 4 March 1916.

CHAPTER THREE **An "unremarkable"**
building on a "fine corner block"[1]

When in, March 1916, Footscray Technical School finally opened
its doors, it was to a community feeling deeply the economic
and military costs of war. Many husbands, sons, brothers and
fathers were absent; at home, unemployment was high, prices
were rising. The export markets which sustained many of Footscray's largest industrial enterprises were severely restricted by
the war's effect on markets and shipping. It was a community in
crisis, but the impulse towards technical education had not
entirely faltered. In late 1914, a deputation from the Footscray
City Council to the Minister for Education was promised that an
amount for a junior technical school would be set aside in the
next budget estimates.[2] From this point, planning proceeded
smoothly. The foundation stone was laid in September 1915 and
the building on the corner of Nicholson and Buckley Streets
ready for occupancy only a few weeks after the official school
year began.[3]

It was in most ways an inauspicious beginning, and not simply because it was war time. The site was central, but clearly too
small. The four-room building was unremarkable and its design
took little account of the "fine corner block" on which it stood.[4]
A junior technical school, with provision for night classes,
under the control of the Education Department was a far cry
from the dreams of the men who had gathered in 1911. Their
model had been the semi-autonomous colleges, such as the
Working Men's College or the Ballarat School of Mines, where
staffing and expenditure were controlled by a council comprised
of local civic leaders and industrialists. The main focus of these
"Council-controlled Colleges" was senior technical work, that is

30

Architects' impression of the original school building 1916

Diplomas and Expert Certificates, though most of them offered courses to bridge the gap between elementary schools and the higher-grade work as well as a range of classes such as drawing, design and commercial subjects. Since the state government provided the essential funding and exercised control over the content of the higher-grade courses, the degree of autonomy was, in reality, quite circumscribed. Nevertheless, newer schools like Footscray, where the Council's role was purely advisory except in the matter of non-academic and part-time staff, felt disadvantaged.

The major difference between those colleges founded before 1910 and those established after that date was probably that the latter had always to deal firstly with a government department, while the former had direct access to the Minister for Public Instruction. More seriously, the Victorian government was still far from committed to providing the full cost of secondary education, let alone the money required for outfitting workshops and laboratories for senior technical work. There seemed little likelihood in 1916 that the School would ever acquire diploma-granting status unless substantial local contributions were made. Since resources were no more abundant in 1916 than they had been in 1911, Footscray Technical School was destined to remain "a chronically poor institution with big obligations" for many years.[5]

Another problem with potential to significantly affect the type of school into which Footscray Technical School might develop, was that the issue of education versus mere 'training' and the appropriate focus of 'technical' schools was still unresolved within the community. Worse still, within the Education Department the Director, Frank Tate, and his Chief Inspector of Technical Schools, Donald Clark, were moving in different directions on the subject. Tate very rapidly came to the conclusion that the technical school curriculum was too vocational while Clark insisted that "general education" was so called because it aimed at nothing in particular.[6] On the whole, Clark was successful in imposing a rather narrow definition of technical education on Departmental schools, yet for many reasons Footscray Technical School would, of necessity, be pressed to fill a far wider role in the community than perhaps either Tate or Clark envisaged, or would have thought desirable if they had.

Footscray was a district which desperately needed a range of educational services, especially for boys *and girls* beyond elementary level. Occasionally, even the *Footscray Advertiser* looked beyond technical training to the need for secondary education and a wider range of choices for children than the assumptions about what sort of schools were good for working-class areas implied. A technical college would, in its view,

> give the boys a chance to excel in whatever calling they adopt; provide a means for acquiring a knowledge of domestic economy that too many girls of today lack, and would be followed by the establishment of higher elementary schools at which the youths of the city would have facilities for learning, and by means of scholarships, opportunities for advancement that would enable the clever, capable and industrious to reach the highest pinnacle of any profession or calling.[7]

The educational opportunities for children in the Footscray were also limited by the inadequate provision of elementary education. Schools in the area were overcrowded, poorly housed and sometimes characterised as breeding grounds for diphtheria more than for trained minds.[8]

Despite all this, those who had remained committed to the dream through all the petty wranglings about a site took comfort in the knowledge that they had the best that could be provided in the circumstances. The quality of human effort expended in the development of Footscray Technical School into a significant institution, both within the western suburbs and the Education Department, is enhanced when considered in this context of insufficient resources and bureaucratic difficulties. Footscray Technical School was blessed from the beginning with a committed and talented Council, a Principal with a clear educational vision and talent for leadership and a staff that was dedicated and loyal. As to the students, the subsequent careers of large numbers of them are testament to both their own qualities and the guidance and instruction offered to them within the School.

The Footscray Technical School Council, appointed in December 1915, included members of the Footscray City Council, the local Labor Party, a group of businessmen, and a few interested individuals. Support for the Labor Party in Footscray had increased over the preceding five years and it was well represented on the initial School Council, if only briefly. Among the more significant members was Jack Lemmon, Labor MLA for Williamstown, who had interested himself in the school idea from the very beginning. His commitment to technical education dated back at least to 1899, when he was elected Victorian Trades Hall delegate to the Working Men's College, and, while he resigned from the Footscray Council in mid-1916, school representatives continued to enjoy ready access to his ear. He was to become an influential Minister for Public Instruction in the Labor governments of 1926–1927 and 1929–1931 and as such profoundly influenced the general framework of education policy within which the School developed. The Hon. W. H. Fielding, Labor MLC for West Melbourne Province, was also a member of the School Council but he died in April 1916, while J. L. Dearie, a Labor city councillor, resigned "due to pressure of business" in November 1916. The only other Labor member of the School Council, Cr A. J. Pearce, who was Mayor in 1916 and Secretary of the Engine Drivers and Engineers' Union, was dropped from the School Council in 1919 for failing to attend meetings. The Parliamentary Labor Party was not again directly represented on the School Council until 1947.

The Footscray City Council was represented from the beginning, frequently by the Mayor, and it provided tuition fees for one year for 15 students.[9] It was always willing to asist the school wherever it could with access to sporting facilities and in putting additional pressure on the government to improve and develop the School's facilities. The Williamstown City Council also provided scholarships[10] and was represented by Cr James T. Gray continuously from 1929 to 1955 when Williamstown acquired a technical school of its own.

Business proprietors were represented by J. H. Hooper, P. R. Richardson, F. E. Shillabeer, J. Jamieson, E. S. Hallenstein and T. F. M. Smith. Hooper and Shillabeer had been amongst the earliest supporters of the school while Jamieson, as the proprietor of the *Footscray Advertiser*, had provided a strong editorial advocacy. Neither Hooper nor Jamieson, however, was a potential employer of higher technical education graduates and even Shillabeer, as a building contractor, was, at best, only a small-scale employer of apprentices. None of these men remained on the School Council for long. Jamieson died in 1922, and Hooper resigned in the same year due to indifferent health and long distance travel. Before doing so, however, he provided £200 to found a scholarship for commercial classes recognising a demand in the community for access to commercial as well as technical subjects.

Shillabeer's interest in technical education appears to have been a strong personal commitment and no doubt grew out of his own 'trade' background. Devonshire born, he had served an apprenticeship as a carpenter and joiner in London before coming to Victoria in 1886 where he eventually established himself as a leading contractor. He relied heavily on government building contracts. His expertise as a builder was of great value to the School but he resigned from the Council in August 1918. Tasman F. M. Smith, a local architect, had attended evening classes at the Hotham School of Design while working as a carpenter. His interest in technical education included a long association with the Mechanics Institute, and, while he resigned from the School Council in 1920 "because he wanted the position occupied by some more influential man",[11] he endowed a scholarship of £10 per annum and made an annual donation to the School library till his death in 1934, when he bequeathed the School £300 for scholarships and prizes.

The Hallenstein and Richardson families were associated with the School for much longer. E. S. Hallenstein of Michaelis Hallenstein, Tanners, remained on the Council till July 1939, though he was overseas for extended periods. Philanthropy, rather than any special need for the type of skills taught at Footscray Technical School, seems to have been his primary motivation. His company donated at least £150 to the engineering equipment fund in the years 1916 to 1918 and was always willing to provide small items of equipment. Michaelis Hallenstein was also represented over a period of many years by senior management, not the least of whom was Edward Johnstone, Assistant Manager at the Tannery. Johnstone, also an executive member of the Mechanics Institute, had been active on behalf of the School since 1911 and acted as first Secretary of the Council. He set up his own tannery in North Melbourne in 1919 and resigned from the School Council in 1925. Two years previously, Isaac Boas, Michaelis Hallenstein's Chemical Engineer, had also joined the Council. He remained till 1939 when he was appointed head of the Forest Products Division of CSIRO.[12] The Richardson brothers of Richardson Gears Pty Ltd were the only proprietors on the Council who were engaged in engineering and metal working. Percy Richardson died of Spanish flu in 1919[13] and was replaced by his brother Henry, who remained on the Council till 1937. The Company went out of its way to provide employment opportunities for boys from the school and like Hooper and Jamieson the Richardson family sent their own sons to the school.

Of the remaining original Council members, the majority were senior managers of local enterprises and most remained involved with the school for many years. E. W. Trend, Works Manager at the Mt Lyell Mining Co, Yarraville, and a graduate of the Ballarat School of Mines had been a member of the 1911 Committee. President of the Council from 1919 to 1932, President of the Technical Schools Association in 1929, and technical schools representative on the Council of the University of Melbourne from 1928 to 1932, he went on to play an influential role in the development of technical education in the state before he resigned in 1932. D. Bayley was General Manager of Colonial Ammunition Works (later Commonwealth Ammunition Factory), which was to prove a consistent employer of Footscray exit students. Bayley resigned in 1922, but the Ammunition Works was continuously represented on the Council by senior management until 1966. Joseph Carmody, Footscray City Electrical Engineer, remained a dedicated member of Council till a few months before his death in 1949. Finally, there was Dr Henry Box, the local doctor, whose interest in technical education began with the Mechanics Institute and whose association with Footscray Technical School lasted until a few months before his death in 1964. In 1919, he endowed the inaugural scholarship with a donation of £200 and for many years acted as the School's medical officer.[14]

Among the more significant early replacement councillors

were Robert Ferguson, Arthur Hughes and Roy Parsons. Ferguson, Assistant Chief Mechanical Engineer with the Victorian Railways, based at the Newport Workshops, represented one of the most important single employers of exit students from Footscray Technical School from early 1917 till 1943, when he resigned due to ill health at the age of 80. As a member of the 1911 Committee, he belongs with those whose own engineering expertise led them to support the expansion of opportunities for others to enter the field. Hughes, Engineer in Chief of Colonial Sugar Refinery, remained active on the Council from 1920 till his death in 1948. Roy Parsons, General Manager of Colonial Gas Association, joined the Council in 1918 and thus there began a long and close association with a man whose energies were directed to many projects within Footscray but whose interest in technical education was deep and influential. President of Footscray Technical School Council from 1932 till 1943 and again from 1951 till 1955, he was also a long serving President of the Council of Swinburne Technical School. He was an active member of the Technical Schools Association, technical schools representative on the Council of the University of Melbourne and a member of the Council for Public Instruction. In these capacities he played an active role in the development of policy regarding technical education throughout the period from 1930 till 1950.

The initial membership of the Council had included categories such as fee-paying parents, and bodies which made a substantial financial contribution were entitled to a position. It seems clear however that 'ordinary' parents and even perhaps the Labor Party men did not feel very comfortable, and by the 1920s the Council was entirely dominated by businessmen, managers or professionals. Since this was more an advisory than a governing body, it was not, except in the most general sense, a representative body. Members did not formally represent any organisation or enterprise, and neither staff nor parents exercised any formal role in the governance of the school.

The new Council turned its attention immediately to the recruitment of students and the appointment of staff. Though they had no real power in the matter of the appointment of a Principal, they had firm ideas. He must be a man with "High grades from a technical institution, organising ability, experience of junior and senior subjects and ten years experience of industry".[15] Their hopes that Charles Fenner, head of the Ballarat School of Mines, would accept the position were disappointed.[16] The position was accepted by Charles Archibald Hoadley who, on the face of it, fitted only a few of the Council's criteria. Under the circumstances, however, they did better than might have been expected in securing anyone to head a junior technical school of 200 pupils in an industrial suburb in the middle of a war.

Hoadley in 1916 was 29, son of the successful businessman and devout Methodist philanthropist, Abel Hoadley. He had degrees in science and mining engineering, and a Master of Science degree in geology. He had worked for two years as a mining engineer for Broken Hill Co Ltd at Port Pirie South Australia before joining Douglas Mawson's expedition to the Antarctic in 1911.[17] At the time of his appointment, he was lecturing at the Ballarat School of Mines. Hoadley's academic background was suitable but his obvious preference for mining engineering and geology was not ideal for the development of a school of mechanical engineering. His teaching background was virtually non-existent. His practical work experience was limited, and he clearly had no experience of administration. He was also a fit, eligible bachelor with no war record.

At first glance, his greatest asset may well have been the aura of Antarctic hero in an era when exploration of the world's remaining wild places had great romantic appeal, inspiring notions of leadership training. One admiring tribute captures the hint of romance Hoadley evidently trailed with the lines:

> From vast eternal snows you came,
> With multi-hued Antarctic skies,
> Deep-imprinted on your soul
> And visions in your eyes. [18]

Another tribute suggested the positive way in which this experience could be seen as fitting a man for leadership:

> The years he spent with Mawson's Party amid the Antarctic ice greatly influenced his character.
>
> Men who share great dangers and hardships develop a stability and a poise, and a quality of comradeship, that stamp them in later years. Archie Hoadley talked little about his Antarctic experiences, but when, on rare occasions, he could be persuaded to yarn round the camp-fire, or to give an illustrated lecture, one felt strongly that his own deep, compelling

sense of comradeship, and his great and generous love for his fellows, were rich legacies from ties forged in Antarctic solitudes.[19]

Wherever he acquired them, Hoadley had qualities that were not easily placed on a career resumé, but his time with the School would be marked by enthusiasm, dedication and inspiring leadership. He may not have been the most methodical of administrators, but he was a man with a gift for warm friendship with people of all ages, a captivating teacher and an acute judge of character. More significantly, he brought to the task a clear and broad educational vision. The School Council of 1915 may not have realised it, nor might they have appreciated it if they had, but what they got in Hoadley was not an engineer but an educationalist, and with him the chance to create an important local institution rather than simply a trade school of the narrow, limiting type that seemed almost inevitable at the time.

Hoadley was joined by eight full-time and eight part-time teachers. One of them was appointed to take charge of the junior boys, thus effectively elevating Hoadley to the position of Principal even though he was not formally classified as such till 1919. Frank Treyvaud brought to the school a distinguished background and a teaching style marked by "skill and intelligence".[20] He had commenced his teaching career in 1893 and by 1905 had sufficiently impressed his superiors to be selected as one of the first group of twenty teachers to undertake studies leading to a Diploma of Education[21] qualifying them for leadership positions in the new secondary schools that were established after 1910.

Principally a teacher of mathematics, a subject essential to a truly technical institution, Treyvaud also brought valuable experience of teaching and the ways of the Education Department that Hoadley lacked. As a team they complemented each other, and the School benefited immensely. Both are remembered as kind, but "Trivo" was more the conventional 'disciplinarian' of his times, as befitted a headmaster no doubt. Few students, however, recall this with resentment. As one observed:

Mr Treyvaud's approach was necessary — at 14 years of age boys did not always understand the full meaning of Mr Hoadley's talks. . . . There was room for the discipline too.[22]

The rest of the original full-time staff comprised S. Birtles (Chemistry), W. H. Nicholls (sheetmetal), C. F. Mudie (art), L. H. Reynolds (English), T. S. Hart (science), R. Spence (carpentry) and C. Morrison (drawing). Of these, Mudie and Nicholls were to remain with the school for almost their entire working lives. These men began teaching 192 day students and 132 evening students with the help of some part-time staff in a two storey brick building that contained three classrooms, and two small offices downstairs and four classrooms upstairs. In addition an old hall on the site was used as a carpentry workshop.

Landscaping the grounds around the school was left to local initiative and the *Advertiser* promoted a tree planting campaign in mid-1917 to overcome their "tip" like appearance and shield the school from the railway line.[23] The placement of the school had been a victory for centrality, and such proximity to the administrative and retail heart of the city certainly gave the school a high profile in the district. Constantly full of people and activity, "the Tech" rapidly became one of Footscray's defining features. On the other hand, the site was woefully inadequate for the needs of energetic adolescent boys, and there was little room for expansion. Indeed, Hoadley considered it an "iniquity" that a school for over 500 boys in the day time should have been established with no playing field whatsoever.[24] This lack of space and amenities, especially lunch shelters or rooms, added a negative element to the relationship between the "Tech" boys and the surrounding area. What was to become a constant theme of complaint about boys wandering and littering in their lunchtime first surfaced in early 1918, when the *Advertiser* noted with distaste that students could be seen "eating their dinners after the manner of blackfellows".[25]

Small as the number of boys displaying interest in studying at the senior level was (only eight of the first 219 went on to the Working Men's College), the development of the School would be severely retarded if such courses could not be offered. The members of the School Council had not abandoned the dream of an engineering school but engineering workshops were essential to a technical school in any case, and they saw the acquisition of these as their next task. The government offered to provide the buildings if £2000 was raised locally to buy equipment.[26] A committee was formed in March 1916[27] to raise the £2000, but once again local money was not immediately forthcoming. On the whole, however, it was easier to promote the extension of a tangible asset than a mere idea, and the required sum was in hand by August 1917.

In a state of considerable excitement, the Principal and Council drew up plans for £8000 worth of buildings but, as was to be so often the case in the future, only half that amount was actually made available.[28] By 1918 a turning and fitting workshop with rooms above for chemistry, mathematics and engineering drawing provided the school with the nucleus of a school of mechanical engineering.[29] The resources the state devoted to education remained very limited, and the School might well have stagnated but for a windfall gain in the form of Commonwealth Repatriation Department funds. Footscray Technical School was chosen as a centre for the retraining of returned servicemen, and a large building sufficient to the purpose of a senior technical school was built in addition to the approved workshops. This reverted to School use in 1922, just as the first diploma classes were getting under way.[30] This was only the first of several occasions when an injection of Commonwealth funds would significantly boost the school's resources and fortunes.

1919, though a year of promise, was beset with difficulty. The classes for returned servicemen imposed great strains on the understaffed and barely established School. Bureaucratic difficulties were compounded by the need to deal with the Commonwealth Repatriation Department as well as the Victorian Education Department. The maintenance of separate budgets and stock records was particularly onerous. Lines of authority for both the staff and the servicemen were confused. A hint of the difficulties encountered is found in the remark of the senior engineering instructor, C. W. Joy, that if the Repatriation classes had

> been under military control there would have been no trouble at all. They are now free citizens and are supposed to be forgiven everything short of murder. They have taken the words of Prime Minister Hughes almost literally. They fix their own time of leaving etc. Unless their pay can be stopped by the Department that is controlling them it will continue.[31]

The Principal was not only responsible for the greater part of equipping his School for the new classes, but also for finding employment for the retrained men once they reached the statutory 40% efficiency of a fully qualified tradesman. Moreover, most of the work they did in the School was supposed to be on a "commercial basis". Hoadley took the task very seriously, and the surveys and contacts he made in this period laid the foundation for a network of contacts with western suburbs employers and industries that would prove of immense benefit the School and its exit students for the next quarter of a century. Hoadley threw himself into this work with special zeal, and while the compounding difficulties of cost over-runs and bureaucratic insensitivity may have contributed to his decision to resign at the end of 1920, his work was recognised by those who observed it closely. The Director of Education, Frank Tate, commended him for willingly accepting the "extraordinary demands" that were made of him, and concluded that

> the enthusiasm and vigor with which you attacked the very pressing problem of providing more workshop accommodation and equipping same, were mainly responsible for the large measure of success achieved.[32]

Wallace Ross, Supervisor of Accounts in the Education Department, also expressed his appreciation in a similar vein, noting Hoadley's unfailing "courtesy and assistance" and his admiration of the manner in which he had

> carried through the stupendous task of erecting and equipping workshops during a period full of industrial trouble. That this was superimposed on his ordinary work and beset with difficulties, not the least of which was the entire absence of a precedent from which guidance might be available, makes his success all the greater. [33]

The difficulties associated with the Retraining Scheme were exacerbated by the the Spanish flu epidemic of 1919. The School's central location and solid structure made it an ideal emergency hospital, and it was so used from January to March and again in May, thus totally disrupting the year's school work. Hoadley himself acted as Superintendent during the first closure, abandoning his planned trip to the United States and submitting to isolation from his friends and family. The Richardson brothers played a primary role in outfitting the buildings for use as a hospital, and Percy, who "for days at a time . . . neglected his private interests in order to meet the needs of the patients", contracted the disease himself and died.[34] The junior boys were accommodated at South Melbourne Technical School, and evening classes were severely affected by both the closure and the epidemic itself.

When, in 1920, the first boys enrolled in a full-time diploma course, the dreams of the earliest planners were almost realised. It would be many years however, before diploma students comprised more than a minuscule proportion of total enrolments, and the School Council remained frustrated at the slow progress and its lack of real power to set priorities. In September 1920, it complained that the only function it seemed to have was that of "advising the Minister of Education and so far no regard appears to have been paid to such advice".[35] The frustration was inevitable. The Minister was chiefly concerned with the provision of educational facilities for those students compelled by law to attend school until they were 14. The Council, on the other hand, displayed little interest in this section of the School apart from providing medals for sports events and the like. Its primary interests were the development of a senior technical school, the provision of day classes for apprentices, action to make this a widespread feature of industrial training, and the night school. These were areas for which the government of the day had either not yet accepted responsibility or expected much local initiative and funding. Even such 'essential' elements of school life as books for the library were funded on a pound for pound basis. The local resources available remained a mere trickle in comparison with the School's great needs, and the bargaining power of the School Council was thereby greatly limited.

Compounding these frustrations was the need to deal with a government department designed to cater for a dispersed and very basic education system whose officers had little experience of, or sympathy for, the different and far more complex needs of an institution like Footscray Technical School. They were also perhaps not used to the energy and impatience of leading industrialists, men used to wielding power and getting rapid results. It was also a department with scant regard for teachers as professionals. Even though the era of payment by results was past, it was a deeply authoritarian system which prescribed in great detail the courses to be taught and the way they were to be taught. Schools and staff were subjected to close and frequent inspections and peremptory interrogations on the smallest deviation from the expected, be it examination results or telephone bills. Headmasters were accorded little more respect by the Department than student teachers, whose progress in examinations was watched in the minutest detail.

Running a school that was even a little different from the norm, as defined by the Education Department, must have been a harassing experience, but for Hoadley and his Council the task was a constant battle to make the Department even understand the nature of the task they were carrying out, let alone provide the resources they needed to do it well. Even where officials began to glimpse the nature of the difficulties faced, there was little inclination to do anything about them. When, for example, the Supervisor of Accounts observed that the amount of clerical work was so heavy that the equipment ledger was kept by the Principal, a task he thought hardly the duty of the Principal of so large a school, he nevertheless concluded that

> as office accommodation is very limited, . . . and as the Princi-pal has made no request for assistance in this direction, I do not feel inclined at this stage to make any recommendation in regard to providing clerical assistance.[36]

The irony of this is that if Hoadley had not in this particular instance sought additional clerical assistance, it must have been a mere oversight. Two of the problems that exercised the Council and Hoadley almost constantly were poor office accommo-dation and inadequate clerical assistance. The Department appeared quite incapable of altering its views on the numbers of clerical staff or salary ceilings in order to accommodate the way in which Footscray differed from a primary school. Lack of sup-port staff would continue to be a problem for the School for most of its history.

Hoadley must have at times been totally exasperated with a department that seemed to care more about rulers and screws missing from stock records and the intricate arrangements of time tables than the welfare of students or staff or the quality of education offered. The task was daunting at times and the risk that Education Department schools would always seem the poor relations of the "council-controlled schools" and indeed the high schools as pathways to high status professions was always considerable. The history of Education Department technical schools in the 1920s was, as a consequence, hardly spectacular, and Footscray's achievements take on greater significance in this context. As the Director of Education, M. P. Hansen, remarked in 1930, "The technical schools founded in Melbourne since 1911 seem to me not to have succeeded very well with one exception".[37] That exception, he believed, was Footscray and in large measure Footscray had established itself as something more that a junior technical school by virtue of the determination of its Council and the quality of leadership of its Principal, Arch Hoadley, affectionately known as the "the Chief", long before he assumed the title officially within the world of Scouting.

1. *Footscray Advertiser*, 4 September 1915.
2. *Ibid.*, 26 December 1914.
3. *Ibid.*, 4 September 1915.
4. *Ibid*.
5. *Ibid.*, 30 June 1917.
6. R. H. Whitely, 'Donald Clark First Chief Inspector of Technical Schools', M. Ed., University of Melbourne, 1980, p 43.
7. *Footscray Advertiser*, 6 July 1912.
8. This is quite a consistent theme of the *Footscray Advertiser* in this period. See, for example, 11 & 18 May & 8 June 1912.
9. These were worth £3. In 1922 the arrangement was changed to 3 scholarships worth £15 p.a.
10. £10 p.a. for three years for a course in Civil Engineering.
11. FTS Council Minutes, 9 September 1920.
12. B. Nairn & G. Serle, *Australian Dictionary of Biography*, Vol 8, 1981–1939, Melbourne, 1981, pp 332–333.
13. See below, p 41.
14. Original members not mentioned are James Millar who resigned in February 1916; C. Walker of the Footscray 'Independent' who resigned October 1918 and S. G. Garnsworthy who was asked to resign due to non-attendance August 1919.
15. FTS Council Minutes, 9 December 1915.
16. *Footscray Advertiser*, 18 December 1915.
17. B. Nairn & G. Serle, *op. cit.*, Vol. 9, pp 312–313.
18. 'A Tribute from Footscray to C A (Arch) Hoadley', typescript initialed RR [?Ron Rankin], FIT Archive.
19. Commissioner W. D. Kennedy, 'Chief', *The Victorian Scout*, 15 March 1947, p 8.
20. Inspectors' Report, 5 September 1904. Victorian Ministry of Education (formerly Victorian Education Department), Records pertaining to Footscray Technical School. These files are in poor condition, incomplete and have not been stored in such a way that easy retrieval of any particular file is possible. Hereafter these shall be referred to as VED Records.
21. See *The Educational Magazine*, December 1965, p 493 for more detail on this first 'Diploma Twenty' who were very much under the personal influence of Tate.

22. Hubert Harris, (enrolled 1916), *Footscray Advertiser,* 13 April 1966.
23. *Footscray Advertiser,*16 June 1917.
24. C. A. Hoadley to Mayor of Footscray, 29 April 1927. Footscray City Council Archives, Box C50, File T4.
25. *Footscray Advertiser,* 13 April 1918.
26. FTS Council Minutes, 2 March 1916.
27. There were two deputations to the Minister in July and November 1916, FTS Council Minutes, 13 July 1916, and *Footscray Advertiser,* 14 October 1916.
28. *Footscray Advertiser,* 21 April 1917.
29. For a report of the official opening of this building, see *Footscray Advertiser,* 27 April 1918.
30. FTS Council Minutes, 21 May 1919.
31. Report of an enquiry conducted by the Footscray Technical School Council into complaints made by Mr Samuel Hampson, 16 March 1920, VED Records.
32. F. Tate to C. A. Hoadley, 9 March 1921, VED Records.
33. *Brown and Red,* 1919.
34. FTS Council Minutes, 9 September 1920.
35. Report of C. Wallace Ross, Supervisor of Accounts [no date but part of a bundle including a letter dated 19 March 1920], VED Records.
36. M. P. Hansen, 'Technical Education. Statement (62 pp) circulated by Mr. Clark. Reply by the Director of Education'; p 11, Typed MS, Victorian Public Records Office (PRO), Council of Public Education, VA 2310, VPRS 10298, Box 62.

CHAPTER FOUR "To educate workers for a life as well as a living"[1]

Principals at this time exercised almost complete executive authority and so can reasonably be credited with the major responsibility for the success or otherwise of their schools. Arch Hoadley brought to his role as principal a degree of commitment, leadership and vision that has lent his period in charge of the School a legendary quality. His clear and strongly held convictions made possible a quality of education that transcended the limited aims of the School's designers and to some extent compensated Footscray for its narrow range of secondary education options. Hoadley also adopted Footscray as his home; soon known to every employer and interested parent, he was also local Scoutmaster and an active citizen in many other ways. When he died in 1947 he was a revered and admired figure, almost as much an 'institution' in Footscray as was the school he had led for thirty years. However the warmth and generosity that explains the depth of affection so evident in people's memories of him should not be allowed to overshadow other more substantial attributes.

Hoadley in 1916 was a young man with no domestic ties who loved the outdoor life. He also loved music, books and academic research. At 29, however, he was still not exactly settled. While he threw himself into the position at Footscray with energy, he does not appear to have immediately accepted it as his life's vocation. Halfway through 1916, he applied unsuccessfully to join the party set up to rescue the men left behind in the Antarctic by Shackleton. Then, in October, he admitted to the Council that he was considering a move to another sphere of work. Much as he had enjoyed his work in Footscray, he recognised that it must necessarily be circumscribed in an industrial area like Footscray. His interest was in research work in geology and minerology, branches of study never likely to be had in the Footscray school curriculum: these he would be able to continue at the college he proposed to apply for, Ballarat.[2]

He was not successful. Not surprisingly, he then attempted to enlist in early 1917. He was, however, told that the Minister considered he could best serve the community by remaining where he was.[3] Then, no sooner had the war ended than Hoadley was applying for six months' leave of absence to go overseas.[4] This did not eventuate for a variety of reasons and for two years he worked at full stretch to establish the School on a firmer footing and make the Repatriation Training Scheme a success.

Both 1919 and 1920 were frustrating and difficult years, marred by the Spanish flu epidemic, an unpleasant conflict with a Repatriation trade instructor, cost over-runs, enormous work loads and escalating bureaucratic difficulties with the Education Department. We can only speculate as to why Hoadley resigned suddenly at the end of 1920 to take up a position as General Manager at Richardson Gears Pty Ltd just as the School began to take on the shape its original advocates had planned. Perhaps he had suffered some loss of confidence in his ability to head an engineering school without further industrial experience, perhaps he saw an inadequate career structure, or perhaps he was simply tired and disillusioned.

Hoadley did not stay long with Richardson Gears, for when E. P. Eltham, who had succeeded him as Principal, was appointed an Inspector of Technical Schools in mid-1922, Hoadley re-applied for his old position. He was re-appointed on a temporary basis, but only after considerable pressure was applied by the Council was he confirmed in the position early in 1923.[5] From this point it seems clear that Hoadley had fully committed himself to Footscray Technical School as his life's vocation, a decision that is hardly surprising when the depth and complexity of his ideas on education and school administration from his very first utterances on the subject are taken into account.

According to its early *Prospectus*, "The Aim" of the School was to educate workers for a life as well as a living. The education provided aims not merely at preparing more skilled workers for the present system, but to develop human beings who are equipped to reconstruct that scheme. It does not assume that the needs of industrial education are met if boys are simply to be trained as plumbers, electric wirers, etc., neglecting as useless for its ends such topics as civics, which make future workers aware of their rightful claims and responsibilities as citizens in a democracy. The school endeavours to equip the student so that he may secure by his own initiative whatever place his natural capacities fit him for.[6]

Whether Hoadley was the author of that statement is not absolutely certain, but it perfectly encapsulates the broad, humane and progressive educational vision that informed his leadership of the school and indeed all his dealings with adolescent boys. Whatever the rhetoric among educationalists and even some supporters of technical education may have been, this was not the view commonly held of the purpose of technical schools in practice, and there were powerful forces pushing for a narrow, vocational and 'efficient' (i.e cheap), focus for schools such as Footscray.

The underlying premise of state technical education remained the assumption that education for the working classes should be distinctly different from that offered in the high schools and specifically designed to provide a better basis for their lifetime employment in manual work. The notion that public money should be spent on educating the 'whole person', or that natural capacities, rather than father's income, might determine a person's place in society was a long way from public acceptance. Indeed, in the post-war years, the dangers inherent in educating a person "above their station" were re-asserted in the public debate. As a 1931 government report claimed,

> the major portion of a boy's time after leaving school will be spent in earning a living, and the way in which he spends that time will have an enormous effect on his happiness. The frustrated and disgruntled man of culture is socially objectionable and politically dangerous. The dictum that education should teach a man how to use his leisure is one of those half truths whose acceptance is so dangerous. [7]

Even the Labor Party was scarcely interested in education as a right or a worthwhile end in itself as distinct from a means to minimise the problems created by what was commonly held to be an excess of unskilled labourers. The Member for Williamstown, Jack Lemmon, for example, argued that the technical schools should not only be efficient but inbued with "an industrial atmosphere" in order to prepare students better for their life's work.[8]

Others opposed a broad curriculum in technical schools out of a generalised belief that applied and theoretical knowledge were inherently separate. This often translated into a contempt for more theoretical and abstract studies which, it was believed, diverted talent from applied studies. The Chief Inspector of Technical Schools, Donald Clark, was obsessed with the idea that theoretical study, even of mathematics, let alone the liberal arts, would divert students from his senior technical schools. Unfortunately, this view too easily resulted in a situation where what was offered in practice was little more than trade training.

That Clark did not envisage many of the products of his technical schools becoming engineers is revealed by his assertion that an "industrial" atmosphere was perfectly appropriate. "Since many boys would work in tin sheds" he saw no reason why they could not "learn how to work in them too".[9] To underscore the harshness, even cruelty, that lurked beneath such statements, it is worth looking into one of those corrugated iron factories through the eyes of a sheet metal shop worker at the McKay Sunshine Harvester factory:

> For heating in this factory up until the War and in most places, after the War, you'd make a little bucket, a fire bucket and if you could get a bit of wood or something, you could have a fire. When I was on night shift, I took the temperature and it was down to zero. Now, you can imagine men handling cold iron when its got down to zero. . . . Holding the cold 'dollies', some blokes' hands would crack. I remember the Sister once, somebody went down about their hands and the Sister said: 'Oh, go back and piss on them'.[10]

Objectively, such an environment seems scarcely conducive to good work, let alone good learning, but an emphasis on creating an industrial atmosphere pervades most discussions of technical education in the 1920s. What it reveals is that the state-funded technical schools were more a product of concern with contemporary industrial conditions than any coherent linking of technical education with industrial development and change. At its worst, talk of an industrial atmosphere masked a desire

"The Door of Opportunity". This line drawing of the front entrance to the school was used on the front of the school Prospectus *for many years*

to provide technical education in the cheapest possible accommodation.

Fortunately, there were some people in the community who viewed the content and purposes of technical education more broadly. Arch Hoadley certainly fought to incorporate this broader view into Footscray Technical School with varying degrees of success over thirty years, even though there were times when classes were conducted in places far less suitable than tin sheds. Under his jurisdiction, the lines between research and application, between scientists and engineers, were not to be drawn too precisely. As he argued in an article on electrical engineering:

> If we trace through the history of science we see that the men who have made . . . great discoveries [the structure of the atom, X rays, etc.] have been pure scientists. It is to be deplored today that we hear so often remarked that we want practice not theory. It cannot be too strongly stressed that without physics, the training of the engineer is reduced to rule of thumb.[11]

Hoadley's aim was to take the students beyond the purely practical and utilitarian. He rejected emphatically the idea that much of what was taught in the junior school was a waste of time because the boys would "only become tradesmen". A full education in their fields was necessary for them to "appreciate what they [did] and why and to answer questions."[12] Subscribing to the view that education was of "value" no matter what a boy did "subsequently",[13] he did not see students as so many cogs to be fitted into an industrial enterprise but as citizens with rights, responsibilities and an important sphere of existence outside the workplace. Just how 'progressive' his thinking was in this regard can be gleaned from his views on the education of girls, an even more contentious subject at the time. In 1917 he told a meeting of persons interested in establishing a domestic arts school in Footscray that

> More than cooking and needlework was necessary to a girl's education, she had to be trained first to become a good citizen — in all the arts and sciences necessary to the fulfilling of her part as a woman in the civic state.[14]

Hoadley was deeply committed to technical education and the advancement of a technically sophisticated society. In this, his vision went far beyond the training of better quality mechanics, though he was seriously concerned to do that also. Hoadley realised that the needs of industry were complex. A narrow industrial education actually threatened the aims of a truly technical education, especially at the higher levels, and therefore the creation of a technologically sophisticated society. As the *Prospectus* made clear, this required "human beings" equipped by their education to "reconstruct" the "system".[15]. Boys trained to accept limited aspirations based on present economic and social conditions would hardly aspire to the senior levels or indeed acquire the educational prerequisites to undertake diploma studies.

Hoadley's statements suggest a genuine insight into the technological dilemma facing the country and the need to increase the level of general and technical education across the entire workforce. That education, he believed, should look to the future rather than the present and seek to raise students above themselves rather than fit them into pre-ordained slots. In this we can see the influence of the ideas of the Director of Education, Frank Tate, who believed that many of the calls for technical education were based on narrow, self-interested motives. Technical education could and should lead to cheaper goods and increased trade, but he believed the

> mere teaching of a trade would be against the best interests of the community since it would lead to stagnation in the factories and industries. A fuller education was needed for all workers so that they would not be content to just use the old methods but would want to experiment with new and possibly better ways of carrying out their jobs.[16]

The prevailing attitudes and conditions acted as a brake on the full development of technical education and probably the whole industrial sector. These affected the attitudes of potential students as well as the provision of resources. Hoadley's annual speech night addresses were full of lamentations and exhortations to take up the challenge and the opportunities his school offered, but always he stressed that

> the very basis of technical education is in giving boys advanced day school training. It is by these means that the best brains among the boys are trained and developed to enable them to qualify and fit themselves for for positions of technical experts and advisers.[17]

This was equally true of the skilled operatives as potential managers. For them too, night school was at best a poor expedient. "The boy of today," Hoadley asserted, "if he shows promise of being able to do things, requires far more education than is possible under such conditions."[18] Moreover, it could not

52

be too much insisted on that Apprentices generally require much more theoretical training than is possible if they only attend at Night School. The failure to complete trade courses of study is largely due to the fact that a boy is not trained enough for the advanced work of the course. . . . Practical work in a subject can be better taught in the workshop than in a school. The function of a school in practical work should be more largely to see that the students learn a variety of operations and latest methods of doing them, than of gaining practical experience.[19]

Unless proper resources were provided to schools and students adequately supported, much natural talent would remain untapped or under-used. Hoadley was convinced after four years that there were boys at the school "clever enough to occupy the very best positions in our industries in later life if they are properly and fully taught now".[20] Even leaving aside the economic constraints on full-time study for working class boys, Hoadley lamented a lack of vision or reward that resulted in poor motivation towards higher technical studies.

For many years past it appears that the youth of our country think to themselves there is no reason why they should waste what they consider is the best hours of their existence in study. On looking round they find that men of brains and culture are being paid less, and very often considerably less, than men at trade, and they think there is no reason why they should spend their time at college. This we emphatically believe is a fallacy.[21]

Hoadley believed his school ought to train managers as well as skilled operatives and he subscribed to the view that the best management came from among those with practical as well as theoretical skills. This aspect of the system was unashamedly elitist. It was "acknowledged that much higher education (i.e Diploma Work) [was] only for the brainy boy who [was] gifted with talent",[22] but the executive positions could "only be filled with men who have passed through the ranks of tradesmen themselves".[23] Therefore the quality of their preparatory education and training was critical. It could not be "done with the limited preparatory education that has, in previous years been thought sufficient".[24]

In all this, Hoadley sought to achieve a balance between intellectual seriousness and practical skills, and he viewed education for leisure as an essential part of a school's responsibilities, though not solely for idealistic reasons. His aim was to encourage a

> true school spirit by trying to lead [the boys'] inclinations out of as well as during school hours. Training in recreation was almost as important as training in the schoolroom. Music had an educational value and he advocated the formation of a boys' band.[25]

Hoadley understood the relationship between poor motivation, low expectations and 'under achievement'. Particularly concerned by the large number of boys who withdrew from courses without completing them, he saw organised sport and other 'non-technical' activities as essential ingredients in creating a school atmosphere that encouraged boys to stay and perform to the best of their ability.

For similar reasons he established and supported the library and gave great personal support to the formation of the Old Boys Association in 1919. Out of his and the staff's desire that "the students of the college should be brought together by other ties than those of mere class study", he instigated a Science and Social Club[26] which arranged lectures, excursions, dances and musical evenings. Such developments clearly enriched the lives of the young men and women of the evening classes who spent so much of their leisure time in the pursuit of learning. It helped in bonding together a support group to sustain members in their pursuit of learning and qualifications in a community which, on the whole, did not value them very highly and was inclined to be suspicious or intimidated by the 'educated'. The Old Boys' Association provided an important sustaining peer group long after many of the "boys", especially the "Dips", were well on their way into their careers.

Hoadley's commitment to his School, his students and his district extended well beyond its walls. He played a central role in the establishment of inter-technical school sporting competitions; his home was always open to students to drop in out of hours. He somewhat reluctantly accepted the position as Scoutmaster in 1919 when asked by First Footscray Troop,[27] most of whom were also Footscray Technical School boys, but eventually he went on to play a significant role in the development of Scouting in Victoria. Such a man could never be content with a narrow, limiting view of education. In all of this he seems to have been amply supported by his staff, who gave their time to coach teams, take school camps and run other sorts of clubs in addition to their allotted teaching loads and frequently in their own time.

Hoadley instituted all the usual structures of a typical school of the time — a 'house' system, prefects and so forth — again in pursuit of the framework which would encourage the development of a School that was something more than simply the sum total of the individuals in it — an *esprit de corps* that would hold and enrich the students in itself. Always he stressed the highest performance, not only in senior technical work but at the craftsman level too, lamenting, for example, the increasing tendency for boiler makers to neglect the more skilled side of blacksmithing.[28] Aesthetics were not to be neglected either. The School was "a place where the beautiful [was] stressed" and the creative faculties nurtured.[29] There was considerable 'streaming' within the school, partly to accommodate the diversity of entrance qualifications and partly to provide maximum opportunity to those who appeared capable of senior work. This was a practice seldom questioned by anybody at the time and students were encouraged to reach beyond themselves, or at least beyond the lowered expectations created by life patterns dominated by economic considerations. Those who did so reach seem to have been richly rewarded especially in terms of the time, effort and commitment of the Principal, his staff and the School Council.

Hoadley was a man of "brains and culture", with a broad and humane view of technical education that could indeed make it the "door of opportunity" for those whose talent or application gave them a chance to move beyond the lifetime employment chances for which the accident of birth had destined them. Under him, Footscray Technical School grew and developed into "the most important technical school in Victoria".[30] The School turned out many tradesmen, but it also provided a path to the non-industrial sectors; for some it even became a ladder to the University, something the advocates of tin sheds scarcely had in mind but for which Hoadley personally must be given considerable credit. Footscray residents had no high school until 1955, and only limited access to other forms of education, but "The Tech" proved to have the flexibility and scope to serve more than the industrial employment requirements of the area. Even those who drifted out to unskilled jobs had probably gained enhanced life chances compared with their prospects had they remained at primary school. They would certainly have benefited from the Principal's wide range of contacts with local employers. Moreover, these boys still had a number of re-entry options that they could take up at a later time and in this, together with its complexity, was the School's greatest source of strength.

1. FTS *Prospectus*, 1925–1926.
2. *Footscray Advertiser*, 14 October 1916.
3. Secretary of Education Department to C. A. Hoadley, 23 March 1917, PRO VA 714, VPRS 10275, Box 130.
4. See above, p 41.
5. See especially FTS Council Minutes, 28 November 1922. F. J. Daley had been nominated as Principal with no consultation with the Council.
6. FTS *Prospectus*, 1925–1926.
7. *Final Report of the Board of Enquiry into the Administration of the Education Department*, 14 December 1931, PRO VA 714, VPRS 2567.
8. Quoted in Bessant, *op. cit.*, p 86.
9. Transcript of evidence given by Donald Clark to the Board of Enquiry into the Administration of the Education Department, 10 July 1931, p 971, PRO VA 714, VPRS 2567.
10. Living Museum of the West, *Sunshine Harvester Diary*, 1987, [No page numbers].
11. *Footscray Advertiser*, 26 December 1925.
12. *Ibid.*, 30 January 1926.
13. Evidence given by C. A. Hoadley to the Board of Enquiry into the Administration of the Education Department, 13 July 1931, p 988, PRO VA 714, VPRS 2567.
14. *Footscray Advertiser*, 24 November 1917.
15. FTS *Prospectus*, 1925–1926.
16. From F. Tate, *School and Power*, Pamphlet, 1908, pp 8–9. Quoted in Robson, *op. cit.*, pp 114 & 142.
17. *Footscray Advertiser*, 31 July 1920.
18. C. A. Hoadley, 'Report to Annual Speech Night', 15 August 1923, FIT Archive.
19. *Ibid.*, p 6.
20. *Footscray Advertiser*, 31 July 1920.
21. *Ibid.*
22. C. A. Hoadley, 'Report to Annual Speech Night', 1927, p 3.
23. *Ibid.*
24. C. A. Hoadley, 'Report to Annual Speech Night', 1923, p 4.
25. *Footscray Advertiser*, 14 October 1916.

26. *Ibid.*, 30 August 1919.
27. He accepted initially with the proviso that he would not wear the uniform, E. L. Walker, interview.
28. *Footscray Advertiser*, 16 January 1926.
29. *Ibid.*, 9 January 1926.
30. Report of the Board of Inspectors, 1947, FIT Archive.

CHAPTER FIVE **Behind "The Door of Opportunity"**[1]

Inside the buildings that quite rapidly covered the triangle of land abutting the railway line, boys ranging in age from 12 to 16 or so stuffed their brown and red caps into bags and back pockets and set to work on a curriculum informed by the precept "Knowledge is Power". No uniform was required beyond a cap and the school badge, but the "coffee and carrots"[2] school colours were a source of grumbling. Born in the depths of war, it is no surprise that the Council had adopted the red and brown colours of the Seventh Battalion, composed almost entirely of Footscray men, which only a year before had waded into history at Gallipoli. The sombre appeal of the colours was, however, short lived. Before the end of the decade boys were wearing the bright blue and gold caps that most former students remember. If the conditions were spartan and the work regimen strict, 'old boys' recall that the sternness was tempered with warmth, and the serious pursuit of knowledge did not preclude moments of hilarity and fun. An unusually colourful account of the first prize-giving night provides a rare glimpse inside a school still very much in its infancy:

Boys Have a Night Out
A stranger passing through the technical school on the night of the 20th inst. might have thought that anarchy had suddenly broken out in that usually peaceful home of learning. The art room had water flooded over the floor and was turned into a skating rink, the upstairs classroom was a stadium for the time being and fierce battles were in progress. In two rooms the master's desk had been transformed into a ping-

First school monogram

pong table and in the English classroom round games, quoits, blackboard caricatures, and blind man's buff were going on to rag-time accompaniment on the school piano. Over all was the shrill pandemonium of the boys' voices absolutely unrestrained. But here, however, the inquiring stranger discovered that the teaching staff was in the thick of the fun — it was prize-giving night for the prize winners. After the boys had had their fill of fun a pleasant little function of prize-giving was carried out. A good number of the school councillors were present as well as Mr Everitt (sic), Principal of the Brunswick College, Mr J Lemmon M.L.A., Mr Drayton (Footscray Harriers), and a few parents. Mr Lemmon and Cr A. J. Pearce, president of the School Council, addressed the grown ups on the future prospects of technical education, and Mr Lemmon told the boys that if they would be masters themselves someday they must perfect themselves in the technical side of their calling. Mr Drayton also spoke to the boys on sportsmanship in work and play. The boys gave ear-piercing welcome to each speaker and yelled their appreciation of the plumbing master's (Mr Bradshaw) exhibition of torch-swinging. Cr Pearce distributed the medals as follows: H. Outen, A. Anchen, Bowls, Stone, Eades, Crellin, Lloyd, Mathews, Newland, Jones, Le Marguand, Edmondson, Williams, O'Hara, Hurst, Thom, McKinnon. The Council medals were designed by Mr Mudie, the art master, and took the form of the school monogram, F.T.S, surmounted by calipers in silver. At the close, two boys (A. Anchen and R. De Coit) thanked the councillors and the Footscray Harriers for their help to the school. The young speakers did excellently, especially in that they knew what many more experienced fail in, enough to stop when they had said all they had to say. A general cheering of everybody was given by the boys and the visitors went down the stairs to accept the hospitality of the Council. The usual toasts brought a pleasant evening to a close.[3]

The junior boys worked at a general preparatory course designed to provide "a broad yet firm foundation of general and technical knowledge".[4] The curriculum covered Algebra, Arithmetic, Mensuration, Experimental Science, English, Civics and Hygiene, Geography, various branches of geometry, Free Drawing, Modelling, Sheetmetal Work, Woodwork and Physical Training. In second year, Mechanical Drawing and Building Construction were added and a wider range of 'trade' subjects such as Blacksmithing and Moulding. In third year, Economics replaced Civics and Geography. Boys entering with their Merit Certificate commenced on a modified second year course. All students who successfully completed two years of the course were awarded the Junior Technical Certificate and those who completed three years were awarded the Intermediate Technical Certificate. Satisfactory completion of the junior technical school course was necessary for admission to diploma studies and had a marked bearing on likely success in other technical courses.

It had been the intention that boys would come into the junior section with Merit Certificate but, in practice, there was little control of entry standards beyond those imposed by the number of places available and, until 1927, fees. In the early years, most boys who did not have their Merit Certificate had passed an entrance test, but there was always a number with no certificates at all. Principal Hoadley remained committed to the wisdom of entry at the later stage. In his opinion, the School declined in the later 1920s when the new regulations forced it to accept boys who had only completed grade 6.[5] There are few reliable records of how many satisfactorily completed the junior courses, but in Hoadley's view, more boys left unqualified after the change in entry policy. He provided dismal statistics for 1927 when, out of an enrolment of 90 students, 30 left after the first year, 26 after the second and ten after the third. None of this 66 had gained his Junior Technical Certificate.[6]

The poor retention rates were not simply a consequence of entrance standards. There were economic and attitudinal factors at work as well. All parents were required to sign a guarantee that they would keep their boys at the school for at least two full years, and if possible, three but this was unenforceable in practice. There were also only a very limited number of scholarships available to ease the financial burden of keeping a boy at school and forgoing his potential income. In 1927, boys over 14 paid £1 a term, while those under 14 were charged were 3s 4d per term for the cost of materials. Charges such as those for books and sports added up to about £2 10s'. The School Council considered that books were "prohibitively expensive".[8]

In 1926, boys with two years "sound" secondary education could compete for one of 20 state scholarships worth £30 per year. The School offered three scholarships worth £10 a year for three years endowed by Dr Harry Box, T. F. M. Smith and the Colonial Gas Association. There was also the J. H. Hooper scholarship of £10 per annum for two years of a commercial course. The Footscray City Council endowed three scholarships worth £15 a year plus free tuition and six providing free tuition for the final year of the Intermediate Technical Certificate. Hoadley was acutely aware that, "In a closely congested district like this all children — both boys and girls — go to work at an early age".[9] He knew that part-time evening school was the only way many could afford anything more than a basic education, but this did not entirely alleviate his disappointment and frustration at the effect this had on his School.

Towards the end of each year, Hoadley visited all the local schools to talk to boys and their parents about the value of secondary technical education, but he fought a hard battle against entrenched attitudes about its value or relevance. His attempts to attract boys were hampered by a general lack of enthusiasm for secondary education among the population as a whole. His quest to attract the "brainy boy" was hampered further by "a strong tendency to draft boys with ability into pure secondary education where the outlook [was] that of the shop, the office, the warehouse and the very much overcrowded professions".[10] That the school did receive talented and motivated boys is clear. Hoadley declared at one point that "students have passed though the school . . . who were equal in brain power to the best who attended university during [my] course."[11] However, these were rather offset by too many "boys who had no brains and who didn't like school", a consequence of the "common belief" that if a boy was not "good with his head he might be with his hands."[12] These boys depressed Hoadley because they had "no idea of personally exerting themselves, no ambition to learn for the sake of learning or for the good it [could] do them".[13] Worst of all, however, were those boys with "talent" who lacked "either the ambition or the spur of parental advice" to undertake higher training.[13] It would be some time before the value of any secondary education was universally acknowledged, and Hoadley's ideas still had a visionary quality 15 years after the School was founded. Yet it was his vision and sense of excitement that offered special inspiration to those boys who chose to follow the path along which he pointed.

The senior school was for the most part throughout the 1920s and 1930s, a part-time and evening institution, both larger and more complex than the day school. All day staff taught throughout this period in the evenings and on Saturday mornings at which times they were joined by a large number of part-time instructors who were practising their trade or profession during the day. For some, evening and weekend work represented a path to full-time employment as teachers, but for the majority it provided valuable supplementary income.

The largest group of students embarked on Certificate courses. These were of two types, Engineering or Trade. The Engineering Certificate comprised basic subjects from the Diploma courses in electrical or mechanical engineering taken three evenings per week over four years. A "strenuous programme that relatively few managed to complete", it was intended to meet "the needs of industry at a level well above that of tradesman but below that of a professional engineer." [15] The virtue of these qualifications was supposed to be that the practical work was completed concurrently, but it was a study regimen requiring remarkable commitment, and for those who had not obtained the Junior Technical Certificate, it had to be prefaced by a year of preparatory subjects. It seems clear that subjects rather than courses had primary value to part-time students. The fact that only 34 Certificates were awarded between 1926 and 1943 suggests that the Technician's Certificate was not in high demand, either because it was difficult to complete or because it failed to meet the demands and circumstances of the time.[16]

Trade Certificate courses embraced "all the theoretical training necessary to turn out fully competent journeymen" in Carpentry, Handrailing and Staircasing, Cabinet Making, Blacksmithing, Coppersmithing, Graining and Marbling, Plumbing and Gas Fitting, Lead Burning, Turning and Fitting, Pattern

Making, Moulding and Boilermaking.[17] The courses claimed to include practical work that would "put them ahead of what they were doing in the shop, and thus help them in their daily work".[18] The fees for these Certificates ranged from 15s in the first year to £1 10s in the later years. The single most expensive course was Electric Welding at £2 14s.

The demarcation between tradesman and engineer was not as strong as it has since become, nor was the training especially theoretical or mathematical. Engineering students in technical colleges at this time spent an average of one fifth of their course on workshop subjects and the development of manual skills,[19] while the level of mathematics achieved by the end of the course was scarcely equivalent to that required at pre-tertiary level in 1967.[20] The line of demarcation between the college-educated engineer and the tradesman was thus more blurred than that between a tradesman and a graduate engineer, even leaving aside the social gulf that probably separated them. In time however, this situation has gradually changed as diploma courses have moved closer to degree courses in style, content and educational prerequisites. By 1967 college courses included almost no trade type work and were, on the whole devoting less time to "laboratory type activities" than the university courses. [21]

The cream of the senior school was, undoubtedly, the tiny diploma stream. Subjects covered in the diploma courses included Mechanical, Electrical, Civil, Aeronautical and Marine Engineering and Architecture. They were intended to be studied full time for three years. In practice most students took out a combined Diploma of Electrical and Mechanical Engineering and all candidates were required to complete a period of practical experience before it was granted. In theory these qualifications provided entry to the

> engineering profession in the capacity of Assistant Engineer, Designing Draughtsman, Power Station Engineer or member of the staff of industrial firms, thus he [was] enabled to get out of the rut and enter on a field of unlimited possibilities".[22]

Not many reached this desired goal in the 1920s. By the end of 1930 the School had only awarded 15 diplomas in a decade when the average number granted per year by all colleges, excluding the Working Men's College, was 14.[23]

The number of full time diploma students gradually increased from five in 1920 to 57 in 1930 while the junior school edged toward 700. This small number was a constant disappointment to Hoadley and his Council. It severely hampered their ability to mount courses of the range and academic standing that would attract larger numbers and consolidate the School as a senior technical institution. Until well into the 1930s, there was always a danger that diploma classes would be transferred to the Working Men's College.[24] During the Depression, Civil Engineering was so lost and a total transfer was seriously considered as a cost-cutting measure. An even greater disappointment was the small number of Footscray boys who comprised the senior day class. In 1928, for example, only 12% of the diploma class of 33 were local boys, that is to say about four students out of the previous years junior school enrolment of 686 were continuing full-time education.[25] Hoadley and others, such as 'old boy' Jack Kepert, newly graduated as a Bachelor of Electrical Engineering from Melbourne University, were inclined to blame parents' lack of "appreciation" of the opportunities offered by the school, but the economic factor cannot be overlooked. Fees for diploma students were 40s a year for three years, excluding books and instruments, at a time when the Basic Wage in Melbourne was £4s 6s a week.[26]

In 1926, the School's *Prospectus* confidently asserted that

> The best opening for the average boy today is an engineering career. Prospects are good; opportunities are unlimited; there is always a wide range of opportunities from which to choose, while advancement depends solely upon the merits of the individual. To enter upon such a career, however, requires a sound training; but, given such a training, the average student is assured of a good, permanent and lucrative position, so that future prosperity becomes practically a matter of certainty,[27]

Notwithstanding this, however, the status of the diploma and its holders was still somewhat uncertain in the community. New, higher-standard diploma courses were introduced in 1924, but diplomates experienced some difficulty in getting suitable jobs throughout the 1920s. "Some employers considered the qualification too good for factory production positions, while others tended to regard the diplomates as potential apprentices and consequently rejected them on account of their age".[28] They did not fit easily into the wages award structure and found little support from the Amalgamated Society of Engineers, who had 200 members unemployed in 1925 and were reluctant to see any variation in their wages award that would increase competition for jobs.[29] Some diplomates solved the problem by going on to complete degrees at the University, while others went overseas. Another group returned after a period of work experience to teach in the technical schools, and as time passed the *de facto* teacher training role of Footscray Technical School took on considerable significance.

While the Institution of Engineers admitted diplomates as professional engineers, professional associations and certain large employers such as the Victorian Railways were slower to accept the school.[30] E. W. Trend, President of the Footscray School Council and the Technical Schools Association of Victoria (a body representative of school councils set up to promote the interests of technical schools), made the point at the opening of the 1929 Annual Conference that

> various institutions, such as Engineers, Architects and Chemists, were of the opinion that the standard taught in technical schools was not sufficiently high, and the result was that the University trained man was sought after for the best positions. He suggested that technical schools must, if they were to turn out students who were to be more than artisans, extend their courses of work to cover the higher grades.[31]

Sadly, this realisation came on the eve of a Depression-engendered slashing of the state budget that reduced even further the meagre resources available to schools like Footscray to enable them to offer those higher levels of training. In the meantime, however, the holders of the qualifications were gradually making a niche for themselves in the engineering world that was the best recommendation the diploma courses could have.

With all the emphasis that the School, its Council and the Education Department placed on engineering and trades, it is easy to overlook the importance of commercial subjects in the evening school. These subjects were almost always the most financially viable, notwithstanding competition from private commercial and business schools, and their high fees relative to other subjects. Second year Accounting cost £2 14s, presumably reflecting the qualifications of the teacher and the potential economic rewards to those who successfully completed the course. The Commercial course, taken part time over four years, "offered a complete practical training for a business career".[32] Both men and women enrolled in these classes, which took the able students to the point of sitting for the Institute of Chartered Accountants, Institute of Secretaries or Licensed Shorthand Writers Board examinations. Students could also take commercial subjects singly and Typewriting and Shorthand were very popular.

Many evening students enrolled for single subjects rather than pursue formal courses, whilst Art and Applied Art carried over in popularity from a time when these had formed a core of technical education. Drawing and Design was strongly emphasised but students could also study Painting and Modelling, as well as various craft subjects such as Leather Work and Wood Carving. The course offered training for careers in such fields as sign writing and commercial art and design for furniture, jewellery, pottery, dressmaking, cement and plaster work.

Once the last of the returned servicemen left in 1923 and diploma classes commenced, the School began to take on the shape that would define it until 1972; that is, it became a large junior secondary school with a technical bias and a senior school that combined full-time day Diploma classes, a wide range of part-time evening classes, and training for apprentices during both day and evening. The day-release apprentice classes remained a small, stagnant area until the Apprenticeship Commission, established in 1928, made this a compulsory element in a larger number of trades. The growing numbers were accommodated in extensions to the school opened in 1925 comprising new laboratories for Electrical Technology and Physics, trade workshops and additional office space. These, however, were barely adequate to meet existing needs. Hoadley had already suggested unsuccessfully in 1923 a move to the Ballarat Road site occupied by Footscray Institute of Technology today. By 1927 he was turning away students and taking temporary accommodation in the Hyde Street Primary School, but Education Department funds were far from sufficient to meet Footscray's desperate overall needs. Overcrowded, under-resourced primary and technical schools were neglected in favour of an equally needed School of Domestic Arts which was opened in 1925. The problem was easing by late 1928, but only because economic downturn reduced the demand for secondary education in the area.

As the years passed and the number of students grew, the proportion of Footscray residents who had some connection with the School increased dramatically. In 1926, the Mothers' Club was formed under the presidency of Mrs Alice Duke, thus providing the school with a consistent source of moral and financial support from parents while throughout most of the 1920s speech nights were important public events. Hoadley moved into Footscray to live and a great many of the staff also lived in the district. School sporting activities took place on public grounds visible to all who cared to watch. Hoadley's role with the local Scout troop made it to all intents and purposes an adjunct to school life with strong ties to the Old Boys' Association. It added complexity to the School's links with local industry because both apprentices and management, such as the younger members of the Richardson family, were involved in Scouting. As Hoadley rose to prominence in the Scout movement,[33] his leadership role in the lives of the young men of Footscray was further enhanced. The School provided important employment opportunities for cleaners, gardeners, office staff and tradesmen as well as teachers, while the Old Boys' Association grew into a social and sporting organisation of some consequence in the district. The *Advertiser* claimed it was the largest old boy's association in Victoria in 1928.[34] By the mid-1920s, the Footscray Technical School Ball had become the "outstanding social event of the year" in the "absence of a mayoral ball or any other such public social gathering".[35]

Nothing, however, better serves a school's reputation than the successful careers of former students. As Hoadley put it, "A school was only wonderful if its product was worthwhile".[36] At first glance the most surprising feature of the "Reasons for Leaving" column in the only surviving Junior School Record Book is the variety of occupations taken up by the boys. There is no escaping the immediate impression that boys entered the school with a far wider range of employment objectives than were encompassed by the prevailing notion of technical. Of the first intake in 1916, some 16.8% entered employment in the metal industries or engineering but a proportion of these almost certainly went as unskilled labourers, often in the agricultural implement making firms. Another 4.1% went to employment in other skilled trades areas, principally carpentry and furniture making, although many of those who took up apprenticeships would have returned to take evening classes at the School. Retailing or wholesaling took 7.3%, Food Processing 3.6% and the offices of professionals such as doctors, lawyers and dentists

8.2%. Nearly 5% became clerks or joined the Post Office, while 6.3% joined the Victorian Railways and 3.1% went into the printing industry. Only 3.6% went on to a senior technical school and many others left for heavy unskilled employment such as bulk handling at the dockyards. A small proportion went to work on farms. At this stage the Colonial Ammunition Works, soon to emerge as a major employer of boys from Footscray Technical School, only attracted six boys. Interestingly, 12, or 5.4%, left to join their fathers, the majority of whom were local small businessmen or farmers.

The trend established in 1916, whereby up to at least a third of the boys went into the commercial or professional sector and about half went into the industrial sector, remained consistent up to 1932, after which no records are available. A comparison of this admittedly rather unsystematically compiled data[37] with the composition of the Footscray workforce in 1921 and 1933, as revealed by census figures, suggests that boys who attended the School were less likely to enter the industrial sector than their fathers, and we can reasonably infer that, of those who entered this sector, a larger proportion would have been skilled and likely to reach managerial level. That a far larger number of boys left to enter the commercial and professional sector than might have been expected, given that only 12% of male breadwinners in Footscray and 22% in the whole of the metropolitan area in 1921 were included in this category, is perhaps even more surprising at first glance. Very many of these boys became messengers, shop assistants and junior clerks, but we can assume that some who went into an 'office' sought higher qualifications in commercial subjects given their popularity in the night school.

Given the absence of a high school, however, and the express concern of the Footscray City Council that "the number of children travelling to other districts to receive high school education is too great",[38] what these findings reveal is that, throughout this period, Footscray Technical School was to some extent acting as a *de facto* high school, even though it did not offer teaching towards the Public Examinations. The School also on occasions provided a route to university, though this path was only open to those studying Engineering. The numbers embarking on full-time senior technical education varied considerably over the period, from a low of 3.5% in 1924 to a high of 13.5% in 1925[39] but a number of those studying at Footscray went on to take out distinguished university degrees.

The diploma students of the 1920s were few in number, but their careers set a pattern that would hold true for several decades. The State Electricity Commission, the Victorian Railways and the Education Department proved the most important employers of diplomates. Indeed, after their initial scepticism, they encouraged and assisted their most promising apprentices to enrol in diploma courses. Of the first 15 who took out diplomas between 1925 and 1930, at least five went to the SEC. By 1946, Douglas Galbraith was an assistant maintenance engineer, John Sullivan an assistant test and protection engineer, Edward Foers was working as a construction engineer while Cyril Smith was District Superintendent for Gippsland.[40] Clifford Callinan became Operational Head and later Chief Operations Engineer of the Snowy Mountain Hydro-Electric Scheme.[41]

Ron Rankin pioneered the acceptance of Footscray Technical School diplomas by the Victorian Railways. He first went to the Railways to train as an electrical fitter but was later awarded one of the three annual scholarships for full-time diploma studies. Until this time, these were taken at the Working Men's College but Rankin, who had attended the Footscray junior school, was able to arrange to pursue his diploma studies at Footscray also. An active 'old boy', Rankin later served the School as Treasurer to the Council from 1955 to 1976.[42] John Chadwick went into the chemical industry, an area that would absorb more Footscray Technical School boys as time passed, and by 1946 was a production engineer with ICI. Eric Richardson went straight to Melbourne University to study for degrees in Electrical and Mechanical Engineering, with the aid of an Education Department Senior Technical Scholarship worth £40 a year and the Simon Fraser Scholarship worth £120 a year. He lived up to the promise of these scholarships, taking first class honours and first place in his final year exams.[43]

The Education Department employed both Harold Tran and Jack Kepert. Tran, from Macedon, went into the teaching profession immediately and by 1954 was foundation principal of Coburg Technical School. Jack Kepert's career, however, stands out particularly sharply. Grandson of a local pioneer, he took out a diploma of Electrical and Mechanical Engineering and then proceeded to Melbourne University, where he was eventually awarded the degrees of Bachelor of Mechanical Engineering, Bachelor of Science, and Master of Electrical Engineering. He then worked briefly for the SEC at Rubicon before joining the

Education Department in 1929 — hardly a surprising decision given his obvious love of study and the fact that both his parents were teachers. In 1938 he joined the staff at Footscray rising to the level of Vice Principal before transferring to Caulfield Technical School as Principal in 1946. In 1963 he reached the pinnacle of technical teaching when he was appointed Director of Technical Education, a position he held until his retirement five years later.

A diploma was not initially necessary to join the teaching staff of colleges, and for many of the enthusiastic early students the line between studying, working and teaching was often blurred. As the demand for trained engineers and technicians expanded, so did the teaching opportunities. Kenneth Tatchell won the Dr Harry Box Scholarship to study electrical engineering in 1920 and in 1926 was awarded his Certificate. In 1927 he was a part-time instructor of Turning and Fitting, and he took out a diploma in 1941. His later career included heading up the Production Engineering Department at Melbourne Technical College,[44] and periods as an Inspector of Technical Schools and Principal of Collingwood Technical School.

Edward L. Walker enrolled in the School in 1919 at the age of 12, though he had been lurking around the grounds for some time before that and had managed to blow out a few windows trying out a new type of firecracker.[45] He left the School to take up an apprenticeship in electrical fitting and mechanics with W. Cumming & Co., but the end of his time coincided with the Depression. Unlike most apprentices, he was not put off quite on the day his indentures expired, but he soon had to start out on his own in particularly difficult times. A keen sporting member of the Old Boys' Association, he was also closely connected with Hoadley through Scouting activities, and in 1937 he was glad to move into part-time evening teaching. Early in 1940 he accepted a full-time position and began 40 years service to the school, firstly as Head of the Electrical Trades Department, then as Trade Supervisor and Vice Principal. Ted Walker exemplifies the type of teacher technical schools sought, combining a good work experience background, a flair for administration and a love of teaching. He was awarded an honorary Diploma of Electrical Engineering from FIT in 1978, but perhaps the best tribute and insight into the nature of his role is contained in a letter from the Director of Technical Education in 1974. Referring to his position as Moderator with the Board of Examiners of the State Electricity Commission, the Director noted that

> Your assistance and support in the recent gratifying progress made with the Electrical Courses and your advocacy with the Chief Electrical Inspector and his staff have transformed an association full of trouble into one which is full of optimism for future development.[46]

There were plenty of less academically daunting role models to hold up before the students. Ern Mollard had not particularly wanted to be an engineer, but circumstances led him into a late apprenticeship with Richardson Gears and he left the School only one subject short of a diploma. Mollard was at first associated with the automotive trade, and his tremendous enthusiasm for the School and the Old Boys' Association was rewarded with his appointment to the School Council in 1925. In 1930 he resigned to go overseas for a period. His later career includes 32 years as Director of Industrial Service Engineers and four years as Chairman and Managing Director of Jamec Tools Pty Ltd. These commitments did not dim his interest in his old school, and in 1962 he was renominated to the Council, holding the office of President from 1970 to 1976 before he retired in 1984.[47]

Harry Hughes was one whose economic circumstances curtailed his education but not his enterprise. Leaving school in 1917 just before he turned 14 to work in a printery to help support a family of ten children, by 1929 he had established his own printing press and founded a local newspaper, the *Newport, Spotswood and Altona News*. At the same time he established a reputation as a footrunner and enthusiastic promoter of all forms of amateur sport.[48] The printing trades absorbed quite a number of Footscray boys, and Bill Jamieson whose father had been one of the early School Councillors, followed in his father's footsteps and continued the *Footscray Advertiser*'s support of the School till the day he sold the paper. Hubert Harris, who left to join the office staff at William Angliss's meat works, went on to establish a wholesale dairy produce business with a turnover close to $41 million by 1970,[49] while Charles Bowles prospered in his father's real-estate business. George Hallet built up an engineering business in Sunshine. Charles Hughes, who left in 1922 one year post Merit Certificate, exemplifies the commercial career opportunities that were buried under the trade and engineering emphasis. He started in the office of Mephan Ferguson's engineering works whilst he studied accountancy and typing at night school. After 20 years he established a grocery business with his brother and then spent the last ten years of his working life with a transport company.[50]

Two artistic careers from the early period also stand out. George Hamilton Sneddon, the first from the School to be admitted to the Institution of Architects, went on to design the Regent and Plaza Theatres, the Atheneum Club and many private homes around Melbourne, while Bill Dargie has won an international reputation as a portrait painter. Finally, we should not forget the women students in the evening school who, along with the office staff and occasional female teacher, suffered without female toilets until 1922, despite a stream of letters from the School Council and the Principal. Gladys Hope (née Carson) first attended the School as an evening student in 1919 and 1920, then in 1921 was offered a position in the School office. After 12 years she resigned to be married, but in 1942 Hoadley asked her to teach typing, which she did for the next 25 years.[51] As with many of the male teachers, the lines between learning, working and teaching were blurred in the manner often seen as ideal by advocates of technical education at the time.

These people were representative of an ever-expanding gallery of local heroes who seemed a living expression of the opportunities that lay inside the doors of "The Tech". They were role models, held up by the staff for later students to emulate, but even better, through the Old Boys' Association, through close friendships established with the Principal and as teachers, many of them were present in person to lead and challenge. The school, of course, produced its share of bookmakers like the Williams boys[52] and postmen, woodcarters and wharf labourers, shop assistants and tailors as well as all the turners and fitters, carpenters, cabinet makers, plumbers and electrical mechanics for which it was specially designed. Of all these Hoadley and his staff were proud. "A Boy might not become a Prime Minister, but if he had put effort into his work he had done well".[53] The deep satisfaction experienced by Hoadley and his staff derived from personally watching the progress of their former pupils within a relatively close-knit and stable community can be measured, at least partly, by the high morale and professional commitment of that staff.

1. Title of FTS *Prospectus*.
2. This is the popular description of the colours by FTS boys. Another was "mud and blood".
3. *Footscray Advertiser*, 28 October 1916.
4. FTS *Prospectus*, 1925–26
5. C. A. Hoadley, Evidence given to the Board of Enquiry into the Administration of the Education Department, 13 July, 1931, p 985, PRO, VA 714, VPRS 2567.
6. *Ibid*. However, 1928 was a year of downturn in the economy and Hoadley himself had remarked at the time that the big "driftage" of students was probably accounted for by the bad conditions outside. FTS Council Minutes, 26 June 1928.
7. FTS, *Prospectus* 1926–1927. Fees for third year are not listed.
8. FTS Council Minutes, as reported in *Footscray Advertiser*, 7 April 1928.
9. C. A. Hoadley to Director of Education, 23 March 1925, VED Records.
10. C. A. Hoadley, 'Speech Night Address', 1925, reported in *Footscray Advertiser*, 26 August 1925.
11. *Footscray Advertiser*, 31 March 1928.
12. C. A. Hoadley, 'Report to Annual Speech Night' 1927, p 3, FIT Archive.
13. C. A. Hoadley, 'Speech Night Address' 1925, *op. cit.*
14. C. A. Hoadley, 'Report to Annual Speech Night', 1927, *op cit*.
15. Docherty, *op. cit.*, p 667.
16. FTS Board of Studies Minutes, 1926–1964.
17. FTS, *Prospectus*, 1926–1927.
18. *Ibid.*, p 26.
19. B. E. Lloyd, *The Education of Professional Engineers in Australia*, The Association of Professional Engineers, Australia, Melbourne, 1968, p 234.
20. *Ibid.*; p 232.
21. *Ibid.*, p 212.
22. FTS, *Prospectus*, 1926–1927.
23. Docherty, *op. cit.*, p 667.
24. The Inspectors' Report of 1925 suggested that disappointing attendance at day classes made costs nearly prohibitive. The school was compared unfavourably with Swinburne and the Working Men's College in regard to both retention rates and costs per student. VED Records.
25. Jack Kepert, Address to Old Boys Association, *Footscray Advertiser*, 18 February 1928. See also Hoadley on the same subject, 26 September 1925, 24 December 1927.
26. *Victorian Year Book*, 1973, p 833.
27. FTS, *Prospectus*, 1926–1927.
28. Docherty, *op. cit.*, p 668. See also FTS Council Minutes, 22 July

1924, which refer to a letter from Diploma student Harold Tran complaining that Diploma students were having difficulty getting the compulsory year of experience due to Federal Arbitration Award for Engineers.

29. Docherty, *op. cit.*, p 668.
30. For example, considerable pressure had to be applied to the SEC before FTS qualified students were granted Electric Wireman's Licence Certificates, FTS Council Minutes, 24 October 1922 and 1 May 1923. The Victorian Railways recognised FTS as one where its employees could study for a Diploma in 1927. The Board of Surveyors did not recognise FTS classes till 1930.
31. FTS Council Minutes, 22 October 1929.
32. FTS, *Prospectus*, 1926–1927, p 32.
33. He was Chief Scout of Victoria from 1928 till 1938 and was closely involved in the development of Gilwell Park.
34. *Footscray Advertiser*, 31 March 1928.
35. *Ibid.*, 30 July 1927. See also 4 September 1926.
36. *Ibid.*, 31 March 1928.
37. On the basis of information in the 'Reasons for Leaving 'column in the Student Record Book covering the years 1916 to 1932, it was possible to determine rough proportions going into the manufacturing, commercial and professional sectors though it was not always clear what work would actually be done by the boys or the level of skill required particularly in the manufacturing area. The figures are a percentage of all those for whom an employment or higher education destination was recorded.
38. Footscray Town Clerk to Education Department, 28 February 1928, Footscray City Council Archive, Box C 38, File E5.
39. I have excluded 1919, the year of the Spanish Flu epidemic (2.7%) and the school's opening year (1.18%). The figures include senior technical schools other than Footscray.
40. C. A. Hoadley, 'Au Revoir', *Blue and Gold*, 1946, p 4.
41. *Footscray Advertiser*, 22 November 1972. He did not formally take out his Diploma till 1932.
42. Interview.
43. *Footscray Advertiser*, 26 March 1932.
44. S. Murray-Smith and A. J. Dare, *The Tech A Centenary History of the Royal Melbourne Institute of Technology*, Hyland House, Melbourne, 1987, p 288.
45. Interview.
46. E. T. Jackson to 'Ted', 30 April 1974, FIT Archive.
47. Interview, *FITIN Orientation Manual*, 1975.
48. *Footscray Advertiser*, 16 March 1966.

49. *Ibid.*, 18 September 1970.
50. Margaret Hughes, Interview.
51. Interview by A. Rosenthal, Tape held at FTAFE.
52. W. Jamieson, Interview.
53. *Footscray Advertiser*, 31 March 1928.

CHAPTER SIX "A chronically poor institution with big obligations"[1] 1925–1938

Once granted diploma-issuing status, Footscray Technical School began to assume a role of strategic importance within the Education Department which enhanced the quality and range of education offered to the western suburbs. By the end of the 1920s the school was cause for considerable satisfaction. The Director of Education, M. P. Hansen, believed it to be "the only technical school founded in Melbourne since 1911 to have been a real success".[2] The School attracted well-qualified, committed teachers. Hoadley led rather than dominated his staff; his administration was characterised by "harmonious relations".[3] The inspectors were

> very pleased with the general atmosphere . . . and the manner in which the teachers . . . co-operate with the Principal and Headmaster in the interests of the pupils.[4]

Against considerable difficulties, Hoadley was more successful than most principals in integrating the junior and senior sections of the School by arranging schedules in such a way that as many teachers as possible worked at all levels and in both the day and night school.[5] Given the rigid rules applied by the Education Department to payment of overtime, this created an administrative nightmare that Hoadley and his staff were apparently prepared to suffer. This task became more difficult as many more boys began entering the junior school at ages 12 and even 11, but Hoadley's correspondence with the Department reveals a sensitivity to the needs of these younger boys and of the young inexperienced teachers that no doubt contributed to his effective management of the School. Hoadley could not, however, quarantine his school from the problems created by the need to establish a new career structure consequent upon the changes brought about by the operation of the 1910 Act, or from the bitterness surrounding the debate over the appropriate age to commence vocational studies. The two issues had become intertwined by the mid-1920s, and several members of the Footscray staff occupied prominent positions in a battle that dragged on into the 1930s.

As they increased in numbers, post-primary teachers acquired a stronger sense of professional distinctiveness, and they began to demand a clear career path marked off from that of primary teachers. The 1925 Teachers' Bill sought to address this demand by creating separate classified rolls for primary, secondary and technical teachers. Before it was passed, however, the Victorian Technical Teachers' Union successfully sought a change incorporating all post-primary teachers on a single Secondary Roll.[6] A very small number of senior technical instructors and principals of technical schools were left outside the system on the Professional Roll of the Victorian Public Service.

On the surface, this move seemed rational enough, since it offered a broader and more complex career path, especially to teachers with academic qualifications in technical schools. The Act, however, was passed in the context of a shift of opinion against the whole concept of junior technical schools. In 1923, after a trip overseas, Hansen, who was then Chief Inspector of Secondary Schools, but would succeed Tate in 1928 as Director of Education, prepared an influential report on systems and administration of education which argued strongly against any form of specialisation before the age of 15.[7] In these views he found the strong support of teachers and many inspectors[8], while the National Party, led by Sir Alexander Peacock, was also strongly in favour of a liberal education at the time.[9]

The Chief Inspector of Technical Schools, Donald Clark, and his senior administrators interpreted this classification scheme as an attempt to eliminate junior technical schools via the medium of a staffing policy which would eventually force on their schools the anathema of a "common curriculum". This would mean that the same subjects would be taught to all students under 15 in both technical and high schools. Clark was particularly afraid of the subversive influence of academically trained teachers on the atmosphere of his junior technical schools and the likelihood that boys of ability would be diverted from the senior technical courses. In this view he was supported by some members of technical school councils and the Technical Instructors' Society, a small group of senior instructors who had broken away from the Technical Teachers' Association in December 1924.[10] The fear was that the incentive to develop a specialist orientation would be lost and "non technical men" be placed in charge of schools, making decisions without regard for "the intricate problems of technical work". "The industrial atmosphere [would] be lost. The technical atmosphere . . . subordinate".[11] These opponents of the Bill launched a determined rearguard action to at least undermine the spirit of the Act if not change it altogether.[12] In the long run, with the strong support of the Labor Minister for Education, the Hon. Jack Lemmon, Clark was successful in protecting the system he had created for good or ill. In the meantime, the issue created serious disharmony within Footscray Technical School.

As the only Education Department technical school in the metropolitan area granting diplomas, Footscray occupied a strategic position in the system of technical education being developed by Clark; it was the only senior school in which he could exert total authority. Clark feared that if the junior schools were weakened, the council-controlled schools would also lose their potential students. From the teachers' perspective, the School represented a desirable apex to a career structure. If Clark had his way, the senior positions of principal and headmaster would be reserved for a tiny elite of technical instructors. Hoadley's views, however, were closer to those of Tate and Hansen than of Clark, and he was not convinced that the theoretical and the practical ought to be so separated in a truly technological education. Hoadley was also sensitive to the aims and aspirations of the the the majority of technical teachers, 95% of whom, including thereby most teachers of trade subjects as well as academic subjects, supported the Act as it stood.[13] It is significant that when the Footscray School Council expressed unanimous concern that if the Act weakened "the continuity of the junior and senior schools" the results would be "disastrous",[14] Hoadley had discussions with Tate and returned to reassure the Council that he believed the Act would bring "real good to the schools".[15] That Hoadley did not take a prominent part in the campaign against the Act, which he could easily have done, suggests that he was not especially opposed to it. It may also explain why relations between him and Donald Clark became so strained that Hoadley began to go out of his way to avoid Clark, and indeed the Department, as much as possible.[16]

A bitter and drawn-out debate between the Victorian Teachers' Union (VTU), with which the Victorian Technical Teachers' Association had amalgamated in 1926, broke out in an atmosphere of mounting paranoia on both sides. The position of Headmaster, responsible for the junior school, was central to the debate, and it is not without significance that F. A. Treyvaud, Headmaster of Footscray Technical School, was President of the Metropolitan Technical Teachers' Branch of the VTU in 1926 and 1927. Headmasters had been placed on the Secondary Roll, much to the satisfaction of the VTU, but the Technical Instructors' Society and the Technical Division of the Education Department sought to have this position either abolished or made available only to a technically trained person, that is, someone on the Professional Roll. Both sides had a vested interest in the position as the second highest rung on a career ladder, but at the heart of the debate was the issue of teacher training and the professional status of educators as distinct from people with other types of professional training. The VTU was unequivocal: "teaching proficiency [was] more important than industrial experience or familiarity" when it came to dealing with 12 to 15 year olds.[17] It set out to protect the Headmaster's position as a bulwark against the aims of the Technical Instructors' Society which was characterised as one proposing that

in every [technical] school there should be an imposing front entrance for "technical instructors" only, an inconspicuous side-gate for trade teachers, while the despised "academic men" might slink in through a hole in the back fence.[18]

The problem for the VTU in the period 1926 to 1930 was that the administration of the Technical Division within the Education Department appeared to go out of its way to try and force "technical" requirements on all teachers in technical schools irrespective of what subjects they taught. This created a mounting sense of injustice that permeates all the transactions of the Technical Men's Branch of the VTU in these years. The details of these matters are not relevant to this study, except in so far as they affected those staff at Footscray Technical School who were key players in the drama. Not surprisingly, the School contained notable activists from both sides. In addition to Treyvaud, William Cremor, teacher of English at the school since 1923, was elected Secretary of the VTU in 1927, while Dr H. J. Schapper, Head of the Electrical Department since 1920, was founding president of the Technical Instructors' Society. The potential for damaging conflict inside the School was high, though significantly it only erupted publicly during Hoadley's absence in 1929. There is also evidence of considerable personal cost. Treyvaud's health suffered badly toward the end of the decade,[19] and Cremor believed he was subject to victimisation.

In 1927, a speaker at the VTU Annual Conference declared that

> more than once it has happened that teachers in Technical Schools had been made to feel that they had incurred the displeasure of certain Departmental Officers because of their outspokenness.'[20]

Some time later, the *Teacher's Journal* reported the case of a technical teacher who had received an "excellent" inspector's report on the basis of his "Notes of Lessons" in 1926. Subsequently, he became prominent in union affairs, and when he presented the same notes in 1927 they were marked unsatisfactory.[21] Whether or not that person was Cremor, something very similar certainly happened to him. By all accounts a 'good' teacher, one whom Bill Dargie[22] recalled especially as opening "up the whole world of literature for me",[23] Cremor had also played a prominent part in school life as Sports Master and a man willing to devote much private time to the boys through holiday camps and involvement with the Old Boys' Association. A returned soldier, he was also active in the local militia. Cremor was not only interested in advancing the career prospects of technical school teachers but also in promoting a liberal, general education for all students under the age of 15.

Clark had been largely engaged in rearguard, defensive action under Tate and Hansen, but the return of Labor to government in 1929 substantially strengthened his hand, for the Labor Minister for Education, the Hon. Jack Lemmon, fully concurred with Clark's views. The temper of the debate sharpened and from his position in the VTU, Cremor mounted an articulate and sustained attack on the narrow vocational function of the system supported by Clark, the Technical Instructor's Society and Lemmon. He argued that the more "industrial" a boy's future employment would be, the more he needed the liberal arts:

C. A. Hoadley, Principal, 1916–1947   J. Aberdeen, Principal, 1947–1951

C. H. Beanland, Principal, 1951–1967   D. R. Mills, Director, 1970–1986

Plate i

First staff of Footscray Technical School 1916
Front: C. Morrison, F. A. Treyvaud (Headmaster), C. A. Hoadley (Principal),
L. H. Reynolds, C. F. Mudie
Back: S. Birtles, T. S. Hart, H. Northridge (Registrar), R. Spence, W. H. Nicholls

Plate ii

Some of the first students at Footscray Technical School [1916?]

Footscray Technical School Ball in the Federal Hall c 1925

Plate iii

Machine Shop Practice Workshop, c 1932

Junior Machine Shop, c 1960

Plate iv

Electrical Technology Laboratory, 1920s

Electrical Technology Laboratory, 1960

Plate v

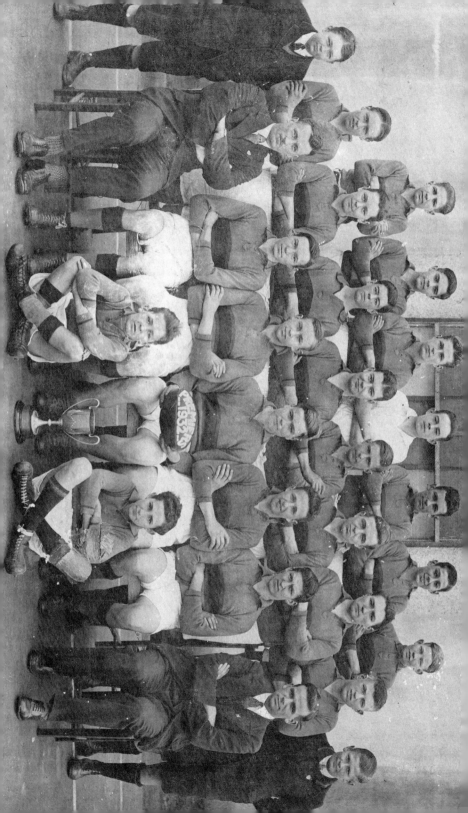

The first building completed at Ballarat Road (A Block) was opened in 1943

Aerial View of the Nicholson Street site looking south east, late 1940s

otscray Junior Technical School Senior Football Premiership Team, 1932
ack Row: S. Knight, R. Hartley, J. Duncan, R. Deeble, C. Nash, C. Daggett,
. McLeod
iddle Row: N. Jones, L. Orr, D. Washington, B. Rochford, S. Butterfield,
. Barker, A. Pascal, F. Ryan, L. Randall, B. Curwood
ront Row: W. Cremor, C. Jamieson, A. Oliver (Vice Captain), E. Luke (Captain),
. Preston, A. Townsend, F. Reid
n Ground: J. Miller, J. Marsh

Plate vii

Cast of one of the many school plays staged in the 1940s and 1950s

Junior boys reading during a geography class

The individual whose life's work [was] to be spent in cutting metal [was] in an occupation where his mentality [was] not occupied to the full. He [was] the individual who should receive at an early age a cultural education that [would] give him, during the hours of rest, something to occupy his mind. . . . Specialisation in industry [meant] narrow and repetitious tasks — unless an individual [was] given a broad cultural outlook at school, he [would] never get it at work. [24]

Moreover, he was outspoken about the class bias inherent in the distinctions between the two types of secondary schools, and objected to the fact that a boy who was to be a carpenter was not deemed to need the same general education as one who was to be a salesman.[25] In practical terms he articulated the problems that arose from making a choice too early in the face of an inflexible system where

a junior technical school boy of fifteen who wants to be a teacher or a clerk, or a high school boy at the same age who desires to be carpenter, both [found] that their 'education' [had] precluded them from their chosen vocations.[26]

Cremor, who described himself as a "plain, blunt man",[27] was a fearless and not always diplomatic fighter for causes in which he believed and he presented Clark and the Technical Instructors' Society with a formidable opponent. It is not surprising, therefore, that Cremor found himself under extreme duress from an administration which was later characterised as "seething with bitterness, discord deliberately provoked, with teachers the victims of rank injustices, blind vindictiveness and increasing obstinacy."[28] As an English teacher, he was particularly vulnerable to Clark's prejudices. Technical teachers were affronted by changes to regulations about inspections, particularly the requirement to keep written notes of every lesson, which was imposed only on teachers in technical schools. Clark saw this as a way of preventing teachers trying to "shovel" a lot of university "stuff" onto him.[29] One teacher later recalled an occasion when, during an inspection, Clark took over a composition lesson on an imaginative topic and made the students write definitions of a nail, a door and other similar objects.[30]

Cremor's problems with Clark were similar, but a transcript of an interview between the two reveals a determination on Clark's part to see nothing good in Cremor's teaching at all.[31] Over the

33/1402

The Footscray Technical School

PRINCIPAL
C. A. HOADLEY, M.Sc., B.M.E

TELEPHONE: FOOTSCRAY 824 - 825

NICHOLSON STREET,
FOOTSCRAY, W 11,

14th August, 1933,

First Official School Letterhead

period 1926 to 1929, Cremor's assessment slipped from A to A minus to B, which left him ineligible for promotion. Furthermore, Cremor was of the opinion that Clark had set the English examination in 1928 in such a way that his students had to do very badly which further reflected on his career prospects.[32] This clearly caused some problems for Hoadley but he was told curtly that the "difficulties" of which he complained did not occur in schools where English had been effectively taught and that he should be acquainted with class room practice and ensure that English was well taught.[33]

The simmering tensions in the School which had been noted by the inspectors might have remained invisible to later observers had Hoadley not taken extended leave of absence in 1929 to lead the Australian Scout contingent to the Jamboree in Arrowe, England, attend a conference on adult education, and make a tour of chemical engineering establishments. Instead of appointing a principal from another school as Acting Principal as had occurred previously, the Department appointed Dr Schapper. Considering that the Headmaster, Treyvaud, was also on leave for the first six months of the year, this left the School substantially under-staffed. In the second half of the year tensions reached boiling point, and the connection with the activities in the VTU and the Technical Instructors' Society are clear. In October Schapper had attended the Annual Conference of the Technical Schools Association which was presided over that year by the president of the Footscray Technical School Council, E. W. Trend. At this time a major issue exercising council-controlled schools was the campaign by the Director of Education, M. P. Hansen, to have them all brought under Departmental control. At the same time, the stand-off between the technical teachers in the VTU and Clark remained unresolved.

Trend had granted the President (Fryer) and Secretary (Cremor) of the VTU permission to attend the Conference as observers, even though the hostility of the VTU towards the Technical Schools Association was public knowledge. The *Teachers' Journal* had described the 1926 conference as "barren" and another as a "junket to the Grampians". There was much resentment that these conferences took place during school time and were subsidised by the Education Department, while VTU activities received little official recognition. More seriously, the VTU deplored the power of a body of "more or less well-meaning amateurs . . . with little or no proved organising or teaching ability", playing such a significant role in determining policy for technical education.[34] The third body actively involved in these issues, the Technical Instructors' Society, always had *de facto* representation at these conferences, since a good many principals were members of both organisations. Schapper added to their number and as a leading member of the Society was a prime target for the author of "Technical Notes" in the *Teachers' Journal*. The November edition carried a report of statements attributed to Schapper disparaging the Director of Education's administrative abilities.[35]

Schapper's sense of siege must have been further strengthened when Trend also allowed Fryer and Cremor to attend the November meeting of the Footscray School Council and put their case again.[36] This seems to have been the final indignity at the end of a very trying period, for Schapper called a special meeting of the School Council to lay before it his views on the School. He began by asserting that he had never come into contact with the administration of the school prior to Hoadley's absence. While Treyvaud was away everything had "flourished and run smoothly," but, since his return, "there had been a marked change; there seemed to be an undercurrent at work which was doing its utmost to undermine the administration of the school". He then gave the report in the *Teachers' Journal* as an instance of this and denied that he spoke even a word at the Conference. He went on the argue that the School "seemed to be the focus of what might be called a 'revolutionary' movement and the result was paralysing".[37] Trend was sympathetic and agreed that there "appeared to be an undercurrent attempting to undermine the school and [that] he personally felt it was time

. . . the disturbing elements [were] told that their propaganda must cease".[38] Since Cremor had also been at the conference, the inference that he was the source of the article was accepted and protesting letters were sent to the Technical Schools Association, the *Teacher's Journal* and the Director of Education protesting that more control should be exercised over what was published in the *Journal*.[39]

The allegations made by Schapper not only exacerbated tensions within the School, they opened up the possibility of an investigation by the new Chief Inspector of Technical Schools, E. P. Eltham. Schapper's position was a minority one, albeit supported by people in powerful positions, and on his return Hoadley received a letter "from practically every member of the staff" repudiating Schapper's statements,[40] while Treyvaud denied emphatically that he worked for disharmony. Respected by all sides, Hoadley poured much-needed oil on troubled waters. Schapper withdrew all the allegations he had made and they were formally expunged from the minutes of the special meeting. The retirement of both Hansen and Clark had taken some of the personal bitterness out of the issue anyway. No-one would ever again dominate the system quite so effectively as Clark had done, while the worsening Depression raised far more fundamental problems.

In 1932 Schapper left the School for 18 months to serve as a popular Acting Principal at Brunswick Technical School. Sadly, he became a victim of the changing tide of fortunes for secondary technical teachers. Schapper applied for, and was formally appointed, Principal, but was successfully appealed against by J. L. Ross, who had been an outstanding Headmaster. The Technical School Branch objected but the Public Service Board upheld the appeal.[41] This was the first time a teacher on the Secondary Roll had been appointed to a principal's position, but when most of the Brunswick Technical School Council threatened to resign in favour of Schapper, Eltham persuaded them that it was best to withdraw their opposition.[42] Schapper returned to Footscray Technical School where he remained until his retirement in 1948.

At the same time, the crisis created by the economic downturn changed the focus of the VTU, and Cremor's radicalism came to suit the VTU less and less. His health had also suffered, and in 1931 he retired as President of the VTU. In 1934 he left teaching altogether to take up a position as Head of the Dried Fruits Board, but his association with his Footscray 'boys' continued. Many of them, handpicked by Cremor, saw distinguished service under his leadership during world war II.[43]

Over this period, the character of the School Council was also changing in a way that might have been of greater significance had the Depression not so seriously retarded the development of education in the state as a whole. Leobard B. Lloyd, a Footscray city councillor was nominated in 1920 and together with other members of his family he endowed the 'LBM Scholarship' with a gift of £600. W. H. Cuming joined in 1921 and remained till just before his death in 1929. William McKinna, a member of the Amalgamated Society of Engineers whose interests also ran to the Worker's Educational Association, was President for the years 1944–1945 and Treasurer from 1932–1943 and again from 1946 till his retirement in 1954. The Footscray City Council had a permanent representative from 1923, firstly Cr J. A. Stephens, and then Cr Duncan O'Toole, who sat until 1936. The Williamstown Council finally acquired representation in 1929 and Cr James T. Gray held his position until 1955 when Williamstown Technical School acquired a technical school of its own. The Education Department was firstly represented by the naturalist, Dr A. J. Leach, who played a very active role in Council affairs, but his replacement, E. R. Davey, rarely attended meetings.

Footscray was, and is, unequivocally an industrial area, but the primary image informing the dreams of the early advocates of a technical school was of a manufacturing area characterised by small, innovative and civic-minded enterprises along the lines of Birmingham. Yet the reality was substantially different. While there were undoubtedly successful manufacturers and engineering establishments in Footscray, the background and interests of the early councillors reflected more the hope than the reality of Footscray's employment characteristics, where so many men worked in relatively unskilled, insecure and unpleasant jobs for large-scale and often impersonal enterprises. Men such as the Richardsons, the Hoopers, the Shillabeers and the older generation of Cumings and Hallensteins were giving way to managers of large and complex operations, many of which only required engineers and even skilled tradesmen in relatively small numbers to maintain machinery and processes that occupied large numbers of unskilled and semi-skilled workers. Footscray is more properly characterised as an area of industrial processing, with chemical processing bulking very large, whether it be in the production of chemicals themselves, fertilisers, leather products, armaments, glass or rubber products. Most of the processing establishments in the area were large and became larger as time passed, and at least some of the local engineering industry developed as a service sector for those establishments of this kind that did not employ a full complement of design and service personnel 'in house'.

Managers and senior staff had begun to dominate the Council by the end of the 1920s, but they were no less interested than proprietors in the local technical school, even if they had fewer personal resources to offer as endowments. E. W. Trend of the Mt Lyell Mining Company was the first of these managers but he was soon joined, as we have seen, by R. G. Parsons of the Colonial Gas Association, Arthur Hughes of Colonial Sugar Refineries and Isaac Boas of Michaelis Hallenstein. Over the next two decades these men were joined by Norman Taylor of ICI; Noel Brodribb, Chemical Engineer in Charge of Munitions, Commonwealth Ammunition Factory; Frank Ayre, General Manager, Parkinson Stove Co; George Simcock of ACI (Glass manufacturing); and Maurice O'Loughlin, also of the Commonwealth Ammunition Factory.

All these men could be grouped comfortably together under a heading 'chemical engineering', and as such they fairly represent the defining feature of Footscray's industrial character. It is tempting to suggest that if Footscray were to have carved out a special niche for itself in the education sector and in the industrial training area it should have set about developing itself as a school specialising in chemical rather than mechanical engineering. Indeed, one of the grander early visions for the School set precisely that scene:

> Perhaps no other school in the state is more favourably situated from the point of view of natural advantages. Situated in the midst of a great manufacturing district, it cannot do otherwise than grow to be a most important institution in the district . . . the day is not so far distant when it will be the centre of investigations into iron and steel working, leather, dye, chemical investigations, glass manufacture, explosives, . . . It will become the seat of scientific investigations into all the great manufactures around it.[44]

It was not, however, until the late 1920s that any active steps were taken to improve the link between the School and the chemical industries nearby. Ironically, the School Council tried to move the focus just at the time when the Education Department decided to designate the school as one "that should occupy a leading place in Mechanical Engineering".[45] In October 1927, the Footscray Technical School Council President, Trend, presented a paper on "The Training of Chemical Engineers" at the Technical Schools Association Conference,[46] and it was resolved that the it would be recommended that the authorities establish a course in chemical engineering.[47] Then, sometime in 1928, the Council began to make specific moves to establish a course and, as we have seen, they succeeded in persuading the Department to allow Hoadley extra leave of absence in the United Kingdom so that he could make a survey of chemical engineering education there.[48]

Discussions were held with the leader of the Parliamentary Labor Party, Mr Prendergast, Jack Lemmon and the Education Department as a result of which local support was actively canvassed.[49] However, despite claims that they had initiated the proposal to establish chemical engineering courses, and that Footscray was located in the heart of the chemical industry,[50] and despite strong support from Footscray and Williamstown City Councils and some manufacturers,[51] it is clear that the Working Men's College had the interest and power to undermine the case. This was reflected in the fact that it was the Working Men's College which put forward the successful resolution at the 1929 Technical Schools Association Conference calling for the establishment of chemical engineering at some suitable centre.[52]

Unfortunately, when Hoadley returned, his Report to the Education Department acknowledged that the Working Men's College already had some of the equipment necessary and overall advantages for setting up such a course. The Education Department then approved the establishment of a *course*, though very specifically not a *school*, of chemical engineering at the Working Men's College in December 1929 with the approval of the Society for the Chemical Industry of Victoria and the Australian Chemical Institute. Whether it was of any consolation to the Footscray School Council, it is worth noting that no Working Men's College students actually completed sufficient preliminary subjects in chemistry to admit them to specialist classes in chemical engineering until well into world war II.[53]

The question that must be asked is why, with the expertise, interest and work experience right at hand, so little came of this opportunity? In the broadest sense it has much to do with the narrow conception of education and industrial development that was pervasive at the time. A chemical engineer is concerned with the design, construction and operation of a plant in which materials undergo chemical and physical change. As a branch of engineering, it is less divorced from science and research than mechanical or civil engineering, and its development in the late nineteenth and early twentieth century had largely taken place outside the United Kingdom. This changed dramatically during world war I, not simply because of the urgent wartime demand for munitions, gas and the like, but also because of Britain's need to supply domestically a range of chemical products previously imported from Germany. The resultant growth and development of the chemical industry and the role and status of chemical engineering there was not paralleled in Australia until world war II, where the similar circumstances prevailed.[54] Typically, Australian industrial and educational objectives were lagging behind those of Britain. Australia's rather retarded industrial development left the advocates of chemical engineering education crying in the wilderness, and chemical engineers saddled with a slightly dubious reputation, as exemplified by the following anecdote: "It used to be said that a chemical engineer was a man who talked to engineers about chemistry, to chemists about engineering and to other chemical engineers about sex".[55] Neither Australian educationalists nor industrialists had yet grasped in any meaningful way that sophisticated technological development implied a marriage of theoretical science and practical application in ways specifically denied by the prevailing attitudes about technical education.

The second part of the explanation lies in a slip between the rhetoric and reality of technical education at a number of levels. Initially the civic leaders of Footscray had wanted a school to create, as much as serve, an industrial base, and their focus on small engineering works and existing trades was rooted more in past processes than any visionary perception of future developments. In one sense at least, the School was an attempt to escape the noxious, smelly, sometimes dangerous, activities that were the nucleus of the modern chemical-based industries. At broader levels, too, technical education was less genuinely linked to specific industrial development than its supporters claimed and was more inclined to follow student demand than actively lead it into new and untried areas. There was, in fact, no point in offering courses students did not want to take, as Hoadley's expensive but abortive attempt to establish aeronautical engineering at the School immediately after world war I demonstrated only too clearly. Just as Footscray was not rushed with students wishing to do aeronautical engineering, neither was the Working Men's College rushed with students wishing to tackle chemical engineering.

A third part of the explanation lies in the 'politics' of education. Footscray was part of a relatively centralised and bureaucratic education system reliant on government funds which had to be shared equally. This inevitably dampened regional aspirations, but the reliance on government was a consequence of the absence of local resources, public or private, to fully develop and control their own special schools. Low population density meant that regional colleges were simply not big enough to support specialised courses unless other colleges were specifically prevented from offering them in competition. No governments proved willing to do this, partly because of their own sectional interests, but also because of the transport problems. Inevitably, the centrality and ease of access to the Working Men's College proved an almost insurmountable advantage, especially when it came to providing what could be classed as experimental courses. It seems that Footscray did not have the chemical societies on side, most likely because it was, in reality, still scarcely viable as a diploma-granting institution. Desperately overcrowded, it was hard pressed to meet existing demand for junior and evening classes, but it may not be without significance that Hoadley was absent from Victoria for almost the whole of 1929 when the major lobbying was taking place. As to location, it was not really possible to argue that the Working Men's College was very far from the chemical establishments in any case.

Finally, part of the explanation has to lie in the fact that Australian industry was still in its infancy and many of the larger organisations were dependent on British capital and/or expertise or were becoming increasingly so. If experts could be brought from overseas and designs, systems and ideas obtained from the same source, there was little urgency to support the development of a local base of highly skilled chemical engineers. The development of technical education was severely hampered by the derivative nature of Australian capitalism and a prevailing tendency to discount the value of education as something associated with 'unproductive' white-collar workers, the professions and the leisured classes on the one hand, and, on the other, a tendency to emphasise the practical at the expense of the theoretical, which was necessary as engineering moved into a far more sophisticated and scientific phase.

Not that Footscray failed to produce chemical engineers in this period. One career history can serve to demonstrate the process by which experience was substituted for education prior to world war II. Fred Giles' story not only reveals much about the haphazard relationship between school, work and 'getting on', but it also provides rare insight into the special qualities of Hoadley's leadership. Giles was dux of Powell Street, Yarraville State School in 1928, from where he went to junior school at the Working Men's College. He completed his Intermediate Technical Certificate in 1930, but family circumstances left him unable to stay at school, nor could he find work as the Depression deepened. Much under the influence of his older brother, he was largely 'hanging about' until a careless decision to try lighting a fire to keep warm under the local scout hall saw a group of eight 'lads' escorted by a policeman into Hoadley's nearby office. Hoadley was firm but kind and perceptive. He asked Giles why he was there, only to be told, "Because my brother was." "Are you", asked Hoadley, "going to spend the rest of your life doing what your older brother does?" Giles believes he began to take responsibility for himself from that moment and willingly took the chance Hoadley offered to sit in on the diploma classes[57] until Hoadley could find him a job. This experience was equally positive and, although a few months later Giles took the unskilled job Hoadley had found for him at Mitchell's Implement Works, he was soon back at night school.

Between 1934 and 1940 Giles studied for a Diploma of Mechanical Engineering while he spent a brief period as an apprentice turner and fitter with the Victorian Railways and then worked as a Detail Draughtsman. A move to Australian Paper Manufacturers set him on the path to chemical engineering. While posted to APM's Maryvale Mill, together with the Chief Chemist, he

> designed and constructed a large circular slide rule for carrying out specific process calculations. This eliminated the need for a shift chemist to be on continuous duty for this purpose and was in use for many years until superseded by calculators. [56]

In 1941 Giles moved to the new Monsanto Chemical Works as a design draughtsman supervising chemical plant layout and

GENERAL SCHEME OF WORK AT THE SCHOOL

The work of the School is divided up into the following sections:—

The Time Table of Classes is exhibited at the School.

Prospectus 1928–29

91

design in conjunction with industrial chemists. In joining Monsanto, Giles was able to ride the huge expansion of the local chemical industry necessitated by the war and Australia's potential isolation. In particular, this heralded the development of an organic chemical industry which, unlike the "simpler, traditional inorganic chemical processes",[57] could not get by simply by cobbling together teams of chemists and engineers. Then, in 1950, he moved to Davis Gelatine (Aust.) Pty Ltd, where he remained till retirement supervising the design, construction and commissioning of new plants in Sydney, New Zealand, South Africa, the USA, South America and England.[58]

As the Depression deepened, students drifted away and the resources of the School were slashed. The maintenance grant from the Education Department which had been £3950 in 1926 was still only £2800 in 1936. Staff salaries, cut by 20% in 1931, were not restored until October 1936. The number of part-time evening instructors was also reduced and the session rates were cut. Full restoration to 1925 rates did not occur for this group until 1943.[59] "The unemployment of fathers and the call upon the earnings of other members of the family . . . resulted in an alarming decrease in the number of applications for trade courses." Many "working people" found it difficult "to raise the necessary fees".[60] Over the period 1930–1933 a number of trade classes were closed down and Civil Engineering was transferred to the Working Men's College. The problem was exacerbated by the tendency, even in the best of times, for a boy not to enrol in a class until he had appropriate employment, despite the good arguments that could be put forward for the reverse approach. However, moves were successfully made to establish some special training classes for unemployed boys,[61] and in one area the School did continue to develop. Having been declared an approved centre for training electrical apprentices in 1930, all subjects leading to an A-Grade Licence were available by 1933.

The severity of the set back to education in this period was intensified by the rise to dominance among non-Labor parties, who held government from 1931, of the view that public expenditure on education should be be curtailed as a matter of principle. The most obvious expression of this sentiment can be seen in both the terms of reference and the report of the McPherson Board of Enquiry into Certain Matters Concerning the Education Department, Victoria, which led to staff reductions, salary cuts, a total cessation of all secondary teacher training and an increase in high-school fees. All these changes appeared to favour technical education, but they seriously undermined the overall quality of education in the state. When called upon to give evidence before this Enquiry, Hoadley argued strenuously for the return to entrance at the end of grade 8. The School Council was called upon to declare where it thought cuts could be made. The possibility that Footscray might lose its senior classes to the Working Men's College as a cost cutting measure was seriously canvassed, but Hoadley and the Council argued successfully against this. No doubt they were assisted by the fact that 26 diplomas were awarded in the years 1930 to 1933 and eight holders of Footscray diplomas were enrolled at the University of Melbourne in 1931.[62] Ultimately, Footscray did not have its technical school downgraded, but it did lose its promised high school, and the overall pressure on educational facilities in the area remained at unacceptably high levels.

As soon as enrolments began to rise again by 1934 the space crisis re-emerged. By 1936 enrolments had reached record levels in both day and evening classes.[63] This time temporary accommodation was sought in the top floor of Caldecott's Buildings in Nicholson Street, and as economic prosperity returned plans for new buildings were approved. In 1938 a two-storey extension along Nicholson Street was completed and a heat engines laboratory established in the basement. The School was ready to enter a new phase of growth and development engendered by the war and the prosperity that followed in its wake.

1. *Footscray Advertiser*, 30 June 1917.
2. M. P. Hansen, 'Technical Education . . .', *op. cit.*, p 13.
3. *Teachers' Journal*, Vol. 13, No. 1, January 1930, p 28.
4. Inspectors' Report 1936. FIT Archive. This is typical of reports throughout the 1920s and 1930s.
5. See, in particular, Inspectors' Reports 1936 and 1943. FIT Archive.
6. Bessant, *op. cit.*, p 239.
7. *Ibid.*, pp 234–237.
8. *Ibid.*, p 237.
9. *Ibid.*, pp 191–193.
10. *Ibid.*, p 241. The major criterion for membership which made this a very exclusive body was that Instructors must have had outside experience in the fields in which they taught. All members of this Society who were in Departmental schools would have been placed on the Professional Roll. It included quite a number of principals.
11. Eltham Papers, 'The Danger to Technical Education', Memorandum issued by the Technical Instructors' Society of Victoria, (undated), p 2. Quoted in Bessant, *op cit.*, p 243–244.

12. The principal means by which this was attempted was the filling of positions vacated by people who had been on the Secondary Roll with persons eligible for the placement on the Professional Roll. In 1926 there were only 26 on the Professional Roll; by 1928 this had risen to 74 giving rise to serious concern within the VTU. D. M. Hudson, 'Post Primary Teachers' Organisations in Victoria 1905–1950', M. A., University of Melbourne, 1971, p 69.

13. See, 'Report of a Special Meeting of Technical Teachers July 1926', *Teachers' Journal*, Vol. 9, No. 14, 1 December 1926, p 407.

14. FTS Council Minutes, 23 March 1925.

15. *Ibid.*, 27 April 1925. See also, *Ibid.*, 24 August & 28 September 1926.

16. In a hand written letter dated 12 February 1930, Hoadley wrote to farewell the retiring Chief Inspector regretting that, 'something had come between us' [about three or four years ago] . . . what it was I was never able to definitely formulate but I have distinctly felt that some misunderstanding existed so I thought it best to keep away from the Department as much as possible.' Clark Papers in the possession of Stephen Murray-Smith.

17. *Teachers' Journal*, Vol. 10, No. 6, June 1927, p 172.

18. Eltham Papers, Report of the Victorian Teachers' Association of a meeting held 24 July 1926 to protest against attempts being made to defeat the provisions of the Teachers' Act 1925. Quoted in Bessant, *op. cit.*, p 242.

19. He had to take six months leave of absence in 1928 and, while he was refused a further six months special leave for 'health reasons' in 1929, he nevertheless took it without pay. PRO VA 714, VPRS 10275, Outward Correspondence, Post Primary Schools 1900–1938, Box 136, passim.

20. *Teachers' Journal*, Vol. 10, No. 2, February 1927, p 41.

21. *Ibid.*, Vol.12, No. 10, October 1929, p 370.

22. See above, p 72.

23. *Footscray Advertiser*, 25 May 1966.

24. *Teachers' Journal*, Vol. 12, No. 2, February 1929, p 28.

25. *Ibid.*, Vol. 13, No. 3, March 1930, p 107.

26. *Ibid.*

27. *Ibid.*, Vol. 12, No. 10, October 1929, p 370.

28. *Ibid.*, Vol. 12, No. 3, March 1930, p 96.

29. Quoted in Hudson, *op cit.*, p 71.

30. J. M. Allen, Monash University, Faculty of Education Oral History Archives, Tape No. 13.

31. Transcript of conversation with Clark re one of his English lessons to Intermediate A class, 29 October 1929, VED Records.

32. Extensive correspondence regarding this matter in VED Records.

33. Secretary of Education Department to C. A. Hoadley, 4 & 22 April 1929, PRO VA 714, VPRS 10275, Box 136. Hoadley's letter that prompted the correspondence about the allegedly unfavourable Inspectors' Report has not survived.

34. *Teachers' Journal*, Vol. 9, No. 13, November 1926, p 271.
35. FTS Council Minutes, Special Meeting, 10 December 1929.
36. *Ibid.*, 26 November 1929.
37. *Ibid.*, Special Meeting, 10 December 1929.
38. *Ibid.*
39. The editor of the Journal replied that he had checked his source and was happy that the words attributed to the acting principal were "true in substance and in effect", but admitted that "accompanying comments were susceptible of causing offence and should not have been printed in the Journal". *Teachers' Journal*, Vol. 13, No. 1, January 1930, p 25.
40. FTS Council Minutes, 25 February 1930.
41. J. M. Allen, *op. cit.*
42. Hudson, *op. cit .*, p 120. See also *Argus*, 26 May 1934, p 11, and 30 June 1934, p 25.
43. After distinguished service in the second world war as Brigadier, Cremor returned to education matters as Guidance Officer to the ex-servicemen at the University of Melbourne and Government Representative on the First Teachers' Tribunal and devoted himself to Repatriation and Legacy matters till his death in 1962. For more detail see *Education Gazette and Teachers' Aid*, 27 July 1962, p 240.
44. *Footscray Advertiser*, 26 August 1916.
45. FTS Council Minutes, 29 March 1927.
46. At the 1923 Annual Conference Hoadley had read a paper prepared by I. Boas on 'The Training of the Technical Chemist'. Programme, TSAV Papers, ACPPIV Archive.
47. *Argus*, October 26 1927, p 27.
48. FTS Council Minutes, 26 February 1929.
49. *Ibid.*, 25 September 1929.
50. *Ibid.*, 25 June 1929.
51. *Ibid.*, 26 November 1929.
52. *Argus*, 17 October 1929, p 11.
53. Murray-Smith & Dare, *op. cit.*, p 290.
54. W. H. G. Armytage, *A Social History of Engineering*, Faber & Faber, London, 1976, pp 263–264.
55. Fred Giles, Interview.
56. Letter to author 24 April 1987, FIT Archive.
57. *Ibid.*
58. *Ibid.*
59. Docherty, *op. cit.*, p 678.
60. *Footscray Advertiser*, 14 February 1931.
61. See *Ibid.*, 24 September 1932, re FTS resolutions for Technical Schools Association Conference.
62. *Footscray Adveriser*, 26 December 1931.
63. FTS Council Minutes, 25 February 1936.

CHAPTER SEVEN **A new school on Ballarat Road 1939–1950**

The 1930s had been a dismal decade; just as the worst of the economic crisis had begun to ease, the threatening clouds of war had gathered. For education it had been a barren decade indeed and the demands of modern war revealed the cost in huge shortages of skilled personnel. A stagnant and highly derivative manufacturing sector was required to modernise, innovate and reach peak efficiency almost overnight. Commonwealth government resources were placed at the service of technical education in particular to upgrade and expand the skills of the workforce in the quickest possible time. Schools such as Footscray became almost 24 hour institutions, moving in shifts of trainees as 'normal' classes left, and working in close co-operation with tightly co-ordinated manpower plans. Normal schedules also expanded while air raid precautions demanded trenches and bricked up windows be imposed on already limited accommodation. Nevertheless before the war was over the long-dreamed-of new school on the Ballarat Road site had become a reality. The 1940s were good years for Footscray Technical School; years of growth and significant achievement during which it finally reached maturity.

Under the shadow of war came a renewed sense of national purpose, and technical education was once again "the favoured child of its age".[1] The demand for every type of course escalated. The junior school enrolment for 1940 edged toward 600 and the 'open night' that year attracted 8000 visitors.[2] In 1941 nearly 300 applicants were turned away.[3] Enrolments in the day diploma classes rose from 13 in 1935 to 75 in 1940 and in the evening school from 539 to 1381. The Nicholson Street buildings were bursting at the seams and the authorities finally agreed that a second site was essential. The Ballarat Road site that Hoadley had recommended nearly 20 years earlier was acquired, and the foundations of a building "with a Swedish tendency and a distinctly clear cut" appearance[4] were laid in September 1941. At first, it was intended that diploma students would remain at Nicholson Street, so 400 junior boys and 200 evening students took occupancy of the new building in 1943 as plans were being laid for further extensions. During 1946 the School acquired a new chemistry laboratory at Nicholson Street, a new draughting room at Ballarat Road, and a special grant of £2500 to buy testing equipment.[5] Then, in 1947, the Commonwealth funds provided £120,000 for additional buildings and equipment at Ballarat Road.

All these new buildings allowed for substantial growth in the senior school, where numbers reached 357 in 1945 and remained at about the 300 mark till 1950, by which time the back-log created by the Depression and the war had finally passed through. Part-time evening enrolments peaked at 2042 in 1945, before stabilising at around 1800 for the rest of the decade. The School became large, complex and potentially unwieldy. As early as 1944, the Inspectors had warned that "future development, unless carefully controlled, [was] likely to lead to considerable complication", and suggested that diploma classes and the junior school should occupy the Ballarat Road site while trade classes would be limited to Nicholson Street.[6] In the event, the Commonwealth building program made this neat arrangement difficult, to the consternation of the Education Department officers, who complained that long-range planning was being neglected.[7]

Undermanning was a feature of the war years, but the administration of the School was made unusually difficult by the early enlistment of the Registrar, W. A. G. Smith[8], who although subsequently killed in February 1942 in New Brittain, was believed to be a prisoner of war until October 1945. His tasks fell to Miss G. McComb, who performed admirably but was denied adequate remuneration or sufficient replacement staff. Treyvaud's retirement as Headmaster in 1941 created a minor catering crisis, as a series of separate functions had to be held to accommodate all those who wished to farewell him. His replacement, J. R. Wilson, came after ten years experience as Headmaster of Geelong Technical School.[9] An "outstanding" junior maths teacher and author of several text books, "he immediately made his presence felt in raising the tone of the school and in effecting greater cohesion between the Junior and Senior sections." "A clear thinker, and fearless in expression", he "won a place for himself in the affections of all" before he left in 1946 to become Principal of one of the newer technical schools.[10] Academic staffing arrangements were improved by the designation of J. L. Kepert as Vice Principal in 1944. Kepert[11] brought youth and administrative flair to the senior school, combined with a capacity to nurture, inspire and befriend.

These were years of considerable change in the structure of courses and the length of time required to complete them. In 1945 the Intermediate Technical Certificate course was extended to four years; correspondingly the Junior Technical Certificate course became three years. The Merit Certificate was abolished in 1947. At the fourth-year level those with professional aspirations were given more mathematics than those planning to take up trades. In 1939 the diploma courses had been lengthened to include a fourth year of part-time evening study. The time devoted to mathematics and English was increased and workshop practice reduced from a quarter to a sixth of the week. In 1946 the Diploma of Engineering was further extended to four years of full-time study and, with the introduction of matriculation English into the course, the diploma became fully acceptable for entrance to university. The path from primary school to university via the technical system had finally been smoothed, and students who took appropriate subjects were entitled to exemptions in Melbourne University's Engineering course.

The range of courses available at Footscray expanded with the addition of the first two years of the Diplomas of Applied Chemistry and Civil Engineering and the Professional Certificate in Building and Contracting.[12] In 1949 the full Diploma of Applied Chemistry became available, though the numbers graduating remained a small proportion of the the total for some time. In the evening school, Expert Certificate courses covered Applied Chemistry, Electrical, Mechanical, Municipal and Structural Engineering and Metallography. Special short courses were available in Foremanship, Air Conditioning, Domestic Refrigeration, Lady Tracers, Jig and Tool Design and Dress Making, and there were also a full range of Trade Certificate courses. Three Commercial Courses were offered: Preparatory, Stenography and Accountancy,[13] while the Art and Applied Art courses had become considerably more specialised.

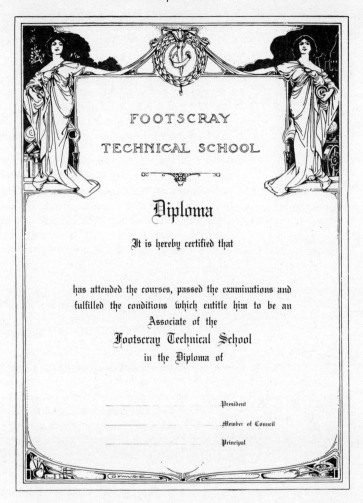

FOOTSCRAY
TECHNICAL SCHOOL

Diploma

It is hereby certified that

has attended the courses, passed the examinations and
fulfilled the conditions which entitle him to be an
Associate of the
Footscray Technical School
in the Diploma of

....   President

....   Member of Council

....   Principal

The changes in the length and content of courses had arisen
largely from the realisation that higher levels of academic performance were necessary to meet the needs of modern industry re-
invigorated by war-time demand. There was finally at this time
also a formal recognition that schools had wider responsibilities
than simply training for certain types of employment. In his
Report to Parliament in 1944, the Minister for Public Instruction,
the Hon. T. Holloway, regretted that in the past specialised

technical training had been regarded as of paramount importance at the expense of "subjects basic to a complete education". Consequently, steps were being taken to increase the emphasis on cultural subjects and "those activities with a high social or aesthetic value". Activities such as sport and music, previously deemed extra-curricular, were to be included in the basic curriculum with official assurances that this did not mean a "lowering of our technical or intellectual standards".[14] Hoadley took up the theme, enthusiastically explaining in the 1947–48 *Prospectus* that education at Footscray had the

> comprehensive aim of promoting the development of responsible citizens, not merely as economic units destined to fall into a prepared place in the present industrial structure, but as the creative and self reliant men of the future who will be competent to play a decisive part in directing, shaping, and improving the industrial system.

Hoadley also took it upon himself to argue the case for English as essential to "complete and assist the student's training in his scientific and practical work".[15] Dr Schapper, Head of the Electrical Technology Department, extended the argument even further. Arguing that science was an essential part of "Culture", he declared

> The magnificent, well-nigh sublime, accomplishment of Art, of Science, of Engineering and of Technology are being prostituted by greed and War to turn this fair world into a slum and shambles. Things are so indeed, because we have no true Culture . . . Art alone is not enough, nor is Science, nor Philosophy, nor Religion. We must strive for a close, intimate link between these so that Culture may become one in the study and pursuit of human perfection.[16]

In the senior school this new emphasis mainly manifested itself in the compulsory study of first leaving and then matriculation standard English, where "training" was given via "discussion classes" in which public questions of importance were debated and the student was shown how to pursue "independent and original study".[17] In the junior school the staff took full advantage of the new status of the humanities which provided an invigorating climate for the development of relevant and stimulating social studies programmes free of the restrictions of a university-dominated public examination system.

Ben "Mother" Howells,[18] Head of the English and Social Studies Department from 1938 to 1964, was a complex man who had been a boxer, a rugby player and a midshipman as well as "a placid conveyor of the English language", producer of school dramatic performances and leader of many 'tramping' expeditions. Initially attracted to the School by its "very unusual" qualities, he flourished in an atmosphere where "the freedom of thought and behaviour in a responsible manner was very marked".[19] Under his leadership the English and Social Studies Department won regular accolades from the Education Department Inspectors. Howells' work was said to be "'marked by a very earnest appreciation of his responsibilities and a close attention to the special needs of his pupils". One teacher was praised for his "keen interest" and the "cheerful atmosphere" of his classroom, another for "bright presentation and close, yet friendly supervision". In marked contrast to earlier periods, the inspectors took the view that "the school magazine" and "the time spent in producing plays and entertainments and in attending to the library is so well spent that it is difficult to assess its final worth".[20] In 1947 the Library obtained a full-time Head, Mrs H. Archer, greatly strengthening its role in school life. At this time, it boasted 2000 reference books, 1600 in the lending section, and an encouragingly high pattern of usage.

The standards of teaching and demonstration throughout the rest of the school were also high. The inspectors, not renowned for their generous opinions, commented frequently on the good organisation, the quality of work produced by students in practical classes and the overall level of interest generated in classes. The main area of concern was the teaching of maths and science, where although the standard in the senior school was generally considered adequate, that in the junior school was far less so.[21] Suggestions for greater co-ordination and interaction between teachers in the two sections of the School were slow to be acted upon but fruitful when they were. The major problem, however, continued to be a general shortage of qualified maths teachers.

It was not the work in the classrooms, however, but in the workshops and laboratories that provided the unique, defining experiences of technical education, and the new workshops were handsome indeed. Here, where students were initiated into the world of machines, chemicals and electricity, much of the folklore and humour peculiar to the School was generated.

Foremost in diploma student folklore were the electrical technology laboratory presided over by "Doc" Schapper and characterised by predictable jibes about sparks and fingers on terminals, and the heat engines laboratory, forever, it seems, the domain of "Johnny" Kepert and always full of smoke and steam:

> The space at the top end of the room seems to be filled by a small "Colonial" boiler, coughing smoke and flame, and a large "Parsons" turbine, which stood grand and motionless against one wall. . . . The remainder of the space was taken up by horizontal and vertical steam engines, in violent motion and emitting great clouds of steam; and the various types of gas, kero., and petrol engines.[22]

The School certainly developed a vigorous extra-curricular life. Music and drama productions, Gardening, Photography, Debating, Chess and 'Tramping' Clubs jostled with the school orchestra, Scouting, sketching, and, of course, sport. The boys participated in a very wide range of sports including cricket, football, tennis, athletics, swimming, hockey, baseball, lacrosse and rugby. Participation in inter-school sport was keen, and Footscray generally acquitted itself well. All this activity found an impressive showcase in the magazine *Blue and Gold*, which not only provided another choice of activity but also engaged members of the revitalised Old Boys' Association.

Music was a special love of Hoadley, and even though there was no music teacher in the School until 1949 it was almost always present in one form or another. The first school concerts were held in 1942 to raise money for the war effort, but they soon became a major event in the School calendar, culminating in an evening performance of the best productions for the benefit of parents. The school orchestra also provided accompaniment for other activities, but perhaps the most famous musical feature of this era was the "Dips Glee Club":

> It all began one day in Room 105 when some of us were trying to warble our divergent ways through various melodies. The resultant cacophony aroused in me the urge to either abolish singing from the class — or better it. We decided on the latter course, hence the formation of the Choir.
>
> We practised mostly in the Heat Engines Laboratory where we were least in fear of interruption. Very occasionally we used the piano in Room 110; but the clang of a spanner against

a nearby engine, or a boy's head, served equally well as a tuning fork in the lab.[23]

In 1944 the Club acquired a wider audience with a successful radio appearance on the Australian Amateur Hour, before going on to do "those half hour [radio] shows they had for servicemen during the war" as well as perform regularly at the Old Boys' dances. Even leaving the School did not break up the act at first. The conductor, Greg Lake, went to the Yarraville Laboratory and two others were at Newport Power Station. Lindsay Davies "used to relieve on the [Newport] switchboard at lunchtime. He could hook up Footscray Tech and Yarraville and we used to practise on the telephone."[24] In 1946, Hoadley himself was acting as conductor, but the Club does not seem to have survived into 1947.

More directly related to the School's role as a technical institution were the Hobbies Club and excursions to local industrial establishments. The majority of excursions to places such as Melbourne Iron and Steel Mills, the Newport Power Station, Yallourn, Bradford Cotton Mills and Monsanto Chemicals were arranged for the senior school, many of them in the war years made in Kepert's famous, charcoal-burning car, 'Lizzie'. Later in the decade regular excursions to local industrial establishments for small parties of junior boys began. The chief attraction at the annual Hobbies Exhibition was usually the model railway, every part of which, excluding the rolling stock, was manufactured at the School:

> The metal rails were shaped in the . . . Sheetmetal Shop, and soldered together in the Woodwork Rooms . . . Besides the rails, there were model tunnels, Loco. sheds, telegraph poles and a host of minor details, all of which were made from scrap wood.[25]

All this social, sporting and cultural activity pointed to the "existence of educational forces" which extended "beyond the school walls" and of which they could "all feel proud".[26]

In 1946 Footscray boys were charged with the "privilege" of participation in "the inescapable task of building a new and better world on the foundations of a just victory". For a time the "younger generation" had the benefit of the presence of young ex-servicemen in the School who, "with an admirable capacity for quick adaption to novel conditions", had "taken a lively

103

interest in all the activities of the School — in sport, in the production of "Integral", and in the concert." This "community spirit", as well as "their serious approach to their studies", was held up as a "stimulating example to their younger school mates".[27] This greater presence of mature young men certainly seems to have instigated the formation of a Students' Representative Council (SRC) in 1946, long before such bodies were especially fashionable. Hoadley was very supportive, always ready with an understanding ear.[28] The SRC comprised 14 students elected by the various forms,[29] under the guidance of F. H. Brooks, the popular Head of the Chemistry Department, who would, in 1965, be appointed Director of Education. Apart from acting as a liaison between students, staff and administration, the SRC published a newspaper from time to time, made contact with various outside bodies such as the the the Engineering Education Research Group and the Senior Technical Schools' Sports Association and organised dances throughout the year.

In the 1940s the diploma school finally achieved the size, status and quality of which its early advocates had dreamed. In so doing, it laid the foundation of the School's long-term development into an autonomous degree-granting college of advanced education at the end of the 1960s. If those interested in technical education in Footscray had sometimes felt over the preceding 25 years that the times had conspired against the School, there was cause for deep satisfaction in the favourable turn of circumstances in these years. Efforts by the School in 1937 to raise the £5000 for new equipment from local manufacturers had been a failure,[30] yet by the middle of the war the school was, for the first time, richly endowed with scholarships and prizes from a wide cross-section of local industry and community groups. The war had not only made manufacturers more aware of the value of training, war-time demand had so lifted production and profits, especially in the industries around the school, that such public gestures became almost obligatory. The number of government scholarships available also increased. Thus, for the first time a truly significant number of boys of ability but limited means could be offered financial support to stay at school. In 1943 there were 128 scholarship holders in the school, 73 in the senior section and 55 in the junior, the total value of the scholarships being £1612. By 1950, there were 57 Senior Government Scholarships and 40 local ones in the senior school and 73 held scholarships in the junior school.[32]

At the same time, to the extent that there remained an insufficient number of places in the junior school to cater for all who applied, the school was able to select on the basis of merit. Once again the age of entry rose till at one stage virtually all first year boys had completed their Merit Certificate.[33] The rise in academic performance in the junior school that this implied[34] had a corresponding effect all the way up the school just at the time when the academic demands of the courses at senior levels were rising. The School consolidated its position as the senior Education Department school[35] and classes in the diploma school were swelled by the arrival of increasing numbers of boys from other parts of the metropolitan area and the country. All this enabled the school to become more finely tuned to the higher standards set in the new courses, thus leading to the enhanced performance and status of Footscray diploma holders, which was, in turn, reflected in the numbers and quality of those seeking admission to the school.

The senior school comprised a broad cross-section of students from city and rural backgrounds, and in the second half of the decade encompassed a wide range of ages, due to the presence of returned servicemen. The number from outside Footscray in the final-year class was well over half in some years.[36] Despite the high enrolments, however, the largest graduation class, that of 1947, numbered 33, which was just under a tenth of the 357 enrolled that year. Even taking account of those who might have gone on to Melbourne Technical College, (formerly Working Men's College), the number actually graduating suggests that a significant percentage of those commencing diploma studies did not complete them. The results for the graduating class itself were good, with only a very small number failing to take out the diploma at some stage during the ten years after they had completed their industrial experience and part-time year of study. The average number of diplomas awarded per year during the war years was only 13 but a total of 200 were conferred between 1947 and 1952. The most academically successful and ambitious took the path to the University, frequently with the benefit of scholarships.[37] In 1941, of the 13 who took out diplomas, at least six went to the University; in the succeeding five years the numbers ranged between three and nine[38] In 1949, Footscray boys won all four Government University Scholarships, the Simon Fraser Scholarship, two Daffyd Lewis Scholarships and five Secondary Teaching Scholarships. Twenty-three students from

Footscray commenced university that year, 13 from the exit group of 1949 and ten from previous years.[39]

Outside the School, in the 'Cold, Hard World', was an expanding economy and considerable opportunity, even if war service and manpower regulations temporarily left the boys marking time. Prosperous times and a substantial commitment to 'development' by Commonwealth and state governments made the times exceptionally promising for well-qualified engineers. For Footscray diplomates, the State Electricity Commission in particular appeared a giant honey pot offering secure and satisfying employment, promotion and further education opportunities. The President of the School Council in 1946, J. R. Wilson, was Power Station Superintendent at Newport, and

> always on the look-out for bright young fellows at the school whom he could get to Newport to help him run things. The whole Power Station was run by an army of "green" engineers.[40]

Electrical engineers generally found their way to the Yarraville Workshops and mechanical engineers went to Newport Power Station before spreading out across the state. By 1950 at least 48 diplomates had commenced their working lives in various aspects of electrical power generation and transmission, as had many others with lesser qualifications. Friendships made at the School endured into working life and if some 'Old Boys' reunions "no longer look like SEC conferences, perhaps they have taken on the appearance of an unofficial retired officers" group.[41]

The diverse and complex career patterns of others provide a glimpse of the range of opportunities available to engineers in this period. Several went to the United Kingdom to work with organisations like Metropolitan Vickers Armstrong and Westinghouse, others to the Ordinance Factory, the Harbour Trust or the Navy. Gregory Mott ultimately went to England and managed the project that launched Britain's first nuclear submarine, the HMS Dreadnought. Several, including a later President of Footscray Institute of Technology Council, John McIntosh, went to Olympic Tyre Co., others to Vacuum Oil and one at least to the Woomera Rocket Range. As always, a small number went to one of the two Richardson establishments. Another group were attracted to technical teaching, including the foundation Head of the FIT Engineering School, Ivan Pellizzer, who attended the senior school after spending his early years at Wonthaggi Technical School.[42]

These young men went out into the world empowered with the sense of themselves as an elite, destined for advancement and success. They could hardly have failed to notice the culling process that sorted and propelled them through ever narrower gates of educational achievement and increased commitment of parental resources. In the senior school they were rewarded with the attention, consideration and high expectations of a small, highly qualified, confident and deeply committed staff. Self-motivation and hard work were taken for granted. The work was demanding; the teaching style was formal and made few concessions to the relative youth of the boys or those who did not 'catch on' quickly. For the country boys especially, the first year in a huge, complex city school could be lonely and daunting.[43]

On the whole, however, relations between staff and the senior classes were warm, encouraging, "family like".[44] Hoadley, Kepert, Howells, and Walker in particular, regularly participated in activities with the boys out of hours. Hoadley's home remained open to students to drop by, and each year the graduating class was treated to an "At Home" where the drinks, food, games and musical items had taken on the character of traditions. Kepert and Walker maintained a high profile in the Old Boys' Association as well. "Johnny" Kepert was ruefully farewelled in 1946 in terms that well capture a student's-eye view of the Vice Principal:

> Perhaps the most cheerful of pedagogues, . . . [he] is possessed of a seemingly inexhaustible supply of patience, . . . which has earned him the respect and admiration of all who have passed through his capable hands.
>
> In going he will leave many gaps; apart from his acknowledged ability as an engineering instructor, Mr Kepert is famous for his biographical notes in *Blue and Gold*. Parted from her most constant attendant, the old Colonial boiler in the lab. must soon pine away and sink into ferric oblivion. At least those hardy annuals, the Heat Engines chestnuts, will be new to the Caulfield lads, but who else could make the iron carbon diagram so easily digestible?[45]

The young men with diplomas left the School with a sense of having been challenged, guided, successful and enriched; but they were only the tip of a large pyramid from which most of the boys had slipped at a much earlier stage in the education process. Of the 200 or so boys who entered the junior school in any one year in the 1940s, only nine or ten at the most would finish the Diploma course. Many, of course, found employment and pursued their studies part time in the evening, and the number taking subjects as part of an apprenticeship climbed. In 1948 provision was finally made for many trade classes to formally become day classes, a development of great benefit to the boys themselves but creating administrative and space problems. These large numbers of trade students occupied a twilight world, slipping in and out of the workshops, barely noticed by the senior day boys or by many of the teachers, and at times proving rowdy and ill-disciplined, but filling an essential place in the rapidly expanding economy.

In these years most Victorian children still did not stay at school long past the official leaving age of 14. Technical schools shared with high schools the characteristic that, although their courses were designed for a particular purpose, the majority of their students did not complete the prescribed program. In 1940, only about 30% of pupils even attempted third form.[46] Footscray generally did much better than this throughout the decade, but the percentage fluctuated between 23% and 63%.[47] The expanding economy benefited all school leavers, but it did not necessarily bring an immediate increase in demand for education. The over-time demands of the post-war period kept many away from evening study and opportunties for advancement through on-the-job performance without great need of formal qualifications were substantial. There was still a plentiful supply of jobs for the unskilled. Working class boys in Footscray could not really benefit from the expanding education sector until the economic climate provided a secure base from which to look up and out: the post-war period finally provided that, but the effects were not felt until the 1950s.

The career of Harry Tribe, President of the Institute Council from 1977 to 1979, perhaps illustrates a more typical path to success in the 1940s than the stories of the senior school boys of that period, though only a few rose as high. Son of a tyre moulder, his primary school results were good enough to attract Hoadley's attention and his mother was persuaded to send him to the Technical School in spite of his father's objections. Tribe performed well but his father remained unreconciled. Circumstances forced him out to work at 15 as an assistant in a local chemical laboratory — a fortuitous circumstance that awakened his interest — and in the early war years he moved to Monsanto Chemicals. After war service with the Navy during which he took courses in Radar Mechanics at Melbourne Technical College, he commenced evening studies in Applied Chemistry at Footscray Technical School and completed his diploma at Melbourne Technical College. At Monsanto, he was able to ride on the new developments in the organic chemical industry that developed during the war, and he benefited from Monsanto's management policies and commitment to local personnel.[48] He subsequently became a director of the company, before ill health forced his early retirement.[49]

The School was closely supported in these years by its parents and Council. The Mothers' Club not only provided several scholarships for junior boys, but improved school amenities by purchasing such items as pianos and books, raising £100 for bike sheds, £250 towards the the an assembly hall and £75 for a first aid room at Ballarat Road. The mothers were also much appreciated for their catering at sports gatherings and other school functions. The Council, meanwhile, developed ambitions on a scale revealed in a 1941 *Advertiser* headline: "Main Technical Education Centre in Australia. Move to Develop Footscray School".[50] Partly spurred by comments made by the Lord Mayor of Melbourne, Frank Beaurepaire, at Olympic Tyre and Rubber Company's West Footscray plant that an engineering university should be built on the boundary between Melbourne and Footscray,[51] and excited by developments at Ballarat Road, the Council probably became over ambitious. While the School certainly grew in size and status, judged against this rather naive ambition that sought to promote the interests of the school as a tertiary institution on almost any front, the 1940s must have seemed a less successful period at the time than they appear in retrospect.

All technical school councils at this time were interested in moves to develop a degree in technical science at the University or an institute of technology to cap the system of technical education. Footscray was well represented in the early discussions on this matter in the person of their long-serving and forceful President, R. G. Parsons, who was also a member of the Swinburne Technical School Council. He was one of three who prepared the 1942–1943 "Report of The Council of Public Education", a progressive and innovative document that was virtually ignored by the government of the day.[52] Early on in proceedings, however, Footscray Council expressed their concern that degrees should not be substituted for diplomas, an opinion some would still be voicing in the early 1970s. "It was felt that the right way of development in technical education was not in the creation of a new degree-issuing university, but to make the Diploma more recognised and more appreciated by industry generally", while smoothing the path to university for the "specially gifted".[53] This objective had been achieved by the end of the war, but it did not entirely meet the need for a post-graduate technical institution — an institute of technology.[54] While all supported the idea in principle, none of the colleges could accept the prospect of such an institution reducing all the other schools to mere feeders. A conference to discuss the idea was arranged for March 1944 and the Footscray Council put its position emphatically to Parsons in February:

> It was felt that such an Institute should deal with post-graduate work only and that, if such an Institute were established, it should not cater for the basic training as at present undertaken by the various schools doing the Diploma of Engineering, Chemistry etc, as it would destroy their value and would ultimately lead to the concentration of great numbers of junior people in such an institution, which would tend to nullify its effect and spoil the usefulness of the Diploma-issuing Technical Schools.[55]

Footscray Council's central, underlying ambition was independence from the Education Department for the senior school and they engaged in considerable lobbying through the Technical Schools Association on this subject. Any bid for higher status arose at least partly from this desire for greater autonomy, and in September 1944 Footscray Council specifically sought to become the new institute of technology on the grounds that it had an adequate site, which Melbourne Technical College certainly did not have.[56] They had not abandoned the hope a year later when, in August 1945, they invited Sir David Rivett and Dr A. E. V. Richardson to assist them in defining more precisely what such an institute should do. They were also much heartened by Parson's opinion that the Minister was "apparently in favour of its establishment in Footscray".[57] Unfortunately, the institute of technology proposal was twice accepted by governments about to topple and therefore toppled with them. The underlying problems of a suitable site and the relative status of the various institutions remained largely unresolved.[58]

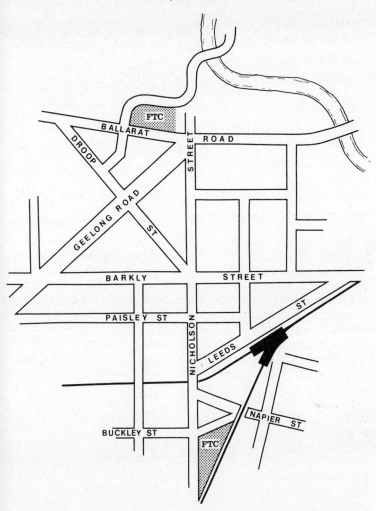

Footscray Technical School Council's ambitions had not been confined solely to institute of technology status. It also bid to have a proposed textile school developed in Footscray arguing, somewhat desperately, that Footscray was the centre of textile manufacturing in Victoria.[59] Local objections to the proposal were raised but Hoadley reassured the City Council that such a school would not reduce the amenity of the local area,[60] and several sites were considered. This idea was not finally laid to rest until well into 1946, by which time rumour had it that the Chamber of Manufactures[61] and/or the Department of Post War Reconstruction[62] were opposed to a Footscray location. Ultimately, the school was established in Pacoe Vale where there was an abundance of vacant land, and the Footscray Technical School Council ought to have taken more comfort in the entirely appropriate establishment of the full diploma course in Applied Chemistry, a course directly related to one of the dominant industries in the region.

In a decade of growth and change the ranks of those who associated the School with a humble four-roomed building at Nicholson Street grew thinner and thinner. By 1949 all but one of the original Council members were gone. Robert Ferguson had retired in 1943, Arthur Hughes died in 1948 and Joseph Carmody in 1949. In their place came W. W. de Steiger, Distribution Engineer, Electrical Engineering Branch, Victorian Railways, James Edgerton, General Manager of Melbourne Iron and Steel Mills, and Cr Ern Sherpherd, the Labor Party Member for Footscray. A number of these men were foundation members of the Footscray Rotary Club, which Hoadley had played a leading role in establishing in 1937, thus inaugurating a relationship that continued into the 1980s.

As well as Treyvaud, a number of other very long-serving staff members such as Dr Schapper and the Head of the Art Department, C. F. Mudie retired, but the most grievous loss of all was the death of Hoadley on the 27 February 1947. It was hard for many to imagine the School without him, and those who knew him were struck with an overpowering need to commemorate his work and personality in some permanent form. His ashes were interred beneath the altar in the chapel in his beloved Gilwell Park, the Scout camp to which he personally had contributed so much. His role in the life of Footscray generally was such that he was genuinely mourned beyond the boundaries of his school. The tributes were many; three will serve to capture the essence of the man and his role. The Education Department acknowledged his success as an administrator who had founded and developed "the most important Departmental technical school in Victoria". "As acting inspector at various times and as a leading member of Departmental committees" he had been one of its "most valued advisers", and, "in the cause of education as in other forms of social service", he had "left behind him an outstanding record".[63] More than respected by his pupils, he was loved. Kindness, concern, accessibility and cheerfulness marked him out for affection. "S.G." of form Eight wrote in the *Blue and Gold* in simple terms that were echoed many times over

. . . any boy taking his problems to Arch. Hoadley was soon made to feel that his troubles were not just another irritating interruption to a busy man. With quick insight he could make a boy feel that his worries were shared by someone else, . . .

To Senior students who came in closer contact with him, he was more than a teacher. He was a real friend who could see our difficulties before we could, and no student ever graduated feeling that he had done with the school for good. Our Principal was always accessible and ever ready with a helping hand.[64]

The images of a cheerful grin and a hand on the shoulder pervade all recollections of Hoadley but perhaps the most eloquent tribute comes from his friend and successor as Chief Commissioner of Scouts in Victoria, W. D. Kennedy:

There is a legion of men working in industrial concerns whose hearts warm at the the mention of Hoadley's name, and to whom his death meant the loss of a personal friend. His help and guidance were freely available to all who sought them, and he was truly the rock on which thousands of worried boys and their parents founded their faith. He lived near his work in the heart of an industrial community, and it is not too much to say that as a trusted guide, philosopher and friend to so many, Footscray cannot find his peer, nor perhaps replace him.

He was a man of power and dignity, but as he understood instinctively that to reign sovereign in the hearts and affections of men is far more grateful to a generous mind than to rule over their lives and fortunes, so he was an ideal teacher. His great humanity attracted confidence; his great charm and talents compelled respect.[65]

Hoadley was a pioneer who steered his school to full maturity. A technologist by training, but an educator by instinct and inclination, he lived long enough to see the 'progressive' ideas of his youth accepted as more or less the norm in technical education.

Hoadley bequeathed a strong school to his successor. It was the end of an era, but Joseph Aberdeen, the new Principal, had the qualifications to guide the School into more prosperous and

DANGER — MEN AT WORK.

Cartoon impressions of some of the staff, 1946

expansive times. Sadly, his untimely death in 1951 robbed him of opportunity. The Council had succeeded in having the Education Department call for a degree in engineering or science in the advertisement for a new Principal, but they were not successful in their request that the new appointee be less that fifty years of age.[66] Joseph Aberdeen, far nearer 60 than 50, took over at the beginning of third term in 1947. Born in Leongatha, he had been one of the original students at Melbourne High School, from where he went on to take out the degrees of Master of Mathematics and Master of Science. He spent four years in research work on heat insulation and completed a Bachelor of Education. A highly qualified teacher for his time, he first taught at Prahran and West Melbourne Technical Schools before going to Bendigo Technical School as Headmaster in 1926. In 1937, Aberdeen moved to Preston Technical School as foundation Principal and was promoted to Footscray just as Preston was about to commence diploma studies.[67]

Considered one of the state's leading educationalists, his loss was a blow to Footscray so soon after the death of Hoadley. The Council acknowledged the loss of guidance, sound judgement and courtesy, and also noted his role in the Victorian Association of Principals of Victorian Technical Schools, particularly as Educational Research and Statistics Officer. "His work on the 'Scientific Approach to the Problems of Technical Education'

114

and 'Education for Industry' all bore the mark of clear thinking and were models of . . . sound education".[68] The School, of course, contained many able deputies, and for the second time in four years George Murray took over the role till a successor was appointed. This time the new Principal did not have a degree, but he was just under 50 and fresh from establishing the diploma school at Preston that Aberdeen had so recently vacated. Footscray Technical School was set for another long period of stable leadership.

1. Murray-Smith & Dare, *op. cit.*, p 133.
2. *Footscray Advertiser*, 25 May 1940.
3. *Ibid.*, 8 February 1941.
4. *Ibid.*, 1 March 1941.
5. This was a 50 ton capacity rather than the more usual 30 ton Avery Testing Machine because they wanted it to help local industry.
6. Inspectors' Report, 1944, FIT Archive.
7. *Ibid.*, 1946.
8. *Footscray Advertiser*, 21 September 1940.
9. *Ibid.*, 8 February 1941. Prior to that he had been briefly at Prahran Technical School and 16 years at Warrnambool Technical School.
10. C. A. Hoadley, *Blue and Gold*, 1946, p 5.
11. See above, p 69.
12. Fees for Diplomas were £2 per term for the first year and £4 per term for the next three years. Day students also paid 20/- per year for Sports, Library, Lockers etc. FTS, *Prospectus*, 1947–1948.
13. Stenography cost 40/- for the first year and 45/- for the second. Accountancy was taken over four years and 40/- for the first year and 45/- thereafter, *ibid.*
14. Minister for Public Instruction, Report to Parliament, 1944, p 33, FIT Archive.
15. FTS, *Prospectus, 1947–1948, p 5–6.*
16. *Blue and Gold*, 1943, p 37.
17. FTS, *Prospectus, 1947–1948*, p 6.
18. Interview, Willcox, Davies & Hall.
19. *Footscray Advertiser*, 3 September 1964.
20. Inspectors' Report, 1944, FIT Archive.
21. Inspectors' Report, 1945,. *ibid*.
22. *Blue and Gold*, 1945, p 16.
23. Greg Lake, *Blue and Gold*, 1943, p 40.
24. G. Lake, 'The Boys from Footscray Tech', *SEC News*, March 1986, No. 312, p 7.
25. *Blue and Gold*, 1943, p 22.
26. Inspectors' Report, 1946, FIT Archive.
27. *Blue and Gold*, editorial [Ben Howells], 1946, p 2.

28. *Integral*, No. 2, November 1946. Name later changed to *Swot*.
29. The foundation committee consisted of I. Schroeter, S. Game, C. Fisher, G. Kerrison, J. Paterson, R. Brett and S. Haines, *Blue and Gold*, 1946, p 5.
30. By 1940 they had only managed £1000, FTS Council Minutes, 27 August 1940.
31. Principal's Report, 1943, FIT Archive.
32. *Ibid.*, 1950.
33. *Footscray Advertiser*, 2 February 1941, p 1.
34. Hoadley spoke to the FTS Council 28 May 1946 of the improvement in the type of student in recent years.
35. The Principal's position was reclassified to Special Class in 1946 thus making it the most senior position in the Education Department technical system.
36. This is based on anecdotal evidence about the graduating class in *Blue and Gold*.
37. For example, *Footscray Advertiser*, 17 February 1940, 22 February 1941, 28 February 1942, 24 March 1945.
38. Anecdotal evidence from *Blue and Gold* and interviews.
39. J. Aberdeen, Principal's Report, 1950, FIT Archive.
40. Greg Lake, *op. cit.*, p 7.
41. *Ibid.*
42. Interview.
43. Interviews, Pellizzer, Willcox and Davies.
44. Greg Lake, *op. cit.*
45. MET. IIC, *Blue and Gold*, 1946, p 39.
46. A. J. Dare, 'The Movement to Establish a Higher Technological Institute in Victoria 1940–1963', M. Ed., Melbourne University, 1976, p 29.
47. Based on figures from Inspectors' Reports, FIT Archive.
48. *Footscray Advertiser* and Footscray City Council, *Footscray's First One Hundred Years, The Story of a Great Australian City*, Footscray, 1959, [No page numbers].
49. Interview.
50. *Footscray Advertiser*, 1 February 1941.
51. *Ibid.*, 16 November 1940.
52. Dare, *op. cit.*, pp 83–84.
53. FTS, Council Minutes, 25 March 1941.
54. For a detailed outline of the various strands in the movement for a higher technical institute see Dare, *op. cit.*
55. FTS Council Minutes, 25 February 1944.
56. *Ibid.*, 26 September 1944.
57. *Ibid.*, 28 August 1945.
58. *Ibid.*, 28 August 1947.
59. *Ibid.*, 28 August 1945.

60. *Ibid.*, 25 February & 26 March 1946.
61. *Ibid.*, 25 June 1946.
62. *Ibid.*, 21 October 1946.
63. Inspectors' Report, 1947, FIT Archive.
64. *Blue and Gold*, 1947, p 57.
65. *The Victorian Scout*, March 15, 1947, p 8.
66. FTS Council Minutes, 11 March 1947.
67. *Blue and Gold*, 1947.
68. FTS Council Minutes, 5 June 1951.

CHAPTER EIGHT **"The best technical school of all"**[1]
1951–1964

Howard Beanland[2] arrived in 1951 to take over the administration of a large, complex institution straddling two sites more than a mile apart. The pioneering days were well past and the School's reputation deservedly high, but it still lacked a truly clear and mature focus as an institution. This was partly an inevitable consequence of the broad range of educational needs it sought to serve and the fact that the vertical integration of the sections was not as great as was often assumed. Generally confident about the quality and place in the system of the secondary and trade training areas, the struggle to achieve viability and status as a senior technical college had encouraged a propensity to try to offer every vaguely fashionable course. While this was a trend throughout the technical system, it was re-enforced by a powerful sense that in such an educationally deprived region the School had an obligation to serve the broadest range of needs possible. The result was much *ad hoc* development, inefficient use of resources and enormous reliance on the willingness of staff to offer services rather beyond the usual call of duty as a matter of course.

The pressures of the war years, rapid growth in numbers, and sparse administrative resources had further exacerbated these tendencies. All this had been compounded by a certain lack of dynamism in school leadership in the years following the war. The result was a busy institution, confident of its usefulness, highly regarded by those associated with it, but lacking a rational overall strategy and urgently in need of strong, clear-sighted leadership. Beanland was apprehensive at the size of the chal-

Second school badge

lenge he faced at Footscray, but his appointers must have been confident that his energy and experience in administration fitted him well to the task.

By this time Footscray was the apex of the Education Department technical school system, and there was little to distinguish the quality of its senior school from the few remaining council-controlled schools in Victoria. As first Principal, Hoadley had pioneered a role in a system struggling to establish a good reputation and battled with a bureaucracy starved of funds and burdened with a remarkably constricted view of the role of the state in education. Hoadley had come to his role rather late in the development of his career path. The models at hand — either the headmaster of a private college or principal of a large, long-established independent technical college — were not entirely appropriate for the small, struggling enterprise that was Footscray Technical School for many years. Hoadley's was a pioneering role, and in no small measure he contributed to the rise in status of the whole state system of technical education through the stature he acquired between 1916 and 1947. The Department had come, with time, to rely heavily on his expertise and advice in many areas and to look on him as a kind of elder statesman.

Beanland, in contrast, had fashioned his career within the state system of technical education from the very beginning when in 1918 he accepted an Education Department 'studentship' to study for a Diploma of Engineering at the Ballarat

School of Mines. After completing two years industrial experience with the Richmond Electrical Supply Company, he taught at Beechworth Higher Elementary School for two years before taking charge of apprentice training at Sunshine Technical School. He then served as Acting Principal of the council-controlled technical school in Stawell for 18 months. Here, he gained "valuable experience" in the operation and administration of a small technical school[3] that he immediately applied to the Yallourn Technical School where he was appointed Principal in mid-1932.[4] In 1943 he returned to Melbourne to establish Box Hill Technical School and then followed Aberdeen to Preston, just in time to administer the introduction of diploma courses there in 1948.

The experience at Stawell had persuaded Beanland that he preferred the Education Department to the apparent independence of a small council-controlled school. By this time, the role of the Department in technical education had become more settled, and with the departure of Donald Clark as Chief Inspector the singular and special emphasis on this form of school management evaporated. Beanland belonged to a new generation of principals who had grown to maturity within the Department. His administrative style and attitude to school councils derived from a clear perception that his most critical relationship was that with the Education Department which controlled financial resources, staff appointments and the curriculum. Under Clark, the Technical Schools Association had served as a powerful lobby group, but the younger principals, especially Beanland, were no longer happy to be submerged in this body which represented a broad cross-section of technical education interests. The considerable power which a principal enjoyed within his school was derived entirely from the Department, not the school council, and his capacity to influence the decisions made at departmental and government level or to act in combination with other principals was severely limited. Beanland's conviction that principals needed to engage more fully in the education community found expression in activities that led to the establishment of the Association of Technical School Principals.[5] As this body grew in influence the principals were able to take a larger role in policy making and the injection of progressive educational and organisational ideas into the process. Beanland, as an executive officer of this body, a member of the VTU and *ex officio* a delegate to Technical Schools Association conferences, was able to establish a broad network of contacts and a formidable reputation for energy and efficiency.

Beanland's firm leadership style, often described as "decisive" and "dynamic", contrasted to Hoadley's warmer, less formal approach. Hoadley had not joined the Principals' Association, satisfied it seems with his regular Wednesday afternoons of consultation in at the Department. The sheer size of Footscray Technical School, the expansion in the number of senior and administrative personnel, and a more rapid change over of staff led inevitably to a greater distancing between staff and administration. The senior administration in 1953 comprised a Principal, Vice Principal, Headmaster and Trade Supervisor. In 1957 an assistant to the Headmaster was added, and in 1961 a second Trade Supervisor. In 1964 a second Vice Principal's position was created. Staff numbers rose from 70 full-time teachers, a librarian, and a support staff of 26 in 1953 to 147 full-time and 50 part-time teachers with a support staff of 34 by 1962. By 1967 full-time staff numbers had reached 203.[6] Greater formalisation of relations was accentuated by the School's physical separation between two sites, while the increase in numbers and changing demand led to a greater demarcation between the three sections of the School that hastened the tendency toward more formal bureaucratic structures.

In close partnership with the Registrar, Jim McDonald, Beanland set about establishing and refining a system of procedures and management practices necessary to contain the overgrown, multi-purpose institution within manageable proportions and expand the range of resources available to it. The public record of Beanland's activities leaves the impression that he concerned himself more with the details of organisation than academic or philosophical leadership. His was a very practical approach, concentrating to a very great degree on buildings, fund raising,[7] resources and organisational structures. His administration was marked by organisational flair, especially in the early years when he inherited a school whose organisation was described as "complex and wasteful, whichever way it [was] approached".[8] By 1954 Beanland had completed a reorganisation of the school which demonstrated his "sound knowledge of various sections of this complex school and the probable lines of development." The day to day administration was "thorough going and keen" and staff and students were "directed and supervised effectively".[9]

As a result of the Commonwealth government's contributions, the School entered this new phase relatively well housed. As the new Headmaster arriving in 1955 observed,

> On coming to Footscray Technical School, the first and strongest impression one gets is of a splendid building, incorporating all the best ideas of modern school design and with ample playing space at the back door. Compared with the older technical school situated close to the City of Melbourne, Footscray is indeed fortunate.[10]

The 1953 *Prospectus* had boasted

> well-equipped workshops for Turning and Fitting, Woodwork, Moulding, Blacksmithing, Metal Fabrication, Steel Construction, Plumbing, Electric Wiring, Electric and Oxyacetylene Welding, and Sheetmetal Working. These workshops comprise the latest types of machinery and tools, and the methods used keep pace with technical developments that have taken place in modern industry. In addition, there are exemplary Chemical Science, Heat Engines, and Electrical Laboratories.[11]

Of particular note was the boilermaking and steel construction workshop opened in 1952. "The only one of its kind in Australia", it covered a floor area of 8640 square feet and included £16 000 worth of the latest equipment.[12] The School also incorporated a registered mechanical engineering testing laboratory for the carrying out of various tension, compression, hardness and impact tests on behalf of industry. Nevertheless, the next 15 years were to see accommodation constantly taxed to the limit and considerable re-arrangement of the spaces inside the school buildings.

Beanland recognised that one of the most urgent tasks confronting him was a rationalisation of the use of buildings and staff. During the early 1950s the Carpentry and Woodwork Department was transferred to Ballarat Road and the Electrical Trades Department at Nicholson Street was converted into a long desired assembly hall. At Ballarat Road the site was landscaped and outside seating provided for about half the number attending there. Most of this work was carried out by staff and students. Over the next few years the senior library was refurnished, and a new junior library established. The Welding Department was transferred to Ballarat Road, a metrology room for production engineering provided and a long desired caretaker's house constructed.[13] By 1959, however, the crisis in basic accommodation could no longer be solved by partitioning and relocation.

The steady increase in enrolments required an additional five classrooms per year, and a building program intended to provide the college with 15 new rooms by 1962 was approved. This was, as Beanland explained, "all part of the programme for the ultimate transfer to the Ballarat Road site, but it appears that as fast as we obtain additional buildings at Ballarat Road, those at our Nicholson Street site are still in demand".[14] The new building to house forms one to five and including a cafeteria was finally completed in 1964. In the same year almost the entire administrative staff was transferred to a new building at Ballarat Road. Further alterations at Ballarat Road provided a new senior library, classrooms and laboratories for diploma students.[15] This completed a rationalisation which left Nicholson Street almost exclusively concerned with trade instruction and Ballarat Road with secondary and tertiary courses. Throughout this time there was also significant upgrading and landscaping of the areas around the schools, and in 1964 a sports centre named for C. H. Beanland was opened.[16]

Unlike Hoadley, or his successor Mills, Beanland did not live in Footscray, but he soon developed a strong working relationship with the School Council, the Rotary Club, the revitalised Mothers' Club and other groups with an interest in the School. At the same time, he brought the benefit of a wide network of contacts inside the education community which continually expanded as Footscray's senior staff members were transferred all over the metropolitan area to new technical schools and into the Department. The School continued to attract well qualified and enthusiastic teachers, and Beanland's energetic leadership built on the strong corporate spirit already present in the School to face new challenges. Beanland's major task was to lead Footscray Technical School into the era of mass secondary education at a time of enormous expansion in the trade education area, and the substantial upgrading and growth of diploma studies. By his retirement in 1967 the School had grown to the size where division into three separate schools was inevitable, and the diploma section was poised to become the autonomous senior technical institution that its founding fathers had envisaged.

The 1950s and 1960s were years of significant change in community views of the role and value of education. The impetus that world war two and the policies of the Chifley government had given to the manufacturing sector produced a sense of opportunity, optimism and, ultimately, affluence that was reflected in an overwhelming increase in demand for access to post-primary education in Victoria. This demand was matched by a greater willingness of governments to fund that access. The Commonwealth government, enriched by the war-time acquisition of wide taxing powers and newly impressed with the importance of its financial responsibilities to education, especially technical and university education, came to provide a level of resources far beyond those available to state governments alone. Unfortunately, this unprecedented demand for education began to make itself felt at the same time as education planners faced the consequences of a rapidly accelerated birth rate and a large-scale immigration program, and so for many years demand always outstripped new resources in some significant way. The result in many schools was enormous classes, much tension and lowered morale among teachers — problems to which Footscray Technical School was not was entirely immune.

Between 1951 and 1964 there were major changes in the relationship between the junior school and the rest of the institution as its role and purpose in the community changed. Despite some years when overcrowding occurred, the junior section remained static at about 800 students, while the senior section continued to grow, thus reversing the relationship of the first three decades and, with time, weakening the special link between the two schools. There was a greater separation of staff into specialist classifications at secondary, diploma or trade level, and a special 'Lecturer' classification for those teaching above matriculation level was introduced.[17] Footscray Technical School junior boys became a smaller and smaller component of the senior school intake. The result was a gradual clarification of conflicting interests between the various sections of the School as each acquired a more powerful sense of separate identity, function and purpose that would become increasingly difficult to contain within a single institution by the 1970s.

In the state as a whole the junior technical school declined in significance in relation to the high schools over the years 1940 to 1960[18] and their nature changed considerably. The idea that their sole purpose was to equip boys to enter the trades and

higher technical colleges had always been subject to some challenge, and over the preceding three decades "general education" had received increasing emphasis. By the 1950s pressure
of numbers forced existing junior technical schools to take even
greater account of their responsibilities to provide a general secondary education and to focus more attention on the needs and
abilities of the students in the classrooms than the demands of
diploma courses.

Concern at the narrow concentration on the small number of
bright boys considered fit to undertake diploma studies had
begun to find a voice as early as 1941 when the newly formed
Association of Technical School Principals published *A Survey of
Curricula in Junior and Senior Technical Schools*.[19] In this Report,
Beanland drew attention to the fact that far too many boys were
taking longer than the minimum time to complete the Junior
and Intermediate Technical Certificate courses. It was felt that
these courses were crammed and unduly difficult and that an
easing would result in higher retention rates.[20]

The low success rate at the final exams raised a further issue
that received little attention until a decade or so later — the
education of the "average" child. Noting that "Directly or indi-
rectly the percentage of passes in the more difficult subjects
determines the percentage of passes for Certificate courses" and
that the student who could not pass these particular subjects
simply dropped out, the Report challenged the view that neither
the teachers nor the system had any responsibility to these
students.[21] Arguing from IQ test results that might be found
simplistic or even offensive today, the Report nevertheless suggested that since children of the professional and clerical groups
had higher "mental ages", on average, than those of the skilled,
semi-skilled and unskilled occupations, and since, "The majority of the pupils in our junior schools come from the three lower
groups", courses needed to fit the ability of the average child if
the junior schools [were] to enable working men's children to
qualify for entry to trades."[22] In terms that heralded a new era,
the Report concluded that

> The main aim in our schools is to see that the child is devel-
> oped physically and socially so that he may take a fitting place
> in the world of the future. We feel that perhaps the examina-
> tion side of our schools is being overstressed at the present
> time and that more freedom should be allowed to the individ-
> ual schools in the development of their curricula and the

awarding of certificates which would show what the pupil had accomplished at the end of a given number of years in these schools.[23]

Over the next decade a number of changes, including the extension of the junior technical school course to four years and increased emphasis on the English and social studies group, revealed a degree of liberalisation and perhaps democratisation of the curriculum. In practice, however, the schools were still primarily concerned to safeguard entry into apprenticeship or diploma courses.[24]

As a consequence of the greater demand, Footscray's junior school gradually lost the exclusivity it had enjoyed since 1916. Until the mid 1950s, it had only to compete with Williamstown, Essendon and University High Schools for ambitious and talented boys, but the rapid establishment of 13 new secondary schools in the surrounding suburbs between 1955 and 1962 undermined its pre-eminent position in secondary education in the region. The junior school gradually ceased to take the cream of the region and shrank to a district technical school that was not even able to accept sons of 'old boys' if they lived out of the "zone".

Even though there were many times in the past when it had been felt that the "right type of boy" was not being attracted, it nevertheless remained true that selection for Footscray Technical School was based on an entrance test or the possession of the Merit Certificate, and its role as a diploma-granting school enhanced its capacity to attract ambitious boys. While demand for secondary education in general had remained low, the self-selection process also acted as a powerful element in filtering out those boys who had little inclination or aptitude for technical studies. As long as this situation prevailed, a demanding curriculum designed to sort boys rapidly into those who could continue with higher engineering work or enter trades and those who could not was relatively satisfactory. As a consequence a certain homogeneity of ability and aspiration shielded the administration and teachers from much concern with those who did not meet the School's standards of academic performance or behaviour.

The Education Department abolished the entrance exam in

late 1951. Henceforth the Technical School was obliged to accept all comers. It was not a move appreciated by the Principal or the School Council,[25] and it is very noticeable in the Reports of the Minister for Education from this point that questions of "differential teaching" and remedial education began to assume an increasingly important place, as secondary schools, and technical schools in particular, began to face problems that had been hidden previously in the primary and central schools. These problems were not made any easier for Footscray, which had to bear rapid increases in numbers while new schools were built. By 1954 junior school numbers were well over a thousand and, while the opening of Footscray High School in 1954 and Williamstown Technical School in 1955 provided some relief, the new Tottenham Technical School students were accommodated at Ballarat Road in 1956 till their buildings were ready for occupancy.

By 1954 there was strong evidence of a move away from narrowly academic organisation. As the Headmaster explained,

> In some respects the system of grading pupils in the various forms according to order of merit has not been entirely successful and in the coming year it is hoped to introduce a modified system, which, while retaining the top sections for the better pupils, will remove from others the stigma of being in the lowest or lower sections. There will be no lower section — after the top two have been made up, the remaining sections will be deliberately equalised. [26]

This heralded a marked increase in concern with the capacities and self-esteem of the 'average' student as the educational system became less meritocratic (that is, concentrated less on encouraging the obviously talented to achieve their full potential), and increasingly sought to raise the general level of education throughout the whole population. This new perspective comes through in 1960, when the Headmaster, C. Green, warned against the "tendency to over-emphasize the achievement of the brilliant student", declaring that

> Many of the leaders in industry and government today, were on their own admission, only average at school. It cannot be too strongly emphasised that the boy who has average ability can qualify for the highest positions. He may have to work

harder and apply himself more diligently than the brilliant student, but in doing so he is developing character traits which will fit him for the most responsible positions.[27]

The School soon had to accommodate large numbers of less than "average" students as well, largely as a result of the decision in the late 1950s that students who had completed grade six would transfer to secondary schools irrespective of the standard reached. Briefly, this tempted the School to try the re-introduction of formal 'streaming' in 1965, on the grounds that boys with special problems could best be dealt with in special classes. When streaming was again abandoned the following year, the teachers reported that "poor performers" were responding better and "discipline problems had been very much reduced" once mixed ability classes had been re-established.[28]

Down at the desk level the old system had often seemed harsh and uncaring, even for those of some ability. William Dick spent four years at the School in the early 1950s, at the end of which he was noted in the School magazine among the "left overs".[29] He had approached the School with a sense of privilege instilled in him by his mother — "You just want to think yourself lucky that you've got a good father who'll send yuh to the tech" — and apprehension — "It had a name for being a tough school but a good school . . . I'd heard of terrible ways they initiated you."[30] Dick, by his own graphic admissions in *A Bunch of Ratbags*, went on to contribute more to the "tough" than the "good" side of the reputation, but he was caught up in the highly competitive grading atmosphere all the same. His story, even allowing for a degree of poetic licence,[31] provides a poignant picture of the destructive side of the system with which the administration attempted to come to terms in the 1950s.

Poor results at the end of 1952 had brought demotion to a lower "section" where Dick found the work easy to do and, as gang leader, the other boys even easier to dominate. His interest in academic achievement was rekindled by the prospect of the book prize, traditionally given to the boys who came first and second in each section. It clearly had special meaning for a boy whose father was an unskilled worker in the local meatworks:

I was really looking forward to the book I would most certainly be getting. It would the first prize I had won in my whole life. It would be marvellous — just imagine getting a

prize, I thought, it's terrific! I had not told my parents anything about it as I wanted to surpise them and show them
how smart I really was — not like last year when I failed and
they were crook on me.[32]

Dick did indeed come top of his section but a break-in and fire in
the administration section of the School[33] robbed him of his
prize:

> We were standing in the line in the quadrangle when the
> headmaster started raving on — as usual.
>   'Owing to the recent fire we had, prizes will only be given
> to the boys in the first four grades in each year who have come
> top this year." He paused and went on, "I'm sorry for you
> other boys, but we do not have the money to buy more prizes,
> after we suffered that great loss . . ." He rambled on, but I
> wasn't listening. I'd heard the worst. He'd just knocked the
> bottom out of my world. I wouldn't be getting a prize.
>   It's the same always, I never get bloody nothin', I thought
> as I hung my head, not listening to what he was saying.
>   All day I worried and worried about not getting my prize
> that I had been counting on so much. It wasn't the value of
> the book that counted, it would probably only have cost
> fifteen bob. But to me, I would have valued it at fifteen million
> quid!
>   Most of that night in bed I cried to myself as I lay there
> thinking: things never change for bums like us, not in this
> joint. Me and the old man, we're meant to get nothin' and be
> poor. We're just bums. Jeez, I wanted to show Mum and the
> old man my prize. Me and the old man against the world!
> That's what the old man reckons, and he's right.[34]

Given the decisions made in the School in the following year to
abandon this rigid streaming, it is clear that some of Dick's pain,
at least in a generalised way, had made itself felt in the School.

Under Hoadley the School had always stressed the need to
develop the "whole" person, but by the 1950s this had become
official policy, along with a concentrated attempt to raise the
status of social studies in the curriculum at all levels. The aban-
donment of strict grading was accompanied by a number of
developments designed to enhance the "pastoral" care offered
to the boys. One important initiative was the involvement of the
School in a pilot scheme to attach chaplains to state schools, and

the Rev. F. Morgan arrived in 1955. Vocational guidance was formalised, with a particular teacher assigned to this role by the Education Department. Another innovative response to these trends at Footscray was the introduction of a 45 minute "social period" for forms three and four. Made possible by the provision of the assembly hall, the time was devoted to vocational and visual education in particular, but allowed for all sorts of matters that were of special interest to the whole of this group to be dealt with informally.

If increased demand and policy decisions were making the junior school population more heterogeneous, the change in Footscray's population was even more significant in both the immediate and long term. With the arrival of large numbers of immigrants from many parts of Europe, the lists of Anglo Celtic names were soon intermixed with German, Slavic and Southern European ones as the new arrivals sought the educational opportunities for their children that had been a prime reason for migration. As the character of the region changed so did the school and with time it would become an increasingly important factor as the School sought to redefine its relationship with the western suburbs. The junior school remained a male domain, but one of the first girls admitted to a day diploma course in 1960 provides a desk-level view of the School and the experience of the immigrant student:

> I shall always remember the day when I walked into a class of twenty six boys. The fact that I was the only girl in the class made me feel scared and lonely, and for this reason I spent many sleepless nights, during which I wished I could cry because this would have made me feel better afterwards. But perhaps I could not cry because I had wept too many tears on my departure from Italy a few months earlier . . .
>
> However, I soon realised that I would not gain anything by indulging in stupid sentimentalities and equipped myself with a high spirit of adaptability and concentrated all my effort and energies towards the attainment of one sole goal: "to become an accountant," which, by the way, has always been my greatest ambition. [35]

At much the same time, the Colombo Plan brought large numbers of students from Asia, many of whom found their way to Footscray to study. Largely confined to the senior school, the

first group arrived in 1957 and thereafter became a permanent presence in the School.

Even though junior school numbers remained static, the age composition changed, as it expanded from three to four and eventually five levels. This permitted the development of a more mature junior school, with its own prefects, personalities, sporting competitions and extra-curricula activities no longer dominated by the demands and preoccupations of the senior school. This helped nurture a stronger separate identity in both staff and students. To the extent that the junior school lost status as a result of the building of so many new schools in the region, the senior school correspondingly gained as its role as a regional college fed by a variety of schools was affirmed and strengthened. In 1958 the School was designated a College under a state wide rationalisation of educational resources which established hierarchies of technical schools within designated regions. This meant that all other schools would send their students to Footscray for senior work and would look to it for educational and administrative leadership. Several years later, Regional Committees consisting of the principals, a representative of each school council and a technical school inspector were set up to co-ordinate the provision of courses and classes and to make recommendations to the Chief Inspector.[36] This, at last, provided a formal and direct means for regional interests to be presented to the Department. The fact that for part of the 1950s, the Member for Footscray, Cr Ern Shepherd, was both a member of the School Council and the Minister for Education meant that, as in the days of Jack Lemmon, the School once more enjoyed rather privileged access to the corridors of power.

Although diploma school numbers were relatively static over this period and statistically quite small in overall terms, its sense of importance and self-confidence strengthened markedly as it became more diversified and separate from the rest of the College. Engineering continued to dominate the curriculum but the seeds of future developments were being sown. The final two years of the Diploma of Civil Engineering were added in 1960, and a new style of course mixing education and work experience was introduced. Students who took "sandwich courses" studied full time for the Diploma of Mechanical or Electrical Engineering for two years, then over the next three years alternated six months' full-time work with six months' full-time study.

Concurrent with this there was an expansion in 'management' courses as the short course in Foremanship of the later 1940s gave way in 1955 to Certificate courses in Supervision, Functional Management or Industrial Management and in 1956 a Diploma of Production Engineering was introduced. In 1959 one of the largest sections of the evening school finally achieved a status comparable with engineering when full day diploma courses in Commerce and Commercial Practice commenced, and with these courses came a brave group of six young women to pave the way for co-education.[37] The rise in status of the Commerce Department was further demonstrated in 1960 when its entry in the *Prospectus* was finally moved from the back to a space between the Trade Certificate section and the junior school section.

In 1962 the College moved into a completely new area with the introduction of a Diploma of Catering and Hotel Administration which Beanland hoped would "result in improved opportunities for the development of Australia as a tourist attraction as well as enhancing the dignity and importance of technical training in a new field". The object of this course, "new to Australia" but "similar in pattern to some overseas courses" was "to provide both basic and professional training for potential executive personnel in the fields of catering and hotel administration". This new course was "greeted with enthusiasm" by the industry which responded with financial assistance and a willingness to participate in the "sandwich" course arrangement[38].

The senior day school developed a stronger sense of separate identity, and with the rise in the average age and variety of the students it gradually acquired more of the characteristics of a mature tertiary institution with a student life independent of staff input. The increase in size and complexity and the more rapid turnover of staff and students meant that the intimate "family" atmosphere of the Hoadley era gave way to greater student organisation and demand for formal channels of communication with the administration. The need to provide a forum for the airing of grievances and a means of communication between students and the administration was great in a school of the size and complexity of Footscray and the SRC expanded its functions and role as the College expanded. The public school model of school organisation with prefects and 'houses' became less and less appropriate and, while senior school prefects continued to exist for many years, as early in 1951 a student of eight years standing drew attention to their loss of status in relation to the SRC, when he declared that the prefects had, during the past few years,

> slipped down to a position where they are a mere name, and play second fiddle to the SRC. Last year they were dispossessed of their room with its many amenities, and are now situated amongst the sporting material at the far end of the school.

This same student, however, quite unselfconsciously ended his complaint about deficiencies in school life with a suggestion that was in fact an argument for an SRC. "It seems to me very desirable that a suggestion box should be set up in the school. Those in charge cannot see and hear all that goes on, and a suggestion from a student can be of value in effecting improvements to the school".[39] In contrast, the SRC Report on the same page reflected great confidence and expressed the view that no senior school could function efficiently without an SRC.[40]

The SRC performed effectively as a 'suggestion box' but it also assumed the student welfare functions that are common to all such bodies in tertiary institutions — arranging entertainment, raising money for various purposes, both inside and outside the school, and orientation luncheons for the many students who were new to the college each year.[41] Even as late as 1958 the SRC felt it was unique in this area, declaring that "as far as we know no other technical College gives its 'freshers' such a pleasant introduction to their new college".[42] As time passed, the SRC expanded its functions and while the appearance of its newspaper was erratic, in 1956 it took on the design of the School pocket books and actually edited *Blue and Gold* for 1958. Increasingly it also began to look outwards. In 1960 it participated in the moves that led to the formation of the Victorian Federation of Tertiary Students and continued to support it thereafter. In the following year the SRC substantially revised its constitution, had SRC stationery printed and recommenced publication of a College news sheet.[43]

By 1964 the SRC had succeeded in having the house sport competition changed to a faculty-based competition, but felt it had reached a crisis point with poor support for its activities apart from the airing of grievances and an obvious loss of morale among the leaders. Several pieces in *Blue and Gold* of that year canvassed the issues. It was suggested that the age of the students and the style of the Technical College did not encourage mature involvement in extra-curricular activities, but the most fundamental problem seemed to be the lack of independent financial resources. "Every other tertiary institution in Melbourne has an SRC levy and they are so far ahead of Footscray with respect to College activities, such as balls, revues, newspapers, etc. that it is not funny".[44] While the administration was obviously sympathetic to the SRC, had provided critical financial support and introduced a procedure whereby a member of the SRC Executive Committee was able to sit in on senior administration meetings,[45] the permission to impose a levy was not forthcoming.[46] Gradually, however, the SRC became the focus of student social, sporting and political activity and its standing in the eyes of the administration went up substantially with its success in raising funds for the College Jubilee Appeal in 1965.[47]

The numbers engaged in trade training grew rapidly and, as day release became the norm, less and less of this was carried out in the evening. This meant that these students could be a little more integrated into College life than had hitherto been the case. This trend was greatly encouraged by Beanland, who personally took a very special interest in trade training. This development scarcely diminished the flourishing evening school where 326 separate evening classes were attended in 1962 by 5641 students each week.[48] The classes included a full range of dress making, millinery, art, craft and commercial courses, and the College also began to function as an evening high school with the introduction of Intermediate, Leaving and Matriculation Certificate subjects. The importance of this aspect of the evening school can be judged by the fact that by the late 1960s there were as many students enrolled in these subjects as in the junior school.

Trade training involved very large numbers of students and remained a primary interest of the college administration. Beanland was keen to see this area receive more attention and recognition. The appointment of Trade Supervisors with special responsibilities for this area and the development of the Nicholson Street site as the near exclusive venue of the trade subjects enhanced the corporate sense of the trade school, even though many boys spent only a small portion of each week in classes. From 1952 an apprentice award night and concert was held annually and a number of apprentices from Footscray were awarded Bronze Medallions for outstanding work in their particular trade. Footscray also included the Outstanding Apprentice of the Year among its students on several occasions. At the Department level, the Chief Inspector, O. E. Nilsson, was especially interested in promoting the status of apprentices through such means as Apprenticeship Week, while Beanland encouraged substantial promotion of this aspect of College work through the annual "Craftsmanship in Industry" exhibition in the College hall. He also played a key role in the establishment of the Victorian Overseas Foundation, a joint venture of Rotary and the Victorian Employers Federation, to provide funds to send a group of promising apprentices overseas for additional experience each year from 1956.

BLUE & GOLD - 1960

Magazine of the Footscray Technical College

Editor: N. C. Porter

Assisted by S. Sweeney

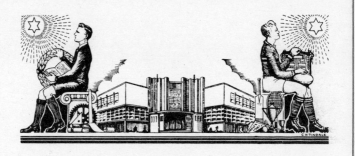

Front page, Blue and Gold, *1960*

Teaching Staff, 1940

Front Row: W. C. Cameron, W. J. Baker, J. L. Kepert, G. Murray, H. J. Schapper, W. A. G. Smith, C. A. Hoadley,
F. A. Treyvaud, C. F. Mudie, W. J. Nicholls, A. Robertson, B. K. Thomson, H. J. Burley, V. W. Palmer.
Second Row: A. McNee, R. Wheatley, A. A. Wright, D. Incoll, J. G. Baker, J. F. Haig, G. McComb, B. I. Johnstone, M. Jacobs,
J. Neate, E. Smalley, H. Slinger, H. A. Poulter, R. E. Appleton, M. A. Lambert, L. D. Danielson.
Third Row: R. A. Vines, C. F. Fenwick, B. J. Willis, J. C. Nuttall, G. B. Hunter, K. B. Mitchell, E. P. Carey, F. L. M. Torode,
F. W. Porter, E. L. Walker, D. C. Spottiswood, B. R. Hames, E. B. Howells, W. Ride, O. J. Soderberg.
Fourth Row: E. H. Sefton, E. J. Sedgley, T. C. S. Barks, S. J. Allan, C. B. Story, H. C. Holyoak, L. R. Travis, J. Rossiter,
A. Aughterson, J. F. O'Brien, J. Stonehouse, W. J. Lonnquist, A. Junowicz, B. W. Pollock, J. A. Douglas, H. C. Smith.

Plate ix

General Staff, early 1950s

Mothers' Club Committee, 1954
Back: Mesdames Storey, Bell, Shaw, Curwood, Grigg, Lumsden, Storey
Front: Mesdames Copeland, Portingdale, Oates, Bennett, Clark

larship holders 1953
es in Appendix, page 278.

Plate xi

Handrailing and Staircasing Class, 1950s

Testing new oxy-acetylene equipment with a group of apprentices, 1950s

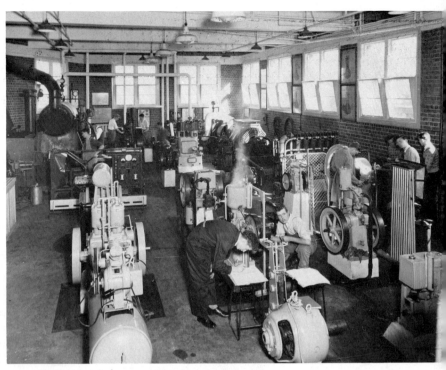

Heat Engines Laboratory, Nicholson Street

Chemistry Laboratory, Nicholson Street

Boiler Making and Steel Construction Workshop, Ballarat Road

Craftsmanship in Industry Display held in the Assembly Hall, Nicholson Street, 1950s

Dressmaking Class, 1965

Typing Class, 1965

In 1959 a new level of trade courses was added with the introduction of Technician courses "intended for persons requiring education above apprenticeship, but closely allied to their particular craft. The courses were of four years duration and intended to be taken concurrently with apprenticeship".[49] This was to become a growth area as new industrial demands emerged, and in 1962 Industrial Electronics, a new three year course primarily designed to produce experts in the construction and maintenance of electronic and electrically-controlled equipment,[50] was introduced. The number presenting for the older-style certificates rose from the earlier period, but not at the same rate as those presenting for diplomas, even though full-time day classes became available. In the long run, the demands of industry for higher qualifications and the increasing preference for full training prior to employment meant that apprentice-linked courses would shrink to a smaller component of the College's curriculum. It was this section of the College, however, which would emerge in the 1970s as "Technical and Further Education", and continue to expand its role and function in non-apprenticeship areas to the point where the pressure for independence from the tertiary section of the College became irresistible.

1. E. P. Eltham, Commonwealth Director of Training, reported in *Footscray Advertiser*, 9 January 1953.
2. Details about Beanland's career, except where otherwise stated, are based on his Education Department record sheet and personal interview.
3. The *Footscray Mail*, 23 March 1967.
4. Acting Principal, June 1932 to 1934 when he was appointed Principal.
5. F. T. Fargher, *The First Twenty Five years Being a Short History of the Association of Principals of Victorian Technical Institutions 1939–1966*, Melbourne, 1969, p 5.
6. Principal's Report, 1967, FIT Archive.
7. Among Beanland's innovations was the introduction of a voluntary contributory scheme which it was doubted would succeed. However, the response was excellent and the amount raised in the financial year 1951–52 was £858/7/1. Principals' Report, 1952 and following. In the five years to 1956 £3593 was raised, *Footscray Advertiser*, 13 December 1956.
8. Inspectors' Report, 1950, FIT Archive.
9. *Ibid.*, 1954.

10. 'Headmaster's Message', *Blue and Gold*, 1955, p 38.
11. FTS *Prospectus*, 1953–54, p 7.
12. C. H. Beanland, *Blue and Gold*, 1952; See also *Footscray Advertiser*, 15 August 1952.
13. Principal's Report, 1952–1958, FIT Archive.
14. *Ibid.*, 1959.
16. This building was the result of a co-operative fund raising venture between the College and the Old Boys' Football Club.
17. FTS Council Minutes, 24 July 1962.
18. Dare *op. cit.*, p 32.
19. This was written by Beanland who was Secretary. The statistical work would have been done by J. Aberdeen, later principal FTS, since the Education Department refused to allow their Research Officer to carry out the research.
20. Docherty, *op. cit.*, p 705.
21. Association of Principals of Victorian Technical Schools, *A Survey of Curricula in Junior and Senior Technical Schools, October 1941*, p 7, FIT Archive.
22. *Ibid.*, p 4.
23. *Ibid.*, p 7.
24. Docherty, *op. cit.*, p 706.
25. FTS Council Minutes, 22 July & 26 August 1952.
26. F. H. Nicholls, Headmaster, *Blue and Gold*, 1954, p 47.
27. *Blue and Gold*, 1960.
28. Report for Board of Inspectors, 1966/67, FIT Archive.
29. 'Billy' Dick 4C, *Blue and Gold*, 1953, p 42.
30. W. Dick, *A Bunch of Ratbags*, Penguin, Melbourne, 1965, p 85.
31. I suggest poetic licence because Dick, in fourth year, was in the C section — hardly the bottom. Secondly he had stayed at school beyond the compulsory leaving age which suggests less alienation than the book presents. Thirdly, if the top four sections were to get prizes — then the top of C class would have got one. However, I am attracted by the emotional truth of this episode.
32. *Ibid.*, p 105.
33. See *Footscray Advertiser*, 26 June and 3 July 1953 regarding the fire. Many school records were destroyed.
34. *Ibid.*, p 106.
35. Leitizia Dedda, 8M, *Blue and Gold*, 1964, p 13.
36. Principal's Report, 1961; Inspectors' Report 1961, FIT Archive.
37. Fees in 1959 were Engineering/Chemistry diplomas 80/- rising to 100/-, Certificate course 40/- to 60/-, Trade courses range 25/-, 40/-, (Welding 75/-). Commercial courses range 40/- to £5/5/-. FTC *Prospectus*, 1959.
38. Principal's Report, 1961, FIT Archive. Students spent four days at Footscray and one day at the William Angliss Food Trades School during the first two years. The course was introduced with schol-

arships from the Australian Hotels Commission, Hospital and Charities Commission, United Distillers and Nation Wide Food Services.
39. Anonymous, *Blue and Gold*, 1951, p 3.
40. *Ibid.*
41. *Ibid.*
42. *Ibid.*, 1958.
43. *Ibid.*, 1961, pp 13–14.
44. *Ibid.*, 1964, p 23.
45. C. Rix, 'Secretary's Report', *Ibid.*, p 24.
46. 'The Facts', *Blue and Gold*, pp 25–26. FTC Council Meeting, 4 August 1964.
47. *Blue and Gold*, 1965, p 3.
48. Principal's Report, 1962, FIT Archive.
49. FTC, *Prospectus*, 1960.
50. Later known as Industrial Electronics and Instrumentation.

CHAPTER NINE **A new name and new status: Footscray Institute of Technology 1964–1969**

The 1960s were years of change, challenge and enquiry in the education sector as the demand for general public education moved insistently beyond secondary education to what rapidly became known as tertiary education. The initial response to this pressure had been the establishment of new universities. In Victoria's case, the advocates of technical education had nearly succeeded in shaping Monash University as a technological university. However public demand for a more general purpose university proved overwhelming and the push to upgrade Royal Melbourne Technical College (formerly Melbourne Technical College) to a higher technological institute stalled. The Murray Report on Australian Universities (1957) had successfully urged increased Commonwealth funding for universities and technical education seemed briefly to languish in the shadows. Only three years later, however, the Federal government was growing apprehensive about the potential cost of this expanding university sector, while still committed to the view that economic growth and prosperity were closely linked to raising educational levels in the broad population. The tide turned again towards the technical schools as the search for "alternative kinds of tertiary education"[1] began with the setting up of the Martin Committee of Enquiry into the future of tertiary education in Australia in 1961.

In the course of the Martin Committee's investigations

it became clear that although non-university courses were the source of supply of a large part of Australia's professional and paraprofessional workforce, the miscellaneous collection of

140

poorly funded institutions (in some cases parts of institutions) responsible for these courses seemed destined to remain as they were unless some organising or co-ordinating concept could be found which would be capable of welding then into a recognizable sector of higher education.[2]

As a consequence, the non-university post-secondary institutions became the solution to the problem of the high cost of further expansion of the university sector.[3] The Martin Report, tabled in 1964, played a crucial role in reshaping Australian tertiary education since, by this time, its future development lay with funding decisions made by the Commonwealth government. Its recommendations provided a significant boost to the technical colleges in Victoria which felt that at last their true contribution to the development of a skilled workforce was to be recognised and appropriately financed.

On the question of status, however, there was a 'catch' for the new colleges of advanced education (CAEs) embodied in the phrase 'equal but different', because they were born under the guiding principle of reducing the cost of tertiary education. The Martin Committee expressed the view that education in the old technical colleges had "long been undervalued because of the overvaluation of the social status of a university degree",[4] and it therefore recommended that efforts be made to strengthen and raise the status of technical colleges. Yet, at the same time, its recommendations were clearly based on the assumption that there were two kinds of 'minds' and two distinct styles and purposes for the education of these minds. There were those suited to the abstract thinking and research orientation of universities, and those who would most benefit from an applied, vocational education. The Martin Committee proposed that the weaker students were suited to the latter and should therefore attend the new colleges of advanced education.[5] There is little reason to dispute the contention that the Committee's recommendations were

> directed primarily at the ways in which increasing numbers of students might be provided with a tertiary education that would maintain existing standards for the best students, and would provide adequate preparation for jobs in the expanding workforce in a reasonably economical way.[6]

The reality of 'equal but cheaper' was the perpetuation of status distinctions between universities and other tertiary institutions which was soon reflected in observations that students in the CAEs came from lower socio-economic backgrounds, had a lower level of educational attainment and were training for the newer, less prestigious occupations than those in the universities.

The Victorian system of technical colleges was the most highly developed and highly regarded in Australia, and it greatly influenced the conclusions of the Martin Committee. Sustained by widely based support groups with considerable influence on education policy makers, it was an evolving system with considerable momentum of its own. While it was boosted by the Martin Report, it could not, however, be entirely constrained within its recommendations. Population growth and demand for skilled workers in Victoria's expanding manufacturing sector increased pressure on the state system overall at the same time as a campaign for upgrading the standard of qualifications began to gather strength. As a consequence, the Victorian government instituted its own enquiry into the development of tertiary education under the former Director of Education, Major General Ramsay, in 1961[7] and set up a State Advisory Council on Technical Education to improve communication between industrialists and education policy makers. Finally, in a difficult electoral climate, the Premier, Henry Bolte, promised to upgrade the big technical colleges to degree-granting status in his June 1964 election speech, only to be pre-empted by the Martin Committee's objections to such upgrading and the power of the Commonwealth to direct finances as *it* saw fit.

Concern to increase the number of tertiary educated people in the community was matched by a desire to raise the standard of pre-diploma education. The suggestion that a fifth year be added to the junior technical course had been made by the Technical Schools Association as early as 1948, and the Principals' Association threw its weight behind the proposal in 1956. The matter came to a head in 1961 when the Institution of Engineers announced that, as from 1971, it would not accept any qualification that did not require three years full-time education at post-matriculation standard.[8] Consequently, a fifth year, leading to a Leaving Technical Certificate, was incorporated into the secondary program as required entry standard to new four year diplomas in engineering and chemistry. The Junior Technical Certificate disappeared and the development of form five became a major consideration in the schools, increasing the demand for qualified staff and accommodation and altering the balance between the junior and senior sectors of the technical system.

It was primarily in the field of Engineering that the Victorian technical schools had established their reputation and they were the major source of professional engineers. The system had drawn its strength from a vertical integration of education that was separated from other forms of secondary education but had, nevertheless, been capped by access to university degrees for the best diploma students. As a flexible, multi-stage and often part-time arrangement, it had offered educational opportunities to young men of ambition but limited means. It had also progressively relieved industry of the responsibility for training and the system had justified itself in terms of its 'practicality' and vocational orientation. However, by the 1960s a convergence of forces was making this style of engineering education inappropriate and irrelevant just as the Martin Committee was seeking to revalue the 'practical' and vocational institutions. The first Chief Inspector of Technical Schools had believed that only specialised junior schools could provide the necessary preparation to feed the senior technical colleges, and that only 'hands on' training could produce a truly useful engineer. These propositions gradually gave way to demands for higher levels of theoretical training and maturity in graduates. One of the clearest statements of the changed view appeared in the Martin Report itself, which argued emphatically that

> even in the routine of present day engineering, competence in techniques cannot replace knowledge of fundamentals. The handbook engineer has no place in the future. The technologist of tomorrow must be capable of interpreting completely the significance of all the elements of a complex system and of developing creative ideas for the solution of its problems.[9]

By the 1960s, the nexus between trade training and engineering had almost completely broken down and much of the rationale for special junior technical schools evaporated. The most graphic demonstration of the changed relationship between junior and senior technical schools was in the shrinking number of entrants to full-time diploma courses who came from junior technical schools. In 1967, 60% came from non-technical schools, and at Royal Melbourne Technical College and Swinburne Technical College the percentage was even higher.[10]

Moreover, since junior technical schools had never really succeeded in escaping the status problem associated with the image of trade schools as places for those of lower ability, many of the former virtues of the system had come to be seen as disadvantages, moving the Principal of the Ballarat School of Mines and Industries to declare in 1962 that

> The first major point is to get rid of that word 'technical'. It is a word which has outlived its usefulness. It has very poor appeal to the general public and is the cause of many students not taking up [the junior technical] course.[11]

Even more significantly, technical schools were no longer the exclusive providers of boys for apprenticeships in a period when the number of male school leavers entering the traditional trades was declining. By the end of the 1960s only about 36% of trade course students subsequently entered the trade on which they had concentrated at school and approximately 40% of apprentices came from non-technical schools.[12]

As the push for full tertiary status strengthened, the vertical integration of the technical system began to appear an impediment to the development of mature senior institutions and the establishment of clearer distinctions between professional and sub-professional categories. In explaining the reasons for the desired upgrading of diploma courses in 1961, the Institution of Engineers had noted disapprovingly

> the highly undesirable but apparently inescapable tendency for the teaching of engineering subjects at secondary school age to be superficial and authoritarian and thus more appropriate for tradesmen and technicians than for professional engineers and technologists.

It was therefore recommended that their study should be deferred until the post-matriculation year because students of engineering needed to be sufficiently mature to benefit from a sophisticated treatment of engineering subjects.[13] The assumption that the technician and the professional were best educated together was under serious challenge.

The Martin Report argued that the presence of apprentices in the diploma schools was inappropriate in the long term and there was growing feeling that the status of the diploma could not be sufficiently raised unless it was more distinguished from technician training and recreational courses.[14] The Director of

Swinburne Technical College, A. F. Tylee, had pointed this out in 1962 when he observed that students who completed a course part time over many years spent a lot of time "engaged in sub professional work". He predicted that the increasing length of technical school courses would 'more clearly divide the professional from the sub professional type, and while this may reduce the number of *bona fide* diploma students, it should enhance the value of the end product.'[15] The overall concern to raise the status of the higher level technical college courses led to a strong move to segment a system which it was once believed had drawn its greatest strength from the integration of various levels of technician and professional training.

Students were similarly exercised by these issues. Les Stephenson, a student at Footscray, forcefully articulated several aspects of the problem of engineering education and the definition of a tertiary institution. In his view there was more to university education than a theoretical orientation and status. A degree was "a qualification attained not only by passing exams, but by experiencing a way of life independent of political control, and free from pressure to conform". The atmosphere of a technical college, however, merely produced a

> student with a fund of knowledge and a lack of worldly experience. There is too much control, authority and misguided methods of teaching in technical colleges. . . . Tertiary students are learning to be Adult Human Beings, not computers.[16]

This may have been a harsh judgement, but the authoritarian atmosphere of the large junior classroom and the industrial workshop was hard to throw off entirely, while the heavy time demands made by courses with a philosophical bias towards 'hands on' experience had necessitated 'cramming' and rote learning for exams.

In response to the demands of the market place and the pursuit of status, engineering courses had been progressively upgraded to look more and more like the university degrees from which they had initially taken great pains to distinguish themselves. As the Professor of Engineering at Melbourne University, C. E. Moorhouse put it in 1960:

> there is a general and apparently ineradicable tendency for institutions which have begun with the sole purpose of training technicians to lengthen and elevate the standard of their

courses — aiming at the prestige which is associated with the granting of a degree or diploma which is 'recognised' — and also to engage in research.[17]

It was unlikely, therefore, that either the technical colleges or the professional bodies would accept anything less than degree-granting status in engineering for very long, and that implied a total restructuring of the technical education system in Victoria.

These new developments had little immediate impact on the well-run, comparatively well-housed Footscray Technical College, where a new building for the secondary section and a new administration block were completed at Ballarat Road in 1964. Form five classes commenced in 1964 and the new diploma syllabuses were introduced the following year. Junior school numbers stabilised at under 800, while the number of full-time diploma students increased from 300 in 1959 to nearly 700 in 1969. The balance of the College shifted markedly and the proportion of diploma school students entering from the junior school continued to decline with more than a third coming from non-technical secondary schools by 1966.[18] This was, nevertheless, still a significantly lower proportion than in the state overall, and was, no doubt, attributable to the large number of junior technical schools in the area, strong regional loyalty and difficulty of access from other parts of the metropolitan area.

While the College was in fact poised on the brink of a new era, much of 1965 and 1966 was overlaid with an aura of continuity and tradition brought about by the organisation of the Jubilee celebrations and the building of a sports pavilion in co-operation with the Old Boys' Football Club, named for C. H. Beanland, on the Henry Turner reserve. The major focus of the celebrations was the raising of £50,000 to build an assembly hall at Ballarat Road to be named in honour of C. A. Hoadley. Unfortunately, the fund-raising fell short of requirements while the potential cost of the building escalated. Worse still, when it came to the point of government 'matching' grants, neither the Education Department nor the newly formed Victoria Institute of Colleges saw an expensive auditorium as high priority when over $2 million had been allocated for a new diploma block. The desire, indeed fervour, for the auditorium derived from a view of the College as a complex, vertical organisation inhabited by students ranging in age from eleven to well into their 20s who ought, from time to time, to be brought together as a whole group. It was a perspective grounded in the era of the Principal after whom they sought to name the building, but it was a sentiment that found little sympathy among the policy makers who had their eyes firmly fixed on a new era of technical education. Eventually, the funds raised were contributed to a joint project between Footscray Institute of Technology, the Footscray Rowing Club, the Footscray City Council and the Department of Youth, Sport and Recreation to build the Footscray Boat Club House on the banks of the Maribyrnong in 1977.

The Martin Committee had proposed that each state set up an institute to foster and co-ordinate the development of tertiary education in technical, commercial, agricultural and liberal arts areas that did not duplicate university studies. Accordingly, the Victorian government established the Victoria Institute of Colleges (VIC) in June 1965. Ultimately, those colleges which affiliated would be able to grant degrees under the auspices of the VIC, provided it could be demonstrated that courses were comparable in standard to university degrees, though not necessarily similar in kind. In practice, the drawing of this distinction proved very difficult, just as the extent of autonomy achieved under the VIC *vis-a-vis* the Education Department for the newly affiliated colleges such as Footscray proved somewhat illusory.

The VIC consisted of a Council presided over by Willis Connolly, Chairman of the State Electricity Commission, with Dr Phillip Law as salaried Vice President and Chief Executive officer, and a Board of Studies to accredit college courses for degree status. The Council comprised representatives of education, government and business interests with a sprinkling of college principals and staff, but was generally viewed by the colleges as under-representing their position and dominated by university people.[19] Footscray was among the first seven colleges to affiliate, but there was little fundamental change to the organisation of senior technical education. The schools had been effectively part of a single system in any case with only minor variations in course offerings and terms of employment of staff. The major effect of setting up the VIC was to channel the new Federal funds into the system while altering the extent of Education Department control very little until pressure from the colleges themselves forced the government to grant greater power to the VIC and greater autonomy to the individual colleges.

On the eve of the creation of the VIC, the College had been judged a successful organisation. Inspectors commented on the "buoyant atmosphere, . . . spirit of enterprise and . . . acceleration of development" throughout the College:[20]

The problem of administering a large and diverse institution has been largely overcome by sensible delegation of authority and by the organisation of regular meetings of various groups or committees to discuss policy, planning and co-ordination of relevant activities. Careful preparation for these meetings is a most important and impressive feature of the organisation, and every endeavour is made to ensure effective subsequent communication of decisions made.

There is ample evidence of adequate discussion and communication within departments. Heads of departments appear to have real responsibility and to accept it well.[21]

They also expressed

unqualified admiration of the dynamic leadership being given by the Principal. His work is marked by foresight and positive planning, untiring effort and refusal to be deterred by difficulties, and his influence is evident throughout the college.[22]

Beneath the surface, however, there were tensions and much of the delegation and consultation was more apparent than real; the habits of autocracy died hard and the transformation would not be achieved without costs to both the institution and individuals. It was as well that the administrative arrangements and corporate cohesiveness were as good as they were; the next few years were to test the ability of the staff and administration to carry out their usual tasks as well as consider their future role and purpose in the face of the upheaval that accompanied the transition to a new system.

Howard Beanland, officially due to retire in 1966, was permitted to remain as Principal until mid-1967, presumably in an attempt to carry the College through to a period of greater certainty as regards the VIC and the Education Department.[23] In fact, the position was little clearer in 1967 than it had been in 1966 and the extent to which the Council, at least, felt unable to dispense with Beanland's services is demonstrated by his employment as a part-time buildings/planning officer by the Council until 1969. In this capacity he continued to shepherd the new 'diploma block' towards completion. The J. L. Kepert Building, which Beanland viewed as one of his finest achievements, was officially opened in March 1971. His last official duty on behalf of the College was to interview one of the applicants for the position of Principal while he was on an overseas holiday in 1969.

He left a fine legacy in new or refurbished buildings and organisational streamlining despite the failure to realise the C. A. Hoadley Hall project. Among the most outstanding features of his period as Principal was the significant improvement in the physical conditions of the College and his success in integrating the apprentices more fully into school life and ensuring that their achievements received suitable recognition. His promotion of the 'Craftsmanship in Industry' displays, the establishment of an annual dinner for the best apprentices of the year and work with the Victorian Overseas Foundation, not only assisted apprentices, but acted as a major means by which industry links were maintained and cultivated with mutual benefit for the College, the students and industry. He continued to serve technical education as secretary of the Technical Schools Association of Victoria from 1971–1977, Careers Organiser for Eastern Region technical schools and through the Victorian Overseas Foundation.

In 1968 the Victoria Institute of Colleges Act was significantly amended. Under the new provisions, each college acquired a greater measure of autonomy and, subject to VIC approval, would be

> responsible for purchasing land and erecting its own buildings, administering finance, appointing staff, planning and introducing its own courses, and doing all those things that are necessary to continue as an educational establishment.[24]

Finance would be provided jointly by the state and Commonwealth governments.[25] In Footscray's case this meant that the tertiary or diploma-granting section was formally 'divorced' from the Education Department, while the secondary school, the trade section and all the courses not considered appropriate to a college of advanced education at the time, remained under Education Department control. On 25 September 1968 the Order in Council necessary to incorporate the College Council as the body to exercise the new powers was gazetted and Footscray Institute of Technology (FIT) came into existence. The Council was expanded from 12 to 22 members, the additional members being a representative of the VIC, a muicipal councillor, a deputy for the Director of Technical Education, an academic staff representative, a member of the Board of Studies and three other persons, one of whom the Council believed should be a graduate of the College.[26]

The change in the composition of the Council was notable. The old Council had included the District Inspector and usually a member of the Footscray City Council. The rest were nominated on the basis of their industry connections, and there was no provision for formal representation of any particular group. While part of the strength of technical education was founded on a notion of 'partnership' with industry, this system, whereby new members were almost inevitably co-opted from the local Rotary Club, also meant that there was little expertise in educational policy as distinct from vocational training and teachers, parents and students were excluded. Under the VIC, the partnership between technical education and industry was structured more broadly. Course Advisory Committees at VIC and Institute level gave industrialists an opportunity to apply their expertise to individual course design, while the Institute Council became the more broadly representative body necessary if genuine autonomy from the Education Department style of centralised decision-making was to be achieved. The new members of the Council provided educational expertise and an opportunity for the interests of staff, community groups, professional associations, and ultimately students, to be coherently incorporated into the greatly expanded planning and decision making roles now invested in it. The new size and power of the Council also demanded greater specialisation within it and greater resources to service it. Consequently, a committee system was established and gradually additional administrative staff were recruited.

The transformation of an institution nurtured under the centralised and bureaucratic regime of the Education Department into an independent, self-defining and self-directing tertiary institution would be a gradual and, at times, painful process. The paternalistic, often plainly autocratic, administrative arrangements and style suitable to a large organisation catering largely to adolescents and offering crammed vocational courses was not appropriate to a higher technological institute catering for adults. Neither, in many ways, were the tight prescriptive requirements imposed by the VIC in its attempt to pull a rag bag of institutions with different histories, orientations and degrees of independence into a coherent system. Such arrangements were certain to create dissatisfaction among the more highly qualified and independent staff that would be essential in the pursuit of degree-granting status, while the broadening of the range of courses offered, and the increased complexity of tertiary functions would require a greater delegation of authority.

The new blue print for technical education also implied a diminution in the dominance of engineering and a belated acceptance of responsibility for the education of young women. The sense that the three major sections of the institution had conflicting, and indeed competing, interests became sharper as the momentum toward degree-granting status gathered pace and inevitably led to something of an identity crisis. In the working out of this identity crisis there was inherent a reappraisal of the relationship between the institution and the Footscray community which it had served and cultivated for 50 years. The principal dilemma was whether to strive for excellence within the tertiary education system or seek to serve the educational needs of the western suburbs, and to what extent could or should these two aims be reconciled.

It was a task that required decisive leadership and a strong presence within the VIC and the Education Department, but for some time this did not eventuate. Beanland had been a caretaker principal from mid-1966. In mid-1967 he was succeeded by an Acting Principal who signalled that he did not wish to join the new CAE sector,[27] but the position was not advertised until March 1969, thus ensuring that a new person would not take up their appointment until 1970. The mantle of authority worn by an 'acting' head is always threadbare and, however skilfully or otherwise an institution is administered, a great deal of important decision making is held in abeyance or considered provisional. To be in this condition for nearly four years was not conducive to the maintenance of the 'buoyancy' noted in 1967, nor to the necessary rapid re-orientation of focus, especially when the administration remained seriously under-resourced to meet the new requirements of autonomy until about the same time as the new Principal took over. Under these circumstances, the role of the long-serving Registrar, Jim McDonald, as a powerful centre of stability was crucial. McDonald's knowledge and dedication provided a solid foundation of continuity from the Beanland years until 1980.

General staffing matters were dealt with more rapidly. The Act setting up the VIC had been framed in such a way as to minimise disadvantage to Education Department staff. Nevertheless, a distribution of staff between the Institute and the Education Department was necessary. Staff had 12 months to decide if they wanted to join the the Institute, but it was under no formal obligation to make an offer to everyone who made themselves available. After discussion and negotiations, 16 vacancies were advertised to make up a full staff of 79 lecturers and five Heads of Departments for the diploma school.[28] Inevitably, some staff felt less than happy with the new arrangements; others were acutely aware that a rapid upgrading of their academic qualifications was essential if they were to justify their appointments in the long term. Throughout the 1970s, a very large proportion of staff took some form of study leave to do just that.

The effect of the new staffing policy was to draw a very clear line between the new 'lecturers', many of whom were quite young, being barely out of teacher training in some cases, and other teaching staff. At the same time, many aspects of the old system geared to the control and organisation of secondary school age boys and the staff structures that went with them remained. The transition from the autocratic authority structures of Education Department days to a more collegiate style was slow, and made slower because they continued to exist in close physical proximity to Department-controlled sections of the Institute. However, the later 1960s were a period of widespread demand for greater participation in decision making and, in the education sector in particular, a growing restiveness with a decision-making framework where 'consultation' more often than not meant simply conveying the content of decisions already made. Moreover, increase in size meant the development of a clearer distinction between administrative and teaching roles and the informal mechanisms for communication that suited a medium-size school became less effective in diffusing frustration and conflict.

Many staff were anxious to break their links with the non-tertiary sections as quickly as possible and a Professional Staff Association was formed in the senior school early in 1967.[29] By the early 1970s it was pushing for improvements in working conditions and representation on the Board of Studies. In the rest of the institution the influence of the Technical Teachers' Association of Victoria (TTAV), which broke away from the VTU in 1967, was very strong and soon took up the cause of those teachers not elevated to the status of lecturer in what became throughout the technical system a period of conflict and strong feelings exacerbated by staff shortages. In 1966 the Council had revealed itself very uneasy with the principle of staff representation, and tried to limit it to a *nominated* staff member, but the pressure for an *elected* member proved irresistible.[30]

While there had always been three, even arguably, four, definable sections of Footscray Technical College, the lines between them had always been blurred, but with time the walls had become less and less permeable and a more distinct separation of staff and students had taken place. Under the VIC arrangements, the process of separation was accelerated at the lower levels, even though administrative unity was maintained at the top. With this separation came a growing sense of competing, even conflicting, interests between the sections. Unfortunately, proximity tended to increase rather than dissipate new tensions, for everyone remained excessively crowded and the various sections often found themselves in direct competition for space and resources. The lack of appropriate playing space for secondary-age boys had scarcely improved since 1916, while the increased number of full-time senior students made the problem even more acute. Classes remained large due to the shortage of classroom space, while special purpose rooms and storerooms often doubled as general classrooms. Student services were negligible and staff accommodation unsatisfactory. The noisy rough and tumble of secondary school recesses was resented as inappropriate to a serious tertiary institution, while both the secondary and middle-level sections began to feel they always came off second best in the allocation of resources, space and staff.

The secondary section had outlived its usefulness as an essential feeder to the senior school and the Council was keen to see the two separated. In most respects, separation would be mutually desirable but only from the secondary section's point of view if it could be relocated, more or less intact, on a new site. From the moment the Council began to consider a new site for the secondary school in mid-1966 the interests of the two sections were in direct conflict in a period when the allocation of resources, the sense of progress and excitement, and the potential for growth all favoured the tertiary section. The process of separation was to be protracted and painful and the efforts to secure a new site nearly as frustrating as the effort to establish the School in the first place.

The Council also agreed in principle that the trade section should be separated in February 1966,[31] though there was less obvious conflict between the tertiary section and the trade/evening school than with the secondary school. In this case, physical separation on two sites over a mile apart had a negative effect on the sense of mutuality, especially as each area became more and more specialised. The feeling that the trade section was the Cinderella of the Institute rapidly gained strength, but a sense of irreconcilable conflict was barely discernible for a long time until the Technical and Further Education section, as it became in the 1970s, began to establish an effective separate power base and acquire greater confidence in itself.

There were also inevitable tensions within the tertiary section consequent on the growth in size and status of subject areas other than engineering and the need to establish an appropriate balance of resources between them. A lament for "The Downtrodden Race" in the 1964 edition of the school magazine captures one undercurrent of feeling on the matter:

It is many years since the Commerce Department was introduced into Footscray Technical College, and it has not lived down being 'the baby', the side-line, the by-product.

Here are some facts: The Commerce Faculty is the largest single faculty in the college. It can boast of having the Chief Prefect, the President of the SRC, the Chairman of the Social Committee, and three members of the SRC Executive, in its ranks. Along with the Chemists, it is the most progressive and college-conscious faculty.

The senior Commerce form, 8M, has four studentship holders out of fourteen students. They are the leading sportsmen — being top of the football ladder, and having the SRC Sports Representative among them. As well as this, they feature the prettiest students — the Commerce girls.

On the other hand, the Commerce Department has the worst facilities in the college, including the basement rooms, the sports store, and a staff room 10 ft × 6 ft for eight or more teachers. Commerce is rarely catered for at assemblies, rarely mentioned, with never a speaker suitable for the course.

How about it? This is no longer an Engineering School, but a Technical College.[32]

If space was tight, the Commerce Department was nevertheless brimming with energy and innovative in its teaching methods, prompting the Inspectors in 1967 to describe it as a "splendid department".

The co-ordinator staff and students maintain close and harmonious relations which produce a pleasing student attitude to study and all are to be commended for their high standard of endeavour to provide a complete education.[33]

Moreover, the future was on its side and the last part of the decade is most notable for the development of this Department. In 1967 the Diplomas of Commerce and Commercial Practice were replaced with a Diploma of Business Studies, a professional course of three or four years duration designed to train accountants, junior executives, private secretaries and system analysts. The diploma could be taken in Accounting, Administration or Private Secretarial Practice. In 1968 a Diploma of Business Studies (Data Processing) was introduced, and in 1970 links with business and professional bodies were formalised through the establishment of a Business Studies Course Advisory Board.

As the Commerce, Applied Science and Management Departments of the Institute expanded, the number of engineering diplomas offered was reduced. Metallurgy, Structural Engineering and the first two years of the Building and Contracting diploma course disappeared, but in 1967 a course leading to a Diploma in Electronic Engineering, essentially a specialisation beyond a Diploma of Electrical Engineering, was introduced. These Departments all offered teaching to a high standard and staff were contributing to the development of engineering education on a wider level through involvement in course design and development.[34] The constant revision and upgrading of engineering syllabuses ensured that the first degree courses would be offered in engineering but the privileged status of these courses within the institution would soon be under serious challenge.

The final tension, affecting the tertiary section at least, flowed from a change in what might be called student mood. These were the years of protest against conventions, censorship, hanging, and above all, the war in Vietnam. By the later 1960s student radicalism and propensity for 'shocking' behaviour as well as their demand for a greater voice in all decisions directly affecting student welfare had become highly newsworthy. For various reasons the level of student activism was far lower in the CAEs than in the universities,[35] and the tiny Footscray campus was no exception. This is not to say that Footscray's students were untouched by the spirit of the times; with the rise in the average age of senior students and the proportion who were full time, the conditions for breeding the degree of alienation necessary for independent student activity gradually appeared, though it could hardly be said to have reached significant proportions even by the 1980s.

FIT student publications contained their share of Vietnam protest poetry and irreverence for authority, and students demonstrated a new ability to unsettle and even anger the upper levels of the administration when the FIT student entry in the 1967 Moomba parade depicting Snoopy and the Red Baron and involving copious flour throwing, led to the banning of an entry in the 1968 parade. The SRC greeted the arrival of full tertiary status in 1969 with a new student publication *Seed*. Combining shock value and idealism in proportions characteristic of tertiary student newspapers in general, it displayed a young, mini-skirted, pregnant woman deep in thought on the front cover and included a fanciful parable about the war between "weeds" and "flowers", the outcome of which was a barren desert just "Waiting for 'seed'".[36]

The SRC had a long history, but if, under Beanland, it had been largely confined to a social and fund-raising role, the desire for a greater 'political' role and financial independence had been growing more insistent for some time. Finally, in 1969, a restructuring of the SRC set the stage for a new style of student politics. The "NEW DEAL SRC of 1970" was intended to improve communication, revise financial and organisational processes and bring "maturity" to its administration. In this way, it was hoped that

> pure politics (politics, that is, devoid of 'social club' image that paternalistic Big Brother policies of the past have propagated, . . .) will be introduced into SRC philosophy, and Graeme Lukey's "NEW ERA" (SEED No 2) will be a closer reality that at present conceivable.[37]

When in 1970 the Business Studies students moved to Ballarat Road, the student body was beginning to develop a more confident sense of itself as 'tertiary' and independent. The demand for a new style of relationship with the administration created tensions that the new Principal had to address along with all the others bubbling under the surface in 1969.

The Principal's job was described as a "challenging position" for an "energetic, enthusiastic and suitably qualified man to control a long-established, modern, progressive institution with an enrolment of 6,300 students" at a salary of $11 000.[38] That 6300 students included 700 students actually enrolled in full-time courses, plus an *equivalent* full-time student population of 1200. The non-tertiary division comprised approximately 800 secondary students in forms one to five, 1800 day release apprentices, 600 enrolled part-time in trade subjects, 1,200 students in part time certificate courses and other subjects and 800 enrolled part time in Leaving and Matriculation subjects. The qualities sought in the Principal were primarily administrative ability, capacity for leadership and "knowledge and experience of tertiary education, particularly as it applied to meeting the needs of business, industry and community services".[39]

The feeling that the new Principal should be above all a skilful administrator was very strong.[40] It was also felt that he should be a good advocate for FIT — "The Principal will project an image of FIT. He should be capable of projecting a forceful and convincing one"[41] — and that local knowledge would be an asset:

> The growth of the Institutes of Technology is taking place against a very complex background. The influences of the VIC, the Universities, the Education Department, Industry and the State and Federal Governments are closely and sometimes conflictingly interwoven. It is felt that while an able man would eventually come to terms with these various forces someone who already comprehends their existence would be at least an initial advantage to FIT.[42]

The issues most exercising the minds of the FIT councillors are revealed in the questions they proposed to put during their interviews with the candidates. These covered the relations between the CAEs and universities, the distinction between education and training, the differences between an administrator and a leader and what style of leader the applicant felt was most suitable. There were questions about student activism, staff and student representation and how the links with the business community would be extended and developed. There were no prepared questions about the applicants' views of future directions for the Institute or course development, but two questions did encapsulate the most critical issues that the Principal and the Institute would face. The first related to the relationship between the various sections of the institution:

Footscray caters for tertiary education, secondary education, and trade work, and has stated its policy that at the appropriate time it will shed the secondary and trade sections. Do you feel that it is possible to carry out this policy? What is your reaction to the suggestion that technician and trade work should be retained in such institutions?

The second concerned the relationship of the institution to an evolving system:

The Principal of the College is the chief executive of an autonomous Council, yet the College is affiliated with the Victorian Institute of Colleges. How do you see it preserving and developing its autonomy under the restrictions imposed by the Victorian Institute of Colleges?

The answers the new Principal gave to those questions would profoundly influence development over the next 18 years.

There were 24 applicants for the position, five from overseas, but it seems clear that local knowledge and intimate connections with the existing technical network had the greatest appeal to the selection committee. Doug Mills was a man from inside the Education Department and the VIC representative on FIT Council. He also lived in the district and included among his referees, the 'old boy', J. L. Kepert, recently retired Director of Technical Education. Born in Ballarat in 1930, Mills took out Diplomas of Electrical and Mechanical Engineering from Melbourne University before going to work as a cadet engineer with the State Electricity Commission of Victoria for three-and-a-half years. Later he took out a Bachelor of Electrical Engineering at the University of Melbourne and a Trained Technical Teachers' Certificate. His first teaching appointment was in the diploma section of Footscray Technical School, but the following year (1957) he transferred to Caulfield Technical School where he stayed till 1964, by which time he was Head of the Computer Department. In 1964 he was appointed an Inspector of Technical Schools, with special duties in regard to higher engineering courses. In the course of his career with the Education Department he had played an important role in the development of engineering and computer education in particular and many other diploma courses in a less specialised way. He certainly considered his close personal associations with officers responsible for the development of policy one of the most valuable assets he could offer FIT.

Mills made it clear that he was not in the market for *any* principal's job but only that at FIT. He had lived in the Footscray area for 15 years and, as an inspector visiting the College and the VIC representative on the FIT Council since 1968, he was well acquainted with the nature of the organisation he was about to take over and many of the key players in the system and the community with whom he would have to deal. Like Beanland, he had made his career in technical education, but his focus had been on the higher level from the very beginning. Mills had not been part of the highly integrated vertical system that was the origin of technical education in the state, nor, despite his educational background, was his interest so narrowly based in engineering and trades as his involvement in the development of computer education reveals. Mills had never been a principal and so he had not exercised the authoritarian style of power that such a position implied. As an inspector involved with senior courses, his role had been principally that of consultant and advisor and, so while he was steeped in the system that was transforming Footscray Technical College into a college of advanced education, it was likely that he had the youth, background and flexibility to bring a distinctive, innovative style to leadership of that institution.

1. Quoted in S. L. Davies, 'Establishing the Martin Committee: A Study of the Setting up of the Committee and its Preliminary Discussions', M. Ed., Monash University, 1981, p 26.
2. P. M. Martin, 'Some Reflections on the Australian Higher Education System, Part I the Colleges of Advanced Education', *Forum of Education*, Vol. 44, No. 1, 1986, p 5.
3. Quoted in Dare, *op. cit.*, p 289.
4. *Ibid.*, p 291.
5. Davies, *op. cit.*, p 85.
6. *Ibid.*, p 124.
7. This reported in 1963. According to Turner there is no evidence that the Minister took any notice of the Ramsay Report. A. Turner, *State Councils for Technical Education in Victoria 1961–1980*, Victorian Education Department, Melbourne, 1984, p 11.
8. Docherty, *op. cit.*, p 712.
9. Quoted in *ibid.*, p 729.
10. *Ibid.*, p 725.
11. H. E. Arblaster to A. F. E. Tylee, Director Swinburne Technical College, 27 March 1962, FIT Archive.
12. Docherty, *op. cit.*, p 768.

13. C. D. H. Harper, Secretary of the Institution of Engineers to C. H. Beanland, 9 January 1961, FIT Archive.
14. Quoted in J. L. Kepert, Chief Inspector of Technical Schools, *Report to Minister of Education*, 1965, FIT Archive.
15. A. F. Tylee, 'Some Thoughts on the Re-organisation of Technical Education', Typed MS, FIT Archive.
16. *Blue and Gold*, 1964, p 22.
17. C. E. Moorhouse, 'Technical and Technological Education in Australia', *The Australian Journal of Education*, Vol. 4, No. 3, November 1960, p 183.
18. Principal's Report to the Inspectors, 1967, FIT Archive.
19. R. C. Traill, 'Development and Perspectives of the Victoria Institute of Colleges', VICSAC pub. no. A72, June 1972, p 5. See also Murray-Smith & Dare, *op. cit.*, p 385.
20. Inspectors' Report, 1965, FIT Archive.
21. *Ibid.*, 1967.
22. *Ibid.*, 1965.
23. There seems to have considerable pressure applied by the Council to bring this about. See for example, FTC Council Minutes, 26 July 1966.
24. W. J. Basset, Acting Principal's Annual Report, 1967, FIT Archive.
25. According to a formula of 1/1 for capital expenditure and 1.85/1 for recurrent expenditure salaries and general maintenance, *ibid.*
26. FIT Council Minutes, 25 February 1969.
27. He later became Principal of Brighton Technical School.
28. FIT Council Minutes, 26 November 1968.
29. FTC Council Minutes, 28 February 1967.
30. *Ibid.*, 22 November, 1966.
31. *Ibid.*, 22 February, 1966.
32. Anonymous, *Blue and Gold*, 1964, p 22.
33. Inspectors' Report, 1967, FIT Archive.
34. See, for example, *ibid.*
35. D. S Anderson, 'The Prospects for Student Power in Australia', *Australian University*, Vol. 6, No. 3, 1968, pp 207–221.
36. *Seed*, Vol. 1, No. 1, 10 February 1969.
37. "Campus 69", News Sheet re SRC Elections, Roneoed MS, FIT Archive.
38. 'Advertisement', New Principal File, FIT Archive.
39. "FIT Position of Principal General Information", Roneoed MS, *ibid.*
40. See, for example, Rex Boschen, Staff Representative on Council, to W. J. Bassett, 9 June 1969, *ibid.*
41. FIT Position of Principal General Information, *ibid.*
42. *Ibid.*
43. List of possible questions to be put to applicants for the position of Principal, *ibid.*

CHAPTER TEN **"A dark tunnel"**[1]
1970–1975

When Doug Mills took over as Principal of FIT in 1970 he faced nearly as difficult a task as Arch Hoadley had 54 years previously despite the progress of those intervening years. Once more the gap between resources and expectations was great. Once more the land and buildings were inadequate, once more the reality of a small institution in an industrial area implied status problems — an uphill battle to establish FIT as a worthy and long term member of the system of CAEs. On the other hand, Mills took over an organisation endowed with several assets denied to Hoadley; a degree of control over budget and staffing that was never possible under the Education Department, a tide of official opinion running strongly in favour of CAEs and tertiary education generally, and a government sector which accepted that such education required substantial commitment of public money. Mills was in a position to plan the necessary moves to place FIT strategically within a clearly defined, if still evolving, structure of education. His task was to identify the opportunities and grasp them. Mills and the Council would be responsible for developments in a way neither Hoadley nor Beanland ever were. In this lay a new 'Door of Opportunity' to at last create an institution with a distinctive character and one which many hoped would genuinely reflect the needs and realities of the western suburbs of Melbourne.

Mills was young, energetic, relaxed and approachable. He was decisive and determined, but willing to listen and be persuaded. There was much that had to change, and a large part of Mills' role was to oversee a transformation in almost every aspect of the old College. Most changes were anticipated with enthusiasm but their actual execution was fraught with difficulties, and if there was general agreement about outcomes in broad design, there was often great tension when it came to working out the detail. In the long run the institution would be substantially remade. The challenge for Mills was to facilitate that remaking. In that task he faced two major obstacles. The first was the slow dismantling of the old system; the second was the fact that not everyone in Footscray was convinced that the expansion and growth of FIT was, unequivocally, a good thing.

Mills spent 1970 establishing lines of communication throughout the organisation and laying the foundations of a more complex administrative structure. A Technical Services Department was set up at Ballarat Road and an Interim Union Board commissioned to draw up guide-lines for the provision of student services. In response to a long-standing SRC grievance, student fees were raised to give it greater financial power and independence. This last step demonstrated Mills' awareness that effective student government was essential to full tertiary status, even if this occasionally meant embarrassing publicity or confrontation with the administration. He also met an insistent staff demand for somewhere pleasant and inexpensive to eat on Campus.[2] Because the canteen was reserved for secondary school use,[3] the senior students and staff had long felt seriously deprived, so Mills agreed that part of an area being excavated under Building C could be set aside as a staff dining room. Its opening in October 1972 prompted one staff member to comment that he and his colleagues were luckier than those in some other colleges in having a Director who was "prepared to lend a sympathetic ear to a just cause" and then do something about it.[4]

Once Mills was established in his role, the Institute rather belatedly began to draw up a blue print for the future development of the CAE — an "Educational Specification". Essential as a basis for funding submissions and course approvals, its preparation provided an important opportunity for the Council to confront in detail the nature of the transition to a college of advanced education. "The change in circumstances brought by autonomy made it imperative that the administration take good stock of the situation and plan wisely for the future".[5] Many of the old councillors were not in a rush to have the Institute achieve degree-granting status. Some would have been content with autonomous control over the old system. Discussion throughout 1970 returned to the proposition that industry was pleased with the diploma system and did not want the sub-professional courses jeopardised, but the tide of events was such that FIT "could not afford to defer applications for degree courses" and risk falling behind other colleges.[6] The Council had to plan for the future, and if the values of the past were not necessarily the best guide, the changed composition of the Council ensured that there were fresh influences at work.

Some members of Council could easily lay claim to being a significant part of the institution's history and they have been mentioned in some detail earlier. Ern Mollard, Ron Rankin, George Thompson,[7] Harry Tribe and Tom Roberts, were all ex-students. Mollard had been a member of the Council from 1925 to 1930 and was re-appointed in 1964. He was President of the FIT Council from 1970 to 1976.[8] As a young man he had formed a close association with Hoadley through the School and Scouting, and in his retirement he worked closely with Mills to build strong foundations for the new Institute. Tribe was President of the Council from 1977–79.[9] Rankin joined the Council in 1950 and remained till 1986, acting as Treasurer from 1955 till 1976.[10] He was also responsible for the establishment of a poetry prize and was the driving force behind the setting up of the Art Acquisition Committee. Roberts, active from 1967 till 1976, had taken out his diplomas in 1942 and was Manager of the Commonwealth Government Marine Engine Works.

Other long-standing members were Roy Parsons, W. J. Cuming, J. A. Smithson, and G. R. Schintler MLA. Parsons had been a member since 1918. His involvement in technical education and Footscray community and business affairs was long and broad, and together with the 'old boys' he provided a deep vein of continuity.[11] W. J. Cuming came from an established industrial family in the district and was the second member of his family to sit on the Council. Closely linked with the chemical industry, he joined the Council in 1953 and was president from 1965 till 1969. He was also a foundation member of the Board of Studies of the VIC. He took a special interest in the problem of student services which was recognised in the naming of the refurished Secondary School building in his honour. He remained active on the Council till his death in January 1986. Smithson, of the Olympic Tyre and Rubber Company, joined the Council in 1957 and was president from 1962–1964. He resigned in 1977. Schintler, Labor Member for Yarraville and a municipal councillor, was a member from 1959 till 1976 and maintained the continuity of Labor representation on Council that began with A. E. Shepherd.

Among the more recently appointed members were J. H. Hood, (1964–1971), Works Manager, Australian Glass Manufacturers Co. Pty Ltd and later Technical Officer for ACI; Peter C. Perry, (1967–1974), Works Manager, Union Carbide; and Wal Beevers, (1970–1982), grazier and Director of Prism Paints. They were joined by those appointed under the new VIC provisions for membership of Council: Cr J. F. Bristow, representing the Footscray City Council; R. Armitage, District Inspector representing the Education Department; Arthur Ferguson of Melbourne University Elecronics Department, representing the VIC; G. J. Lowe the elected staff representative; and Gordon Murray, Vice Principal of FIT, representing the Board of Studies.

The *Educational Specification* set out the philosophy of FIT and the changes and developments necessary to achieve its educational goals in terms of student and staff welfare, responsibility, decision making and campus development. The role of FIT was to

(a) provide at a professional level an education appropriate to the needs of a complex industrial society.

(b) act as a Regional College by providing a logical extension of the education offered by technical schools in the western metropolis and an avenue to technological qualifications for the students of secondary schools.

(c) act in close concert with industry, assisting it to solve its technological difficulties and, by encouraging its interest and participation in technological education, helping to make more meaningful the vocational bias of the courses.

Its primary educational objective was to

provide at a tertiary level an education which will be an equivalent alternative to that offered by the universities, and which will assist in the intellectual, social and personal development of students, so that as graduates they may acquit themselves worthily both as professional officers and members of the community. The courses should be vocationally oriented and intrinsically attractive to those contemplating post-secondary education.

Specifically this meant offering "diploma and degree courses in the fields of Engineering, Applied Science, Business Studies and

General Studies", and ultimately "post-degree courses in specially selected areas".[12]

There had been a retreat from the desire to separate from the trade section; the *Specification* placed strong emphasis on retaining "institutional unity" and FIT's continued functioning as an integrated whole. It was expected that most students would and should study full time, though part-time courses would still be available. The emphasis in staff recruiting was, in theory at least, to be more on teaching expertise and industrial experience than academic achievement, working conditions were to be improved and academic and student services greatly expanded. The relationship with outside employers was to be fostered, though not to the point where course standards were *dictated* by them or professional bodies, and consulting work with commerce and industry was viewed as an essential component of Institute activities.

While not always realised in effect, embedded in the traditions of the Institute was a desire to serve the local community above and beyond the clearly defined task of educating its children. The vocational emphasis and the notion of partnership with local industry dovetailed with this aim. The close relationship maintained with the City Council, Rotary and other local groups was seen as a means by which members of the Institute made a contribution to the community as well as receiving valuable support. Historically, many members of staff had lived locally and involved themselves in local affairs. Mills continued this tradition, aided by a greater interest throughout the community generally in the concept of "community colleges" and the special relationship between community and college that might be developed. Martin, in the course of his preliminary investigations in the early 1960s, had ultimately rejected the concept for Australia, but the ideas were still exercising a strong influence among educationalists, especially those in provincial or 'deprived' areas like the western suburbs of Melbourne. Many FIT staff felt a special responsibility not only to provide education but also to try and compensate for perceived deprivations. Such sentiment was nicely captured in a report from the Union and Staff and Student Services Building Committee which declared that, while the Union Building should become the centre of campus life, in line with FIT's policy of community involvement, it should also be made available in such a way as "to destroy the moat that almost always isolates all educational institutions from the outside world".[13]

Once the parameters of future development were outlined, planning for the new buildings and courses began. Site development was handed over to the architectural firm Bates, Smart and McCutcheon who presented their "Campus Plan" to the Institute in 1971. Unveiled in a blaze of publicity, the proposed complex required the expenditure of $21 million over about 15 years and would cater for 4000 equivalent full-time students. Much stress was laid on the "Complete Involvement of the Community" and the aim that "the campus should be a community within a city . . . freely open for the general public to use". By that it was meant that the library, auditorium and physical education centre should be available to the public when not being used by the Institute. Landscaping and design features were incorporated to take account of local topography, and there is no evidence that anyone expected anything other than local approbation. The Deputy Director of the VIC endorsed the project enthusiastically as "most impressive". The old campus had "presented a number of problems which, it seemed, would condemn it to mediocrity", but these had been "solved by the architects in a novel and exciting way, opening up completely new prospects for developing the campus".[14]

An essential feature of the Plan was the diversion of Farnsworth Avenue to a point further north where it would meet Ballarat Road and Droop Street in a realigned intersection. FIT would then acquire the old road reserve and part of the abutting parkland which sloped steeply to the Maribyrnong flood plains. At the same time properties along Nicholson Street, the west side of Geelong Road and the south side of Ballarat Road would be acquired to allow for expansion and for the Country Roads Board to widen Ballarat Road without encroaching any further on the Institute on the northern side. It was a neat, logical, indeed clever, solution to FIT's site problem. Unfortunately, several features of the Plan had a direct impact on nearby residents, particularly those immediately to the north west. There was also a lack of clarity about just how much public land might be incorporated into the Institute, and possible cost implications for the Footscray City Council in respect of the re-aligned intersection at Ballarat Road. A storm of controversy erupted almost overnight that left supporters of FIT gasping in frustration and disbelief. Absolutely, and on the whole properly, convinced of the value and merit of FIT's expansion for the community as a whole, the administration at first failed to take sufficiently seri-

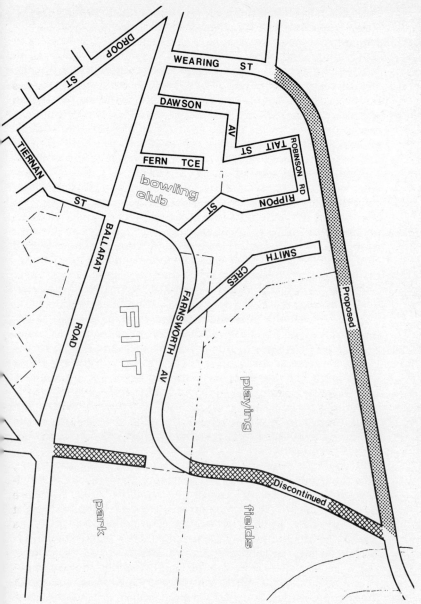

Proposed Farnsworth Avenue diversion to allow for expansion of FIT Ballarat Road site

ously the potential of these apparently trifling objections to provide the foundation for an escalating campaign against FIT which, while not successful in the long run, seriously frustrated the Institute's progress and damaged its public image.

The temptation to credit the objections to the Plan as merely self-interest on the part of nearby residents was, and is, strong but it obscures a genuine conflict of interests that helps explain the turbulent aspects of FIT's relationship with its host community in the early 1970s. A tertiary institution versus parkland in an area acknowledged to be deprived of both was not the black and white issue of local amenity versus rampant development that might have been aroused if, for example, FIT had been a chemical plant or even a shopping complex. However, the opportunities presented by a tertiary college were, perhaps, less appreciated than might have been expected in an area that even in 1987 had a much lower than average number of tertiary qualified people.[15] The FIT administration seems to have felt so confident of success that it took few public opportunities to 'sell' the Institute on philosophical and educational grounds and only after a series of hard fights were concessions made on particular details. In particular, FIT was slow to calm fears about loss of open space just at a time when the potential for the area along the Maribyrnong River to provide attractive parkland was being recognised. If we are to understand the force of objections to FIT's plans they must be seen in the context of the early 1970s when large bureaucracies were impinging on local amenities with freeways, land re-zoning and large-scale 'planning' by 'experts' and community organisation to resist was gaining momentum and sophistication. Under the circumstances, the headline, "Institute wants parkland'[16] could rally a significant degree of opposition.

FIT issued an invitation to local residents to bring any objections to it but at all times the residents preferred to channel these through the City Council and later the Town Planning Appeals Tribunal. No sooner had the Plan been submitted to the Footscray City Council than nearby residents asked to be heard.[17] A deputation of 30 presented their objections on 15 November and successfully delayed acceptance of the Plan.[18] Mills' reaction was dismissive, he simply asserted that parkland would not be "lost in effect" without going into detail, and made the dubious suggestion that the FIT Council was an adequate representation of local opinion.[19] Early in 1972, in response to continuing pressure from FIT, the City Council approved the Plan with the proviso that the new intersection be at no extra cost to it. The relationship between the institution and the City Council had always been supportive, and, as G. R. Schintler, ex-Mayor and ex-Member for Footscray, argued,

> The Labor Councillors have shown an appreciation of the scope of this expansion of FIT — with which Footscray Council has been associated since the opening of the college in 1916 — and they are to be congratulated on their support. This is going to reflect greatly on the reputation of Footscray. It is going to put Footscray 'on the map' in educational circles. I'm sure that in considering their verdict the Labor councillors realised that they were giving a decision that would result in the greatest good for the greatest number, far outweighing any parochial considerations.[20]

The two Independent councillors, however, had voted against the approval and, when it emerged in the local press that the vote in the Labor Caucus[21] had, in fact, been very close, the objectors campaigned to have the motion rescinded.[22]

Deputations, petitions and media campaigns continued throughout 1972. Encroachment on open space remained the central issue in the public arena. It fed on a vague sense that the College and now the Institute had been gradually reducing the open space for some time. As the buildings had spread over a larger and larger portion of the present site, some houses were purchased on the south side of Ballarat Road, the C. H. Beanland Sports Pavilion was built down on the parkland, the students dominated the day-time use of the sports fields and parked their cars along the nearby streets. It enabled opponents of the Plan, such as R. C. Stanhope, to argue that "Nibbling away at this parkland has been going on for many years . . . the time has come to say 'hands off'".[23]

> The Footscray City Council is being asked to support annexation by the Victoria Institute of Colleges of several acres of prime open space zoned as such by the MMBW, in an industrial suburb with only a fraction of the MCC's parkland. It is proposed to bodily move a roadway about ¼ mile northwards at an estimated cost of $1 million. Presumably Commonwealth and State education grants will be used for the purpose at a time when country colleges are crying out for a larger share of available funds.[24]

Another letter to the local press tapped a less elevated vein of hostility. The writer attacked student supporters of the Plan, labeling them selfish, because "most of them" came "from suburbs well endowed with parkland", and were over-indulged by their trendy tutors.[25] Along the same lines, another writer concluded, "Most members of the FIT Council live outside this municipality and cannot be expected to show that much concern over the loss of our open space".[26]

A petition of 350 signatures objecting to the Plan was presented to the Footscray City Council in May,[27] prompting the FIT Council to complain that the City Council was continuing to meet with residents but not the Institute.[28] Conceding that fears about the cost of the intersection realignment at Ballarat Road was a major problem, FIT submitted an undertaking to the City Council that municipal liability would not be in excess of that normally applicable.[29] This did not succeed in quelling the campaign of opposition. The attempt to rescind the approval also failed but, in October 1972, the Footscray City Council requested that FIT sign a Covenant setting out a broad range of concerns about the Plan that were not limited to the desire of the Smith Crescent residents to retain their existing access to Ballarat Road.[30] FIT took no action until July 1973[31] after the Smith Crescent residents had once again sought to have the approval rescinded, this time because the Covenant was not signed.[32] It seems, however, that the City Council was still dissatisfied, and in November it felt compelled to pass a motion insisting on a formal guarantee that Smith Crescent would not be encroached on in any way. Supporters of FIT were defeated in their attempt to have this motion deferred by eight votes to six.[33]

In March 1974 the Campus Plan went on public display as required to obtain the necessary rezoning.[34] It incorporated some critical concessions, such as agreements to eliminate the proposed student housing on the south side of Ballarat Road and to buy part of the Standard Quarries site to hand over eventually as new parkland and assurances regarding Smith Crescent access to Ballarat Road.[35] In July the *Advertiser*, which strongly supported FIT on this issue, carried the jubilant headline "They can't stop this new FIT Plan. It's Carry on Campus", and declared categorically that the education of tertiary students was "infinitely more important than the surprising objections of a few Footscray councillors and a handful of residents".[36] Those "surprising objections" which had grown to 570, were lodged with the Town Planning Appeals Tribunal where they appeared to get a sympathetic hearing, and the *Mail* beat up the story with the headline "Park 'Grab' to Make Floods Worse on River Flats".[37] The rezoning was finalised by October 1975, but with the proviso that the new road be at ground level to obviate the effects of flooding on areas to the north.[38]

If the process of obtaining approval for the rezoning and acquisition of land was drawn out and frustrating, there were other factors delaying the actual implementation of the Plan in any case. Not the least of these was uncertainty of funding and the need to relocate the secondary school. Information presented to Council by Mills in February 1973[39] revealed serious gaps in funding commitments yet great optimism regarding completion dates. At the same time, the size of the projected expenditure coupled with a growing realisation of the extent of educational deprivation in the western region of Melbourne led to the floating of the idea that the tertiary section rather than the secondary school should be relocated. The Western Regional Commission[40] argued that FIT and the Mercy Teachers' College (Ascot Vale) were the only tertiary education establishments to the west of a north/south line drawn though Melbourne, whereas to the east there were ten VIC colleges, three universities, eight state teachers' colleges and seven other tertiary institutions. Students entering FIT were restricted to nine possible courses whereas several hundred were available in the central and eastern areas[43] Even though this was rather over stating the case, especially in regard to the location of Royal Melbourne Institute of Technology, the Melbourne Teachers' College and Melbourne University, the need for teacher education and the provision of a wider range of course choices within the region was indisputable. "The majority of students" were obliged to travel out of the region if they were "to undertake the course of their choice",[42] yet the Victorian government's policy had been to allow a proliferation of small institutions in provincial areas on the basis of such arguments.

The Joint Report of the Australian Universities Commission and Australian Commission on Advanced Education presented to Federal Cabinet in May 1973 noted

the possibility of re-establishing the Footscray Institute on a more suitable site either to the west in Sunshine or further south-west toward Werribee. Such a development could desirably include teacher education as a new activity as well as continuing the present functions of the Footscray Institute.[43]

FIT Council immediately protested that investigating such a proposal would cause harmful delay to its plans,[44] but the Commission replied that it was important that the present site be seen to be clearly to "the satisfaction of the people of the western region" as "the best for its purpose". If FIT's case was as strong as they felt, it should "not object to reassessment".[45] An independent committee recommended in January 1974 that the FIT site should be retained and developed as proposed.[46]

A more serious setback to FIT's Plan came in the form of reduced funding. Victoria's CAEs had their budget proposals for the 1973–1975 triennium slashed by both Commonwealth and state governments. Overall capital expenditure for buildings was reduced from $111 million to $51 million and recurrent expenditure for salaries and running costs cut from $120 million to $95 million.[47] FIT's projected recurrent expenditure was cut from $8.5 million to $5.171 million precluding any significant increase in new courses and services during that triennium.[48] The special needs of the western region were, nevertheless, seen to be a basis for separate consideration and a meeting was arranged in July 1974 with Dr J. F. Cairns, Federal Labor MHR, the Assistant Director of Technical Education, state and federal MPs and the President and Secretary of the Technical Teachers' Association of Victoria in order to request a special allocation of funds for the "relocation of Footscray secondary school, the development of the College division on the Nicholson Street site, and the tertiary development on the Ballarat Road site". The outcome was a promise from Dr Cairns to strongly support a special submission to the Minister of Education if it were "based on established priorities for the total requirements of the Western Region" and agreement that the "Tertiary and College requirements were the top priority when considered on a regional basis, but the development of Sunshine Technical School should take precedence over the secondary school relocation".[49] Shortly afterwards, an amended submission providing for the *concurrent* development of Sunshine Technical School was forwarded to the Minister for Education. In accepting low priority for relocation of the secondary school and calling tenders for Stage 1A of the Campus Plan,[50] the seeds of future conflict and delay to the building program were planted, but in the meantime FIT was moving ahead with planning new courses.

Law's fear that the Institute was in danger of being condemned to mediocrity extended to more than a cramped site.

Over the course of the 1960s, with the expansion of technical colleges in general, Footscray came to draw on a smaller geographical base for students than it had in the 1940s, while the increased availability of high school and university education meant that some who had made their path to the university via a diploma now by-passed the technical system. Subtle, and not so subtle, status hierarchies among institutions tended to place Footscray down the scale, at least partly because it was situated in a low-status area. FIT would have to achieve greatly in order to overcome that bias, but it was further hampered by its small size, which left it vulnerable to amalgamation or deletion from the system. If FIT was to survive, it had to grow bigger, diversify its course offerings and find a niche for itself within the system of colleges of advanced education. As the problems with the Campus Plan had demonstrated, the magnitude of these tasks could not be underestimated. Morale was not especially high, the transition in itself produced mixed responses, and the problems with the Campus Plan added to the burden, but the leadership was optimistic and determined that any setback would be only temporary.

Planning for new courses, and up-grading old ones, occurred within strict guide-lines set down by the VIC, but this was a situation which old Education Department schools found familiar and even rather comforting. The Institute began by building on its existing strengths and rationalising certain functions. Moulding was transferred to RMIT in 1970 and strong Course Advisory Boards on Chemistry, Business Studies and Civil, Electrical and Electronic Engineering set up. A degree course in electrical engineering commenced in 1972 and the first degrees were conferred in 1974. Degree courses in accounting, civil engineering, chemistry and mathematics soon followed. These courses, however, were widely available in other colleges. There was a critical need to find at least one distinctive area in which to offer courses[51] not only in order to compete effectively with other institutions, but also because numbers studying chemistry and engineering were dropping.[52] One possibility was within FIT's ambit — catering and hotel management. The course had been conducted jointly between FIT and the William Angliss Food Trades School since 1962 but had not really flourished. Despite an agreement in 1968 that the Angliss School would take over the course, FIT's involvement had actually increased,[53]and by the end of 1970 the situation was in need of further resolution. Some were sceptical of its potential to enhance the academic status of the Institute. On the other hand, it presented an opportunity to provide a unique course and pioneer the development of a distinctive management course oriented to an industry just beginning to expand.

The Report from the President of the Australian Hotel and Catering Management Association based on a survey of diplomates made a very strong case for FIT control. It was generally felt that the present course was unsound and provided no real foundation for future development. More significant than content or the inconvenience of the dual arrangements, however, were the status implications of association with "the food trades school". The Report was remarkably frank about the problem. Employers, it was argued, generally regarded the trade school as

> an institute for producing purely trade, craft, personnel. When a student or graduate applying for a position mentions an association with the trade school, the employer does not look upon him as a prospective employee with management orientation.

Furthermore, a diploma from FIT had more status anyway because, within a VIC college, there was the potential for the course to achieve degree status and thereby, ultimately, international recognition.[54] Like the students, Mills favoured keeping the course for FIT, but negotiations proved difficult at a time when many other problems were occupying his energies. In early 1973 he seemed prepared to abandon the course if a satisfactory agreement was not reached by 30 June 1973.[55] At this point, Brian Wise suggested that this would be foolish in the extreme.[56] Mills took up the challenge, and three years later the Degrees of Bachelor Business Studies (Catering and Hotel Management) and Bachelor of Business Studies (Tourism) were available. FIT was on the way to both a distinctive place in the Victorian tertiary sector and international recognition for these courses. By the mid-1980s, with burgeoning hopes for the role of tourism in the revitalisation of the economy, the decision to back the development of these courses was particularly fortuitous.

The second opportunity that FIT exploited was in physical education and recreation studies. In the early 1970s the University of Melbourne was preparing to abandon its Physical Education course and FIT established a Course Advisory Board in 1971 to prepare a new type of course. Diplomas of Physical Education and Recreation Leadership were accredited and, despite the lack of appropriate accommodation, they commenced in 1974, making use of the nearby Footscray Youth Club buildings till the Campus Plan began to take shape. These courses were a relatively new development in Australia, based as they were "on a social science foundation rather than the more traditional biological-science foundation." Consequently, the academic content, laboratory work and movement experiences were "designed to emphasis the total understanding, and the ramifications, of play-activities in contemporary society". Importantly, in terms of future developments, these course were not designed specifically for teacher training, and elective and sub-major streams allowed for a wide range of career options including "administration, sports journalism and facility construction and planning". Students taking Recreation Leadership were

assured of employment by the recently stated policies of the Department of Youth, Sport and Recreation. This department estimates an immediate need for some four hundred recreation leaders to serve local governments and communities throughout Victoria. Training in Recreation Leadership is also ideally suited for leaders in such agencies as Y.M.C.A, youth clubs and playground associations.[57]

The third new course development was in the Humanities Department, previously only a service department providing English and social studies subjects for the engineering, applied science and business studies students. Under the new structure of colleges of advanced education there was a requirement to develop applied arts courses. After a certain amount of bargaining among the various CAEs, FIT found itself providing courses in urban studies — a particularly fashionable area in the early 1970s and one with promise to contribute a distinctive character to the Institute. A Diploma of Arts in Urban Studies commenced in 1974, with the prospect of a degree in the future. The special place for this course arose

from the fact that our society is one of the most urbanised in the world. As a consequence of the urbanisation process, a new physical environment has emerged, and with it have arisen new social and political problems of great significance to the future of the country and the world in general. The introduction of such a Diploma at FIT, the only government tertiary institute in the west of the metropolis, is important for local reasons. The western side of Melbourne is often described as "the deprived West" but its citizens are becoming vocal and active in their desire to improve the quality of life. As much of the action with regard to urban redirection and renewal will take place in Footscray and neighbouring suburbs, the Footscray Institute of Technology is an appropriate place to develop a course with an Urban Studies bias.

In line with the best intentions of the designers of the new system of tertiary colleges, this course was also intended to be innovative in style as well as content:

> Since this urbanisation process has been a recent one, those Institutions of learning with traditionally compartmentalised fields of learning have not been able to neatly fit the urbanisation process and its social consequences into their existing structures. At FIT a new multi-disciplinary course free from traditional structures has been established to deal with urbanisation. The Diploma is unique in Victoria in providing a more complete framework for understanding the problems of the urban environment . . . In these courses students will analyse the factors which have produced the urban environment, the land use and socio-economic patterns which make it up, and the social, political and town planning conflicts which have emerged.

Finally, as with the Physical Education course, the employment opportunities were closely related to the expanding and changing role of government in the community. The most important employment outlets were in "Federal, State and Local Government research" and "planning and policy-making fields in departments that are involved in urban matters and in ancillary town planning services", but the course did not preclude teaching and other positions normally occupied by arts graduates.[58]

In 1976 a student wishing to attend FIT could choose from a far wider range of courses than had been available ten years earlier. The Institute offered the degree of Bachelor of Applied Science (Chemistry or Mathematics), Bachelor of Business Studies (Accounting), and Bachelor of Engineering (Civil or Electrical). Diplomas were also available in all these areas in addition to Arts (Urban Studies), Business Studies (Electronic Data Processing and Catering and Hotel Management), Social Science (Physical Education) and Mechanical Engineering. Associate Diplomas were offered in Recreation Leadership and Secretarial Practice and Preliminary Year (form six) courses appropriate to qualify students for entry to all Schools were also conducted. These new tertiary courses clearly addressed a significant area of previously unmet student demand. Full-time enrolments grew significantly, while part-time enrolments remained static. The increase of approximately 100 full-time students in 1973 was "entirely due to the introduction of the two new courses in General Studies and Physical Education". Growth in the number of students studying Business Studies was inhibited by the application of quotas, while courses in applied science and engineering suffered declining popularity.[59] As a result of past decisions and demand, resources, such as the new wing for engineering and science courses opened in 1971,[60] were concentrated in the area of declining demand, while it seemed only too apparent that future growth would be dependent on the introduction of further new courses and the availability of adequate staff and accommodation to permit an increase in the numbers admitted to business and general studies courses.[61] It was possible that "a major effort on the part of the College, Industry and professional organisations" might help to "arrest the trend of declining numbers in the Engineering and Applied Science areas,"[62] but the major imperative for the Institute was the rapid execution of the Campus Plan.

Award winning design in the FIT logo competition

Unfortunately, the struggle to get the Campus Plan approved dragged on and reduced allocations of finance truncated many plans, but in the meantime attention was paid to some important details that would enhance FIT's sense of becoming a more mature organisation. A competition provided a striking new logo in the familiar blue and gold, and, while degrees were conferred at VIC ceremonies, Mills arranged for the diploma-conferring ceremonies to be transformed into grand, formal occasions held in the Great Hall at the Arts Centre in full academic dress "with a view to improving the image of the Institute". The move was considered an "outstanding success",[63] but not one which sought to gloss entirely the underlying reality. The editor of the Staff Association newsletter noted with approval that "The Director in his address avoided the platitudes common to such occasions and chose instead to speak with some edge on the educational deprivation of the western suburbs".[64] A further break with the psychological links to the Education Department style was the decision to change the title of Principal to Director in 1973.[65] In 1971 a policy on "Staff Involvement with Industry" designed to encourage "all staff to develop a maximum reciprocal involvement with Industry and Commerce" was formalised[66] and involvement in joint projects such as the development of a laser radar project improved its image as a technological institution.[67]

At the end of 1974, work finally began on Stage 1A of the Campus Plan — a new building to house General Studies — and the feelings inside FIT had begun to belie some external impressions. When the Committee on Advanced Education visited in October of that year, it apparently still doubted the viability of FIT, but Mills reported happily that

> It was generally felt that as the discussions progressed through the day the attitude of the members of the Committee changed from being somewhat pessimistic concerning the future of the Institute to one of optimism and enthusiasm for further progress. They were clearly impressed by the contribution made by the staff and students and several complimentary references were made to the 'team spirit' which exists within the college.[68]

FIT had maintained intact much of the strength of the old Technical College, and Mills had established himself with the staff and Council as a leader who would attend to the needs and interests of FIT with tenacity and foresight. With new found confidence, FIT gave renewed public expression to its determination "to concentrate its teaching and research efforts on matters of *practical* value not only to industry but society at large", to only offer courses where it was clear that the graduates would "have a useful place in Australian life," to build good relationships with local government, educational and business agencies, and to tailor many courses specifically to the needs of "the immediate community".[69] It was a statement that bore a close resemblance to the ideals that had always underpinned the technical college and as such connected the future constructively to the past.

1. I. M. Herrman, "Statement on FIT's Future to Policy and Resources Committee", 28 May 1980.
2. *Fits*, Journal of the FIT Professional Staff Association, Vol. 1, Nos. 1 and 2, 1971.
3. Mills stated this in a meeting with staff, 12 February 1970, *ibid*, No. 2.
4. *Ibid.*, Vol. 3, No. 14, October 1972.
5. *Educational Specification*, 1970, Preamble, p 3, FIT Archive.
6. Gordon Murray, Vice Principal, FIT Council Minutes, 25 August 1970.
7. Retired Head of RMIT Moulding Department.
8. See above, p 71.
9. See above, pp 108–109.
10. See above, p 69.
11. See above, pp 36 and 109.
12. *Educational Specification, op. cit.*, pp 9–10.
13. *Fits*, Vol. 3, No. 10, 1972.
14. Double page publicity spread probably reprint from *Footscray Advertiser*, 15 December 1971, FIT Archive.
15. *Age*, 16 November 1987. A report based on the 1986 Census figures showed that only 2% of people in Footscray held a university degree compared with the Melbourne Metropolitan average of 6%.
16. *Sun*, July 18 (undated clipping), FIT Archive.
17. Footscray City Council Minutes, 1 November and 8 November 1971.
18. *Ibid.*, 15 November; *Footscray Mail*, 17 November 1971.
19. *Footscray Mail, ibid.*
20. *Footscray Advertiser*, 8 March 1972, p 11.
21. *Ibid.*
22. Footscray City Council Minutes, 27 March 1972.
23. *Footscray Mail*, 4 December 1974.
24. *Age*, 29 July 1972.

25. *Footscray Mail*, 29 March 1972, p 5.
26. *Ibid.*, 3 May 1972.
27. *Ibid.*, 3 May 1972 p 7; Footscray City Council Minutes, 1 May 1972.
28. Footscray City Council Minutes, 8 May and 6 June 1972.
29. *Ibid.*, 26 June 1972.
30. Attachment to FIT Council Papers, 24 October 1972.
31. Footscray City Council Minutes, 23 July 1973. FIT told the City Council that it would accept any decision in regard to Smith Crescent that it made, but added that they still thought entry to the new road would be in the best interests of the residents.
32. *Ibid.*, 26 June 1973.
33. *Ibid.*, 23 November 1973.
34. FIT Council Minutes, 26 March, 1974.
35. *Footscray Advertiser*, 3 July 1974.
36. *Ibid.*
37. *Footscray Mail*, 4 December 1974, p 3.
38. *Footscray Advertiser*, 25 June 1975.
39. FIT Council Minutes, 27 February 1973.
40. Western Region Development Bureau was reported in January 1973 to be working on a submission to Canberra. Mills was chairman of the Education Committee. *Footscray Advertiser*, 24 January 1973. See also, 21 January and 7 February 1973.
41. Extract from Western Region Commission Report reproduced in Principal's Report to Council, 27 February 1973.
42. *Ibid.*
43. Extracts included in Director's Report to Council, 22 May 1973.
44. FIT Council Minutes, 22 May 1973.
45. Extract in Director's Report to Council, 26 June 1973.
46. Director's Report to FIT Council, 26 February 1974; *Sunshine Mail*, 16 January 1974.
47. *Age*, 17 June 1972.
48. Director's report to FIT Council, 27 February 1973.
49. *Ibid.*, 23 July 1974.
50. *Ibid.*
51. FIT Council Minutes, 25 May 1973.
52. *Ibid.*, 22 June 1971; Director's Report to Council, 26 February 1974.
53. Principal's Report to FIT Council, 25 August 1970.
54. *Ibid.*, 24 November 1970.
55. *Ibid.*, 27 February 1973.
56. B. Wise, Interview.
57. FIT, *Handbook*, 1975, p 98.
58. *Ibid.*, 1976, p 77.
59. Director's Report to FIT Council, 26 February 1974.
60. Named for J. L. Kepert who died a few months before the opening.
61. Director's Report to Council, 26 February 1974.
62. *Ibid.*

63. FIT Council Minutes, 23 May 1972, Principal's Report to Council, 22 August 1972.
64. *Fits*, Vol. 14, No. 5, 1973.
65. FIT Council Minutes, 27 February 1973.
66. *Ibid.*, 24 August 1971.
67. Jointly funded by FIT, Radio Research Board, Richardson & Sons Pty Ltd, Monsanto Australia Ltd, Colonial Gas Association, Olympic Tyre and Rubber Co. and ICI. *Footscray Advertiser*, 12 September 1973.
68. Director's Report to Council, 22 October 1974.
69. FIT, *Handbook*, 1976, p 2.

CHAPTER ELEVEN **Metamorphosis**

By the middle of the decade growing confidence offset many of the obstacles created by the budget stringencies and planning problems, but the secondary school still had to be relocated, and there were internal tensions that had to be addressed. There were some obvious advantages in transforming the old diploma school into a college of advanced education, but FIT began with a structure, staff, and even a group of students whose orientation and purpose was not unequivocally focused on a new system. Mills was certainly committed to the creation of a new type of institution, but the very nature of his aim made a dictatorial imposition of his personal preferences untenable. At the same time, the old structures, commitments and expectations continued to exert considerable influence. An important part of Mills' role was to facilitate a shift in the allocation of resources and the development of more open and participatory forms of organisation.

Most of the foundation staff of FIT were former Footscray Technical College teachers; the new recruits for the college of advanced education (CAE) section of FIT were increasingly indistinguishable from applicants for university positions. With the acceptance of the Campbell Report in 1973, salaries for CAE staff rose dramatically in contrast to those in the secondary and trade sections. With the enhanced professional status that this implied, and the greater responsibility for course design and budgetary planning required of CAE staff, came an increasingly insistent demand for access to information that had previously been the preserve of the administration, and greater participation in the decision-making and resource-allocation processes.

At the same time, the growth in student numbers in business and general studies courses demanded a change from past administrative practices and assumptions. What was required was a restructuring of administrative arrangements and resource allocation which in turn would foster a new kind of collegiate spirit — one that embraced a complex community of interests based on factors over and beyond similarity of background. While the traditions of Footscray Technical College provided the foundations of an indentity, future cohesion could only come from the commitment that flowed from shared responsibility for policy formulation and implementation.

Staff solidarity was strengthened by the formation of Professional and General Staff Associations in 1968 and 1971, and pressure for increased staff representation on the Council gathered strength. The single staff representative allowed by the original Constitution could not realistically represent the variety of interests that emerged as FIT developed into three separate Schools — Engineering, Applied Science and Business and General Studies. The volume of Council business and growth in the committee structure was such that the work load for one representative was excessive. More importantly, staff desired a full acknowledgment of the *principle* of 'representation'. It was, as David English, staff representative on Council from 1974–1976, explained, "quite consistent that staff who have committed themselves to the welfare of their students want to play a part in educational decision-making". The proposition that good policy could only come from 'dialogue' between teachers and administrators was gaining popular currency, but it had special relevance to FIT because tertiary education was

a self-governing enterprise. Academic staff [we]re "members", not just employees, and all administrative decisions [we]re also educational decisions — all ultimately affect[ed] the quality of learning and quality of student life.

Far from threatening the independence of Council, representation was crucial to harnessing the institution to a common purpose. The presence of staff was "desirable not because the interests of staff [we]re different from those of the Council and administration but because the interests [we]re identical."[1] The request for two additional staff members on Council was accepted in June 1976,[2] though not without serious dissent from several members. An attempt to include a member of the non-academic staff was defeated, and Mills had to argue strongly against the proposition that the additional staff members be "selected" rather than "elected". Roberts felt so strongly on the matter that he resigned six months before the expiry of his term.[3] Two months later Peter Green and Jack Rankine began to attend Council meetings as observers until the new Constitution was officially adopted in 1977.[4]

The inclusion of additional staff members on the Council reflected an increasing diversity of membership that not only more properly represented interests within FIT, but also the changing nature of the courses offered. As a governing body with real power and responsibility, it needed such diversity to enhance information flow and improve the quality of involvement with the institution below the senior administrative level. From 1972 there was a clear attempt to recruit new members for Council who were unequivocally identifiable as 'local' and to expand the expertise in line with the changing nature of the Institute. Geoff Longbottom, Marketing Manager with Michaelis Bayley, joined the Council in October 1971 occupying the positions of Vice President from October 1976 till 1979 and President from 1980 till 1981. Briefly, the Council acquired the services of another successful 'old boy', W. de Campo, Assistant General Manager (Administration) of the SEC and Chairman of the Electrical Engineering Course Advisory Committee. In October 1974, Robert Fordham, MLA for Footscray and shadow minister for education, joined the Council and he brought with him not only an essential link with community interests and local political organisations but a broad expertise in educational matters. He resigned in 1983 on becoming Minister for Education, thus continuing a long tradition of Labor members of the Council taking up this portfolio.

Attempts to involve the hotel and tourist industry directly in Council were not very successful in the 1970s but Ian Secomb, Footscray City Solicitor, brought valuable legal expertise in late 1976 and remained till his death in 1983. Further local links were made with the appointment of George Thoms, an obstetrician at the Western General Hospital, Frank Trimboli, a local real estate agent, and Jim Betson, a senior administrator in the Education Department. In 1978 the Council was joined by Norm Hartmann, General Manufacturing Manager and a director of Dunlop Olympic Tyres, and another 'old boy', John McIntosh.

An executive with ICIANZ, former President of the Western Industries Association and a director of the Westgate Bridge Authority, he subsequently joined the Waite Consulting Management Group. Throwing himself into the task with great enthusiasm he was Vice President from 1980 till 1985 and President from 1986 till 1987. Between 1974 and 1978, students were represented by Larry Perry, A. J. Galea, Ian Malloy, Des Blake and Sergio Ruffini.[5]

It was also necessary to bring the Council and the rest of FIT together in other ways. Principally, the Council continued to rely on senior administrative staff to guide them in their understanding of the organisation and how policy might best be applied, but both formal and informal lines of communication needed improving. A bulletin of notes from Council meetings was established in 1974,[6] and simply increasing the number of staff representatives made for greater access to Council activities. From the early 1970s there was also a conscious attempt to bring the Council and senior staff closer together. It began with occasional informal meetings,[7] developed as Council members joined Course Advisory Boards, and led to the practice of inviting the deans of the three Schools to dinner with the full Council from time to time.

While access to Council was an important issue, of far greater significance to staff in general was the composition of the Board of Studies which advised Council on academic policy and budget allocations. Decisions made there most crucially affected staff at all levels. Initially composed exclusively of *ex officio* members, principally heads of departments and senior administrative personnel, late in 1970 the Council agreed that the staff member elected to it could also serve on the Board of Studies.[8] Many staff, however, were seeking a radical redefinition of the relationship between administration and staff in general and, as with Council, the central issue was the principle of representation and rejection of the old paternalistic style of management. A token member of the Board of Studies was not sufficient to quell simmering dissatisfaction — the minimum demand was three members, one to represent each of the three schools. The proposition that the presence of the head of department was adequate representation was rejected, especially when there was no *formal* requirement that staff be consulted.[9]

The Council was slow to concede the right to representation. It initially tried to counter these staff demands by amending the

Constitution of the Board of Studies to the effect that no-one *represented* anyone, though they would seek to present "opinions on relevant matters of staff or students who are non members", and tighten the ruling on confidentiality.[10] This engendered a certain amount of cynicism as well as frustration among most staff, especially when the right to elect three staff members to the Board of Studies was granted anyway early in 1972.[11] 'We're all anxious to know", declared the editors of the Professional Staff Association Newsletter, "why we took part in an election of staff representatives if those two people are forbidden, by the Constitution of the Board of Studies, from representing us", and further, "if the Board of Studies is not a representative body, why is every department represented on it?'[12] Denial of participation in a more collegiate style of administration left staff feeling under-rated and mistrusted, as reflected in a bitter editorial in the Staff Association newsletter in 1972:

> Now that the outside world has recognised our abilities (Staff Bulletin 11/5/72) we're all anxious to hear of a similar recognition from within our Institute. You know the kind of thing; something really daring, like implementing the prescriptions of the Educational Specification and appointing members of the academic staff to the sub-committees of the Institute Council and the Board of Studies.[13]

Appropriate responses to these demands were essential for good staff morale. Not only did the new system offer opportunities and impose new demands that were often simultaneously exhilarating and stressful but, whereas once staff morale had depended on firm, authoritative leadership, it now required participation and consultation. Until staff were welcomed as active members of all committees, their influence on the main bodies remained circumscribed, yet their input was essential to the determination of workable policies.

From the staff perspective, representation on the Board of Studies was only the first step towards more fundamental reform of the policy-formation and budget-allocation processes. Not surprisingly, the desire for change existed in proportion to the perception that some areas in the Institute received less than their fair share of resources. The setbacks to the Campus Plan impinged most heavily on the new course areas. The Schools of Engineering and Applied Science were housed in a new building, the various Business Studies departments occupied A Block at the other side of the site while the Departments of Humanities, Physical Education and Student Services were located in old houses around the perimeter. The administration was scattered throughout various locations. The Director was in A Block and the Assistant Director in D Block and, there were few places on campus for informal mixing of all sections of the Institute. The budget was tight and many resources went into buildings and real estate when staff in the new areas felt that they often lacked the barest of educational resources. Heads of some departments felt that their student numbers were being artificially kept down, further weakening their bargaining position. Staff mood was restive and prickly, and tensions were compounded by a sense that it was "not always clear to staff what factors influenc[ed] the allocation of priorities for funding" causing "unpalatable and often erroneous conclusions to be drawn". This arose at least partly because of some inadequacies in "Management of Resources".

> While acknowledging the excellent work done by our senior administrative staff there still remains an expressed concern that at the very least there is a lack of vertical communication and probably a need for additional staff to share the load.

The problems were seen to be related to a certain loss of focus within FIT, and Lowe suggested that in the area of general "educational and resource planning", there was "a need for a continual review of our purpose and plan as a tertiary institute. Again it is not enough that this be done but it must also be seen to be being done".[14] Despite this plea however, nothing of substance occurred in this area for several years, and reform came very slowly.

The desire for change was strongest in the new School of General Studies but by no means absent in Engineering and Applied Science. Heads of department seem to have been particularly disgruntled, and while these frustrations are not easily retrieved, especially with the expansivess that comes with later success, glimpses are possible. Formerly, heads of department had reported directly to the central administration. Under the new structure a Dean of School had been interposed, but this was only one factor contributing to frustration. John McLaren was appointed Head of the Department of Humanities in 1976 and spent the first six months convinced that rational and equitable planning in his department was simply not possible. The impression that everything was designed to favour engineering courses and that the non-technological areas were deeply resented and disadvantaged by a system designed before they arrived was widespread. It frustrated McLaren intensely:

> Everything is *ad hoc*, with consequent advantages to engineers and scientists. There really seems little feeling for the Institute as a whole . . . There seems to be no forum or centre of consciousness.[15]

He soon learned, however, that this was a simplistic view of internal relations, as he was caught up in a new push to reform the Board of Studies that manifested itself in, among other things, an informal group of heads of departments, self-titled "the Mushroom Club".

Several issues were intertwined in this frustration at the 'middle management' level. Some of them were vague and ill-defined, some were largely the result of external factors, particularly the tight control exercised by the Victoria Institute of Colleges (VIC) over all new course matters, while some centred quite directly on the need for a different formula on which to allocate resources. There was certainly an impatience with lingering habits of authoritarianism and paternalism and the slow dismantling of the old technical college structures which seemed to favour the old subject areas. Under these circumstances, Mills was seen as the man of the future sufficiently committed to the creation of a multi-purpose institution to push and pull the old administration into a new shape. His approachability and informality of style encouraged a conviction that most grievances could be addressed if only heads of departments could have formal access to the administration and bypass the Board of Studies.

The later part of 1976 was taken up with a struggle by some heads of departments to have some sort of administrative liaison committee with direct access to the Director established. McLaren, who had initially felt that it was only the newer areas that were disgruntled, was "impressed" after meeting with the "Mushroom Club" that all heads of department "shared common concerns about [their] exclusion from decision making and the inadequacy, or rather total lack of, rational planning and accounting". While he was sceptical as to how long the concern would survive the "competition by conflicting interests for scarce resources", he was "impressed by the calibre and determination" of his colleagues.[16] Mills was not prepared to challenge the pre-eminence of the Board of Studies, but he agreed that heads of department could meet regularly as an advisory panel to the heads of school and that this committee "should receive full information and be able to participate in full discussion prior to the determination of policies and resource allocation".[17] This was a long way short of direct access to the administration, and by early 1977 it was clear that the reform had been very limited.[18]

For the School of General Studies, which included Commerce, Business, Management, and the fledgling Humanities and Physical Education Departments, there was a deeper issue at stake in the fight for a revised administrative structure. The VIC imposed tight restrictions on individual institutions in the interests of creating a stable and viable system in the state as a whole, but the effect of this was that new departments were often forced to bargain for essential senior staff positions at the expense of old ones. The numbers on all the decision-making bodies favoured the old subject areas, and the view that resources were not being fairly allocated to new areas was a festering sore, even though it only occasionally erupted into the public record. The central issue was the formula on which internal budget allocations were made. Any formula based purely on class-contact hours rather than, for example, student numbers, disadvantaged the humanities and many of the business studies subjects, but for some time in the mid-1970s the major problem seems to have been to extract a public definition of any sort of formula at all. There was also concern that allocations made by the VIC for particular purposes were being diverted to other activities and that earnings on unused funds did not flow back to departments.[19] Keith Lansley, Head of the Department of Physical Education, was upset enough to complain to Council that, "although the Physical Education and Recreation Department generated income for the Institute from the VIC, his allocation for 1977 did not include all this income". The reply merely noted his concern, explaining that the Finance Committee could not see "any immediate solution to the problem" because it felt that, while funds were indeed allocated on a VIC formula, "it was not appropriate at present to allocate these funds on the same basis to departments".[20] At this point, Lansley, who been enticed from a secure position in the United States by the prospect of setting up a unique and exciting program, became somewhat despairing and began to consider whether he could take the degree program to some other institution.[21] Fortunately, with the gradual reform of the Board of Studies and the enhanced power and status for the new areas that came with growth and popularity, the adjustments were gradually, if sometimes most begrudgingly, made.

These problems were far from unique to FIT and were largely a manifestation of growth and transition in a period of changing values and uncertain finance. A new assertiveness among younger members of staff and the ability of new subject areas to 'prove' themselves would ultimately assist in the forging of a changed collegiate identity that would position FIT, small though it was, quite strongly within the advanced education sector. In all this, the personality, and indeed the youth, of Mills was crucial in minimising damaging head-on confrontations. His approachable style gave the impression that the worst log jams of the system could be eased and further, quiet avenues of negotiation and compromise discovered. Mills was confident that problems could be solved with discussion and goodwill, preferably in a relaxed social atmosphere, but he also displayed a firm set of views on how matters ought to be arranged and he rarely promised more than he could deliver. Above all, his strong commitment to the necessity for FIT to offer a wide range of courses, his efforts outside to gain resources for those subjects and his confidence in his staff, provided an atmosphere in which morale generally remained high despite the obvious difficulties.

Mills was a man who relied on networks, negotiation and goodwill to solve problems. Within technical education generally and FIT in particular, where everyone had fundamentally the same goals, there seemed few problems that he could not quietly resolve. Outside that sphere, however, particularly where there was a fundamental and irreconcilable conflict of values, he was less successful. Indeed, in both the case of opposition to the Campus Plan and the relocation of the secondary school, he appears to have been caught by surprise at the strength of the opposition and slow to realise that a quiet word here and there would not resolve either issue. Staff restiveness in the middle years of the decade, therefore, pales in comparison to the escalating crisis associated with the 'divorce' from the secondary school during the same period.

1. David English, Attachment to FIT Council Minutes, 22 June 1976.
2. Director's Report to FIT Council, 23 March 1976.
3. FIT Council Minutes, 22 June 1976.
4. *Ibid.*, 24 August 1976.
5. Students had no voting rights until 1977.
6. FIT Council Minutes, 26 March 1974.
7. *Ibid.*, 24 March 1970.
8. *Ibid.*, 24 November 1970.
9. 'Report of FITPSA Executive Meeting', *Fits*, Vol. 2, No. 2, [1971], p 7; *Fits*, Vol.3, No. 7, [1972].
10. FIT Council Minutes, 22 June 1971.
11. *Fits*, Vol. 3, No. 3, [1972].
12. *Ibid.*, Vol. 3, No. 7, [1972].
13. *Ibid.*
14. Director's Report to FIT Council of a meeting between heads of department and the executive committee of Council arranged by staff representative, Graeme Lowe, 26 March 1974.
15. John McLaren Diaries, 10 May 1976.
16. *Ibid.*, 1 October 1976.
17. *Ibid.*, 11 November 1976.
18. *Ibid.*, 20 December 1976.
19. McLaren recorded a conversation with Rowsell about the failure to allow earned funds to flow to any departments, *ibid.*, 14 October 1976.
20. FIT Council Papers, Finance Committee Minutes, 28 September 1976.
21. McLaren Diaries, 7 October, 11 November 1976. See also 6 April, 9 & 23 June 1977.

CHAPTER TWELVE **Breaking the ties with the secondary technical school 1970–1980**

At first sight the forging of a new relationship with the secondary school must have appeared uncomplicated and therein perhaps lay part of the problem. The junior and senior sections had been drawing apart since the late 1950s, but in 1968 the Education Department handed over the buildings on the Ballarat Road site to FIT without taking any decision on the future of the secondary school. The old Council had rarely concerned itself with the affairs of the secondary school and there was even less incentive to do so now. It was a matter for the Education Department to deal with, and disengagement from the subject increased as the complexities of running FIT absorbed more and more energy. The clearest evidence of this disengagement comes in a statement in October 1970 that Mills saw "little value" in Council discussing motions listed for the Technical Schools Association annual conference which he was about to attend, since they related "primarily to building and finance problems associated with non-tertiary education and other items of general interest concerning secondary school operations".[1] In a few years time those buildings and finance problems were to impinge heavily on FIT's plans for growth.

From the secondary technical school's point of view, the lines of communication and authority had been fragmented and weakened by the changes that had created FIT. Normally, a school principal was appointed from within the Education Department and he was the school's advocate within that Department. He would also usually be supported by an advisory council drawn from members of the local community with a

Ballarat Road Site at the commencement of building E Block

Students leaving Dallas Brooks Hall after an FIT Diploma Conferring Ceremony

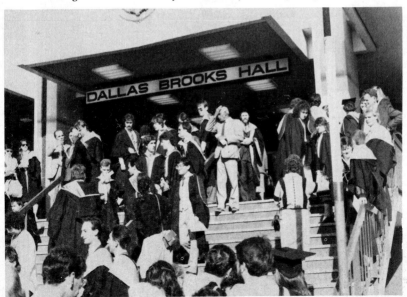

ORIENTATION
WEEK '71

SEED

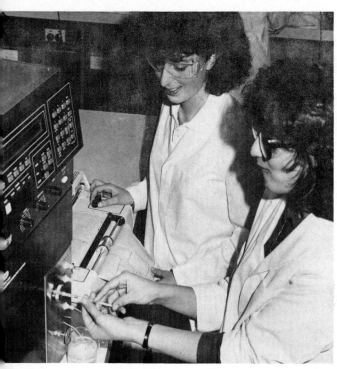

Chemistry students with an ion-chromatograph

Nursing students in anatomy class

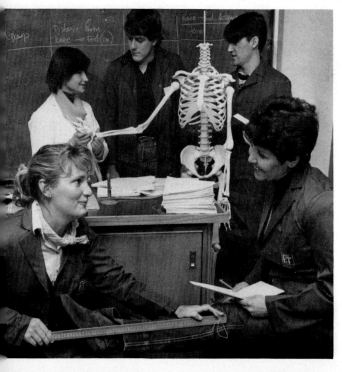

Plate xix

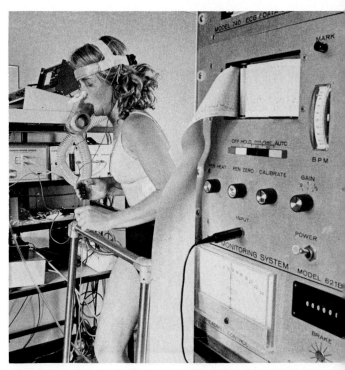

Physical Education student being tested for heart and lung fitness

Catering and Hotel Management students enjoy their Chinese meal

Plate xx

FIT Education student observing a class in a local primary school

"The forum", Ballarat Road

Final year Electrical engineering student writing a computer program to control the movement of a model robot arm

FIT Engineering students with successful entries in the "mouse-trap"-powered vehicle competition

Examinations

Electrical engineering students' design project

Plate xxiv

Recreation students at play

Chemistry laboratory

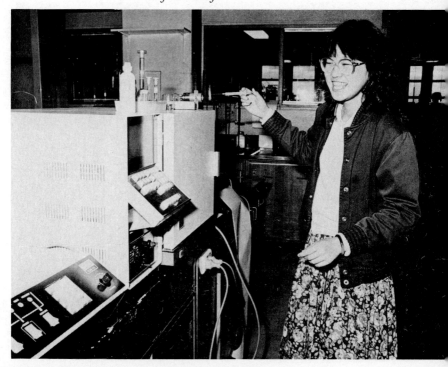

particular interest in secondary technical education. Footscray Technical School, however, found itself with a Principal appointed by a Council specifically constituted to govern a CAE, though he had Education Department approval. The FIT Council, for all its goodwill towards the secondary school, had poorly defined legal and administrative responsibilities for it, but total ownership of the buildings and site it occupied. The Headmaster, who was forced by the circumstances to assume role of Principal as well, could not exert the same authority as a Principal, and if Mills did not pursue the secondary school's interests to its satisfaction there was little it could do. The secondary school was in a most anomalous situation while the Principal faced the potential of unresolvable conflict of interest unless the Education Department acted on its responsibility for the provision of new buildings and/or the VIC made some form of compensation for the acquisition of the old ones. Unfortunately, this did not occur until the conflict reached crisis proportions. The growth and development of FIT therefore, must be set against a background of turbulence, bitterness and recrimination.

The early 1970s were years of staffing difficulties for many secondary schools. Teacher numbers continued to lag behind increased enrolments while unions successfully bargained for reduced class sizes in the interests of higher quality education. A serious staff shortage struck the secondary school in 1971[2] and resulted in some confrontation between teachers and parents who wanted students to be rostered until extra teachers were provided, and Mills, who opposed the idea.[3] In a precursor of later events a group of parents and staff sought to take their case directly to the Minister for Education. Mills denied them official Institute recognition because "every effort" was being made by FIT and the Education Department to obtain additional staff, and it was "unlikely that their representations [would] assist in alleviating the situation".[4] By May the staffing position had improved,[5] but parents and staff still felt a need to put their own case, and a deputation to the Director of Technical Education in July received a sympathetic hearing. Later in the year Neville Hamer, Technical Teachers Association of Victoria (TTAV)[6] metropolitan councillor and staff member at Footscray Technical School, publicly explained the outcome of this deputation and thanked parents for their co-operation. Over 100 parents had supported the roster plan, and in a year when the Mothers' Club went into recess owing to apparent lack of interest,[7] others were taking pride in "the establishment of a good parent-teacher relationship. The understanding gained by all concerned had been most valuable" and staff expressed "the hope that if events in the future required similar action" then parents and teachers would be

> quick to realise that meaningful negotiation and joint action is the only way to overcome mutual problems, and the avoidance of disruption of students' education is a prize worth the effort of all parties.[8]

Over the next five years this alliance between parents and staff emerged as a major strength of the secondary school, and its constituency of support diverged sharply from that of FIT.

Overall, the secondary school suffered little in material terms in the early years of FIT, and it received substantial assistance from the Commonwealth government's Supplementary Grants for Disadvantaged Schools scheme.[9] This at least partly helped the school to cope with the large number of children of recently arrived immigrants who entered it. One special source of pride was the establishment of a Migrant Centre under Mrs Glen Barnes.[10] This was the first of its kind in Australia and most necessary in a school where 38% of students in forms one to three had been born in one of 18 non-English speaking countries.[11] Barnes was a dynamic force in obtaining support for the venture, and the Centre played a significant role in forging links between the school and its parent community through classes for parents and informal gatherings on Saturday afternoons.[12] Throughout the school, an innovative and committed staff worked to deal with an educational environment considerably removed from the academic demands underpinnng FIT; for various reasons only a very small proportion of its students were destined for tertiary education.

One aspect of the the secondary school's anomalous position was resolved with administrative separation from FIT and the elevation of the Vice Principal, W. C. Moore, to a newly created position of Principal of Footscray Technical School, on 1 July 1972. A former English and social studies teacher with a commerce degree and a Bachelor of Education, he belonged to the new breed of technical administrators who came from a wide variety of backgrounds and took a broad, democratic view of education.[13] However, the school still lacked a council of its own, notwithstanding the FIT Council's assurances that it would "give every possible assistance to the new Principal dur-ing the period that the school remain[ed] on our site and in the establishment of a new school".[14] Moore proposed that a special committee of FIT Council be set up to do just this, but there is no evidence that it was.[15] The lines of responsibility and authority had been clarified, but the school's legitimate claim on the atten-tion of the Council had been weakened, while it was not bal-anced by a community support group of its own.

However well intentioned the FIT Council may have been, the reality was that, with the opening of D Block, the secondary school had been effectively sandwiched between two parts of the Institute to the mutual discomfort of everyone. A year later the publication of the Campus Plan revealed that the initial expansion was to be at the expense of secondary school accom-modation. In a very real sense, FIT had become a rather hostile landlord. The difficult search for a new site and the funds to purchase it proved that little had changed since 1916. Two sites — the Standard Quarries site in Wearing Street to the north west of the present site or the river flats leased from the Common-wealth to the Myer Emporium — were canvassed by FIT Coun-cil. The Myer Emporium was not co-operative, which left only the Standard Quarries site. This was not only on the edge of the municipal tip but, since it was private property, the cost was substantial at a time when the Education Department had many calls on its resources for the establishment of new schools and upgrading of schools in serious disrepair, such as Sunshine Technical School. Enrolments were falling and the Education Department gave some thought to simply dispersing the school among others nearby such as Tottenham Technical School, but this was politically untenable. FIT was bearing the cost of a legacy of inadequate planning by the Education Department, compounded by a special quality of neglect for the western sub-urbs of Melbourne.[16] Nevertheless, for quite some years every-one in FIT laboured under what proved an illusory belief that the school would soon be relocated. Mills regularly assured gatherings that the school would be gone "in two years". FIT Council applied what pressure it could,[17] but the new site was still not purchased until late 1975.[18] Even then very little of substance occurred until secondary teachers and parents forced the issue. Coupled with the delay to the Campus Plan this severely retarded FIT's development.

When the Wark Committee on Advanced Education had suggested in 1973[19] that perhaps the Institute rather than the secondary school should be relocated, it must have had some inkling that every move FIT wished to make impinged on some other interest. FIT was caught in a web of sectional interests amongst which it could not always easily claim priority. However, as the most dynamic, clearly focused and best funded section of the institution, FIT assumed an appearance of power that at times had the effect of putting those interested in the secondary school or the TAFE college desperately on the defensive. As each of these acquired a clear focus of its own, the Institute found itself impeded in the prosecution of its plans. In a strict sense, the Institute could not be 'blamed' for the way its growth affected other sectors of the education community. It was so positioned as the agent of change, however, that, at various times, it found itself under bitter attack and forced to act as an intermediary in situations where it had much to both gain and lose but little formal power.

In 1973 FIT unveiled the architect's model of its first new building under the Campus Plan[20] driven by the desperate need for accommodation and the VIC requirement that allocated finance be spent within certain time limits. This stage of the project required demolishing the apprentice workshops and moving some secondary classes into portable rooms[21] on the south side of Ballarat Road. Mills attempted to smooth potential difficulties mid-way through the year in discussions with the Minister and the TTAV, but there was little concrete action.[22] Early in 1974, just as the first moves towards purchasing a new site were made, a committee of teachers began to draw up plans for a new co-educational secondary school of 1000 to 1200 students in forms one to four.[23] Shortly afterwards a new Parents and Citizens Association was formed[24] and there is a strong sense that the school, faced with the prospect of demolition teams by mid-year, had finally grasped just how vigorously it would need to pursue its own interests with both the Education Department and FIT.

The ingredients for a desperate showdown were all present in 1974. The Technical Teachers' Association was militant, with a very broad base of support. Its links with the trade union movement were strong, not only because many technical teachers were, or had been, tradesmen, but because the TTAV, in pursuit of greater industrial muscle, had affiliated with the Trades Hall

Council. The genuine overlap of interests implied in this relationship was clearly revealed by the situation in Footscray. Conflict between the TTAV and the Victorian government resulted in state-wide strike action in 1974,[25] and the situation in Footscray served as a dramatic example of a wide-ranging and serious problem. The state government was vilified for the planning crisis in Footscray, and the involvement of apprentices as well as secondary students, made the issue one of legitimate concern to the trade union movement, irrespective of its relationship to the TTAV. As the secretary of the Furnishing Trades Society put it: "For far too long apprentices, their trade training and their education in the broader sense have been the last considered in educational priorities".[26] In this period, when the trade union movement was developing a much broader view of its role in the community perhaps best exemplified in the 'green bans' imposed in the Sydney "Rocks" area, several unions were only too willing to place black bans on all work until more satisfactory arrangements for apprentices were made.[27]

Careful negotiations in early September provided a solution to the worst of the secondary school's problems by severely limiting the extent of the proposed site works and the black bans were lifted,[28] but the question of apprentice classes remained unresolved.[29] What was certain was that a most useful alliance between teachers and several building unions had been formed. Unless the state government moved with uncharacteristic speed it was inevitable that FIT would be the target of similar industrial action again.

Late in 1974 the secondary school finally acquired a Council of its own, with Dr John Stearne, Head of the FIT School of Applied Science as President.[30] The Principal was invited to attend FIT Council meetings as an observer from time to time, but a siege mentality was breeding within the secondary school as its focus and orientation diverged from FIT and its base of parent support strengthened. On the other side, irritation at sharing a very crowded space with what was mostly seen as an unreasonably noisy, ill-disciplined, and at times personally threatening 'grey horde' of schoolboys, became magnified among Institute staff who resented the retarded pace of redevelopment. It was not easy to lecture in rooms with footballs bouncing off the windows; it was not easy to occupy boys during lunch periods on a small square of asphalt. Once the actual building began however, matters became infinitely worse.

During 1975 cabinet making and boat building apprenticeship classes were relocated to an annexe in Berry Street. This was a significant concession to the union demands in contrast the temporary use of a Yarraville factory. Plumbing, sheet metal and metal fabrication classes, however, still needed a new permanent location and when work began on a second building at Ballarat Road the issues flared again.[31] Stage 1C of the Campus Plan, the physical education building, involved the demolition of more workshops and further reduction in the secondary school playing space. Predictably, the unions re-imposed black bans on the site works until further guarantees were made in regard to apprentice classes and secondary school accommodation.[32] This time the issues were not so easily resolved, as a deepening sense of desperation made negotiation more difficult. The Berry Street site was purchased by FIT in early 1976[33] and other temporary premises obtained till all the facilities at Berry Street could be brought up to standard. The black bans were lifted long enough for work to begin excavating the northeast corner of the Ballarat Road site but the activity was short lived.

Mills' perception that the secondary school was being "inconvenienced" by the construction work on building E seriously underestimated the depth of feeling among staff and parents.[34] It seemed to the secondary teachers that any possibility of achieving their educational goals was being undermined by the physical environment. Unfortunately, it appeared that the only hope for change lay in the application of maximum pressure to FIT, and with the beginning of work on the second building site the situation reached flash point. There was no suggestion that FIT was to blame for the lack of a new school, but anger at the conditions prevailing as a result of the building activity was directed at the Institute. Once school resumed in 1976 the combination of noise from the overhead crane and heavy traffic on Ballarat Road became overwhelming. It was measured at two-and-a-half times acceptable Environment Protection Authority levels. Then there was the problem of shepherding boys back and forth, without pedestrian lights, across Ballarat Road to the portable classrooms. Teachers held a stop work meeting on 25 February, and when the Education Department did not respond to requests for a new school and up-grading of the existing conditions, a second was held on 2 March. The result was dialogue in which certain undertakings were given that FIT would soundproof the crane and perhaps assist the Education Department with modifications to the existing buildings, but feelings of frustration and distrust were not dispelled.

In the following weeks, two accidents — a student knocked down by a car in Ballarat Road, and a truck loading rocks on the FIT site careering out of control and smashing seventeen cars in an area used by secondary students at recess times — injected a note of hysteria into the situation and the teachers went out on indefinite strike on 31 March. At a public meeting on 5 April parents declared solid support for the staff action. Once more the unions were called to assist, and this time the Trades Hall Council itself imposed black bans until a satisfactory agreement had been sealed unconditionally.[35] Parents and teachers were "up to the neck",[36] but their ambit claim for, amongst other things, the use of A Block until a new school was ready, angered FIT staff, who felt that the demands had become altogether unreasonable. Secondary teachers were attempting to make FIT "pay" for the failure of the Education Department to provide their new school. It was action which, as they tried to explain to the Trades Hall Council, jeopardised provision of adequate tertiary education facilities in the western region of Melbourne, which was already lagging at least ten years behind that of other metropolitan regions:

> The building on which your Council has placed a ban is intended to provide both essential teaching resources and also *community* recreational facilities. Should your ban continue the money will be spent on colleges in some other region. A further loss which the West can ill afford.[37]

Footscray, it seems, was still being forced to trade one form of education against another just as it had always done. Tactically, the interests of the secondary and tertiary sections were the same, yet the presentation of a united front to the Education Department was apparently not tenable. Any commonality of interest between the senior and junior school had evaporated as the tertiary staff of FIT moved inexorably into a 'tertiary culture', with only sentimental vestiges of commitment to a special relationship with any particular technical school.

Promises regarding a new school were quite readily forthcoming, though many queried the wisdom of building the school next to a partially-filled rubbish tip. Changes to Education

Department policy gave the new Technical School Council considerable control over the design of the new buildings, and planning to create a "model" school began immediately. The aim was a school that did not "look like a school" with the maximum participation of the community in its planning and use.[38] The cohesion and interest generated by the dispute made it likely that this would be a successful enterprise from the point of view of the participants, though, with the benefit of hindsight, it can be seen that there were some serious weaknesses in the planning.[39] The new school was ready for occupation in May 1980, and the move was made with great relief by all concerned. Relations between FIT and the secondary school returned to the natural cordiality that usually exists between such institutions. In the meantime, however, the conditions for students who would never attend the new school and apprentice workshops remained the subject of protracted and bitter negotiations.

Aware that the only truly powerful weapon at their disposal was the black ban, neither staff nor parents were prepared to call for its lifting until soundproofing and other safety measures had been carried out. The Trades Hall Council also had its own agenda of demands regarding conditions for apprentice classes. Meanwhile, the physical education building remained simply a hole in the ground — a symbol to FIT of all its deepest frustrations. When FIT Council tried to make the sound proofing conditional on the lifting of the black ban tempers frayed again in the secondary school. During a half-day stoppage in November 1976 a delegation of parents and 24 teachers hired a bus to take them to the Education Department. Denied access to the Minister, 85 people sat down in the foyer determined to stay until they were heard. At seven o'clock that evening, nine were arrested and charged with trespass. The following day Mills wrote to the Special Projects Officer, Mr H. S. Hobbs, with a list of the firm commitments that FIT, its Council and Staff Association were prepared to make in regard to the intrusion on secondary school space, use of workshops, soundproofing and safety.[40] This proved to be the basis of a satisfactory compromise which was finalised early in 1977. The lifting of the black bans, however, did not occur until the Trades Hall Council was satisfied with the facilities at the Berry Street Annexe for apprentice classes. The dispute was not fully resolved until July 1977.

The completion of building E, named for the president of the FIT Council and 'old boy', E. A. Mollard, gave much-needed breathing space to the expanding general studies and humanities area and ended the site works in the immediate vicinity of the secondary school building. Work recommenced on the physical education building, named most appropriately for C. A. Hoadley, and it was officially opened in 1981. At the end of 1977 Mills breathed a sigh of relief and hope into his usually sparse reports to Council:

> The year 1977 will be remembered as the period in which the major problems associated with the physical development of the tertiary campus were overcome. Regrettably, this situation has not yet been reached with the College Division but the forthcoming consideration by the Footscray City Council of development proposals will, hopefully, advance activities in this area.
>
> Financial constraints currently imposed on physical development and student enrolment will retard our growth and development in the immediate future but there is every reason to be optimistic concerning the realisation of the longer terms aspirations of the Council.[41]

The optimism was appropriate enough, but there were more problems ahead with regard to the trade section of FIT than simply buildings and resources. Yet another shift in emphasis at the Commonwealth-funding level would soon remove the 'Cinderella' status of Technical and Further Education and with this would come a desire for control and autonomy within that section that would lead to yet another painful separation.

1. Principal's Report to FIT Council, 27 October 1970.
2. *Ibid.*, 23 February 1971.
3. *Footscray Advertiser*, 3 March & 7 April 1971.
4. Principal's Report to FIT Council, 27 April 1971.
5. *Ibid.*, 25 May 1971.
6. The technical teachers had broken away from the VTU in 1966 to form a separate union.
7. *Footscray Advertiser*, 29 September 1971. FIT Council Minutes, 27 July 1971.
8. *Footscray Advertiser*, 27 October 1971.
9. For example, Footscray Technical School Report to FIT Council, 24 June 1974.
10. *Footscray Advertiser*, 4 June 1972.
11. Footscray Technical School Report to FIT Council, 24 October 1972.
12. *Footscray Advertiser*, 23 May 1973.

13. Undated clipping, FIT Archive.
14. Principal's Report to FIT Council, 22 February 1972.
15. Footscray Technical School Report to FIT Council, 26 September 1972.
16. For a general overview of educational 'neglect', see Tom Roper, *The Myth of Equality*, Melbourne, 1970.
17. Director's Report to FIT Council, 26 February 1974; FIT Council Minutes, 28 May 1974; Footscray Technical School Report to FIT Council, 8 July 1975.
18. Director's Report to FIT Council, 27 April 1976.
19. See above, pp 171–172.
20. *Footscray Advertiser*, 14 November 1973.
21. Footscray Technical School Report to FIT Council, 26 November 1973.
22. FIT Council Minutes, 24 July 1974.
23. Footscray Technical School Report to FIT Council, 26 March 1974.
24. Footscray Technical School Report to FIT Council, 28 May 1974.
25. *Ibid.*, 23 July 1974.
26. Ken Carr to FIT Principal and FIT Council, 20 June 1974. Mills files. Secondary School/TTAV File, FIT Archive.
27. See cuttings, leaflets, etc. in *ibid*; also *Footscray Mail*, 12 June 1974.
28. Director's Report to FIT Council, 22 October 1974.
29. Letter D. R. Mills to A. Marriage, TTAV President (An FTC Old Boy), 10 September 1974. Secondary School/TTAV File, *op. cit*. See also Director's Report to FIT Council, 24 September 1974.
30. Other members were E. A. Curwood MBE, R. C. Fordham MLA, B. M. Morales (President, Parents Association), J. H. S McDonald (FIT Registrar), F. O'Donnell, A. O. Wallace, the District Inspector.
31. Director's Report to FIT Council, 24 June 1975.
32. *Footscray Advertiser*, 8 October 1975.
33. Director's Report to FIT Council, 23 March 1976.
34. Insight into this can be seen in TTAV *Associate News*, "Up to the Neck at Footscray Tech" 7 July 1974; 'Footscray Dispute Flares", 12 April 1976; and "The School that was Given Away", 6 May 1976; also *Farrago*, Melbourne University Student newspaper, "Footscray Tech Forgotten" [undated clipping], *Axis*, AUS Paper, 26 April 1976, "Footscray School Strikes'; Kathy Tyson, Letter to the Editor, "Look After Young tech Students Now" [undated, unsourced news clipping], Secondary School/TTAV File, *op. cit*.
35. *Footscray Advertiser*, 19 May 1976.
36. TTAV *Associate News*, Vol. 10, No. 5, 12 April 1976.
37. K. Peard, Secretary FITPSA, to K. Stone, Secretary THC, 28 May 1976. Secondary School/TTAV File, *op. cit*.
38. *Footscray Advertiser*, 28 July 1976.

39. For a sympathetic treatment of the dispute from inside the technical school see J. Ingleby, 'Participation: Action Research and the Politics of Change in Working Class Schools A View from the Inside', MA, FIT, 1985. For a less favourable perspective on the success of the planning and building process, see T. Thomas 'Footscray Tech's Object Lesson', *Business Review Weekly*, 8 March 1985, pp 80–86.
40. D. R. Mills to H. S. Hobbs, 25 November 1976. Secondary School/ TTAV File, *op. cit.*
41. Director's Report to FIT Council, 22 November 1977.

CHAPTER THIRTEEN **The development of TAFE at FIT 1972–1979**

The later part of the 1970s was a period of re-examination of tertiary education not unlike the early 1960s, but the emphasis was on reduction and rationalisation rather than expansion and growth. Three enquiries, two Commonwealth and one Victorian, had far-reaching implications for technical education in Victoria. The first of these — the Australian Committee on Technical and Further Education chaired by Myer Kangan — sought to give some coherent form to the multitude of courses and institutions that fell somewhere between secondary and tertiary status, and to determine their significance in vocational and educational terms. Its Report, presented in 1974, not only dignified this sector with a name TAFE, but provided a clear rationale, a distinctive identity, and an objective basis for increased Commonwealth funding. Taking the view that recurrent education was an essential national priority best achieved through unrestricted access to post-secondary education for all adults, the Kangan Report invigorated the whole sector with a renewed sense of purpose, and proved to be as far reaching in its implications for TAFE as the Martin Report had been for advanced education. Under its new terms of reference, TAFE was to be regarded as

> describing all organised and sustained programmes designed to communicate vocationally oriented knowledge to develop the individual's understanding and skills. It should include all programmes of education with a vocational purpose, other than those supported by other Commissions, whether the individual is using the programme with employment as a primary aim or with the aim of gaining additional specialised

knowledge or skills for personal enrichment or job improvement. It includes what is usually known as 'adult education'.
It does not include activities which have no direct educational
purpose.[1]

Far from narrowly vocational in its emphasis, the Report cleared
the way for technical colleges to develop a broad range of
courses in the humanities and social sciences, as well as the
more traditional areas, and begin to acquire the greater institutional strength that comes with a larger proportion of full-time
students. Even though funding never reached the anticipated
levels, significant progress was made towards refurbishing a
sector that offered a wide range of educational and training
opportunities to students who had not completed a full secondary course.

The TAFE sector's financial dreams were not realised, largely
as a result of rapid deterioration in the Australian economy and
a widespread acceptance of the need to curtail federal expenditure. The same circumstances prompted the setting up, in
September 1976, of a Committee of educationalists and industrialists under Professor B. R. Williams to examine post-
secondary education facilities and the relationship between the
education system and the labour market. The length of the enquiry — it did not report until February 1979 — created largely
by a philosophical *impasse* within the Committee,[2] left the CAEs
marking time in a period when adaptation to changed circumstances was imperative. More importantly, it reduced the
impact of the Report on the Commonwealth government's
determination to cut its funding commitment in order to contain
the budget deficit.

In Victoria, with a proliferation of small institutions and an
unwieldy separation between teacher-training colleges and
other colleges of advanced education, the pressure for change
culminated in the establishment of the Victoria Post-Secondary
Education Committee of Enquiry under the chairmanship of
Professor P. H. Partridge in July 1976. This Committee reported
in March 1978 and successfully recommended the establishment
of the Victorian Post-Secondary Education Commission
(VPSEC) to incorporate most of the functions of the VIC, the
State College of Victoria[3] and some co-ordinating role in respect
of universities. It was intended by this means to further ration-
alise the courses offered across the system and allow greater

autonomy to individual colleges. The Committee also recommended that the TAFE sections of CAEs be removed from Education Department control and placed under some form of co-ordinating body of their own. The result was the creation of the Board of Technical and Further Education in July 1980.

One of the major outcomes of these enquiries was strong pressure to reduce the number of institutions in Victoria and minimise duplication of courses. Situated as it was in an area relatively deprived of educational resources, FIT was not seriously threatened with amalgamation, but it lacked power and prestige when it came to arguing for a greater share of the diminishing resources. It was a hard climate in which to seek resources for expansion when most institutions were facing reduced funding and staff redundancies. Politically, it was easier to delay the introduction of new programs and buildings than reduce existing ones, and FIT continued to labour under a funding formula that left it worse off than many other institutions. Nevertheless, much of the course-development work of the early 1970s began to bear fruit with the introduction of the new degrees of Bachelor of Arts (Urban Studies), Bachelor of Business (Catering and Hotel Management; Tourism), Bachelor of Social Science (Physical Education), Bachelor of Engineering (Mechanical) in 1976–77, and Bachelor of Engineering (Civil-Building) in 1978.

This period is also characterised by the introduction of a new tier of courses known as graduate diplomas. These short, applied courses, such as Graduate Diplomas in Digital Control, Municipal and Water Engineering, Remote Sensing, Communication Systems, Industrial Relations and Vacuum Technology, were designed to meet specialist needs not easily covered in the broader, more generalist degree courses. In part a response to a genuine demand in the community, these courses also provided a means for increasing student numbers in ways that quite efficiently used existing resources and helped deploy staff threatened with redundancy as demand for engineering and applied science courses among school leavers slumped. From FIT's point of view, they also had the virtue of capitalising on the relationship with industry that was part of a CAE's rationale. The courses could be tailored to specialist needs, closely involve the expertise of members of Course Advisory Boards, and respond quickly to technological developments. They also helped solve the dilemma that faced educationalists and industrialists about the balance between generalist and specialist content in curricula which always threatened to overload the students. Finally, they provided FIT with a larger group of mature and experienced students to balance the undergraduate student population. In all senses, it was a move back towards the complex type of institution that the old technical colleges had been at their best — responsive and flexible, with a broad mix of part-time and full-time courses offering several levels of professional certification.

The development of graduate diplomas also signalled the approaching end of the old-style diploma courses which, in the early 1980s, gave way to degree courses as the basic professional qualification. This did not mean that a case could no longer be made for shorter, less academically demanding courses to provide training to sub-professional level, and herein lay the development of a demarcation dispute between the advanced education sector and the TAFE sector. In the heady days of new status as a college of advanced education, many at FIT had happily watched the retreat to Nicholson Street of trade subjects, certificate courses and various other short courses which catered for new and as yet low status employment areas. So strong was the desire to draw clear distinctions between true tertiary work and the twilight 'middle' level occupied by the College, that even the Tertiary Orientation Program in Engineering and Applied Science was removed to Nicholson Street in 1978.[4] Thereafter no staff at Ballarat Road were teaching students who had not satisfied the entrance requirements of a CAE. The developments that were taking place as a result of the Kangan and Partridge Reports, however, were such that some would soon have cause to regret their haste in ruling off so firmly the line between advanced education and all the other things technical colleges had done previously.

When in 1968, Footscray Technical College became a college of advanced education, it chose to rename itself Footscray Institute of Technology, presumably to make as clear as possible its change in status within the Victorian system. For some time after this, the non-CAE section continued to be referred to as the Trade Section, but the name Footscray Technical College retained powerful associations and was not easily discarded, either formally or informally. What was left of the old Technical College gradually came to assume ownership of the abandoned name and this was formalised in 1973 when the it was officially designated — Footscray Technical College, a Division of Foot-scray Institute of Technology. By this time it had become usual to refer to Nicholson Street as the College Section or the College, and while this was potentially confusing for some outside the system, it was a distinction that was broadly accepted in other similar institutions and was generally confirmed by the transformation of college sections throughout the state into colleges of technical and further education in the mid-1970s. After the adoption of the Kangan Report, it rapidly became common practice to refer these sections as the TAFE college. Throughout the rest of this study, College will be used to refer to the TAFE section of FIT.

The developments flowing from the Kangan Report proved a mixed blessing for those CAEs with a college attached, because the climate of economic crisis into which this new concept of post-secondary education was introduced was such that an increase in funding in one area was more than likely offset by a reduction somewhere else. As with the implementation of the Martin Report in 1963, governments were tempted to focus on the new concept in terms of its 'cheapness' rather than its intrinsic value. Technical and further education was thus born in a climate of competition. Many directors soon found themselves facing a conflict of interest between the advanced education and TAFE sections, while the TAFE sections began to demand independent control over the increased funding that became available. That the TAFE sector embraced a wide area of need not covered coherently by universities or CAEs was not in doubt, but whether separate institutions were necessary to deliver these educational services was debatable. The problem was further exacerbated in places like FIT, where the TAFE section remained under Education Department control, because its relationship to the CAE was poorly defined. For all the goodwill, both historical and current within FIT, it was not enough to prevent an enervating, distracting and in some respects, destructive battle for control of TAFE in the region. This battle can only be understood in terms of the process by which the TAFE sector came to see institutional links to FIT as a positive impediment to its full development.

The drawing apart of the diploma and trade sections predated the establishment of the VIC and the Kangan Report. In one sense, it was a product of a tension always inherent in the status distinctions society made between engineers and tradesmen, between qualifications based on academically demanding courses and those based on the acquisition of practical skills. The CAEs, because of their history and their sense of themselves as more technological, more vocational and more 'practical' than the universities, had not yet fully come to terms with the fact that the gap between CAEs and universities had become narrower than that between the CAEs and their former trade schools. This was especially so in colleges still largely led and staffed by men who had begun their careers in the old system of technical education. When the TAFE colleges began to criticise the CAEs as elite institutions rushing headlong to 'copycat' university status, there were understandable protests and expressions of resentment. At FIT, this tension was heightened by physical separation, where contact between the staff and students of the two divisions diminished and they began to develop new institutional identities largely in isolation from each other.

In the 1970s the sense of tradition and identity that had characterised the old Footscray Technical College divided into two streams under the influence of prevailing ideas and bureaucratic arrangements. Though each contained many common elements, collegiate identity at Ballarat Road was re-shaped in terms of autonomy, degree-granting status and greater diversity of courses. At Nicholson Street, the traditions were re-defined along the lines elaborated in the Kangan Report. While the Institute began to acquire staff with a stronger academic profile, the College was attracting staff with a commitment to a distinctive educational sphere and a strong sense of vocation. Distinctions were further underlined as salaries and conditions in the advanced education sector began to outstrip those in the TAFE colleges. With separate employers and awards, the staff no longer had a common industrial relations position from which to act as a cohesive force countering physical separation. By 1974, the two sections not only had separate staff associations, but separate students organisations as well, indicating just how weak most of the horizontal links were becoming.[5]

Further, as diplomas began to assume a relationship to degrees similar to that which certificates had previously held in relation to diplomas,[6] the academic nexus between advanced education and TAFE was weakened. This was hastened by the inclusion of CAEs with universities in a joint admissions scheme for students completing secondary school which further reduced the importance of technical sixth year courses in CAE intakes. Increasingly drawing their students from different pools with different career aspirations, the values and focus of the two sectors inevitably diverged. On the whole, Footscray Tehnical College remained closer to the local community since short courses, apprentice training and night school must be taken closer to home and work than full-time studies, and the College retained most of the role of filling in gaps in educational and industrial opportunities that had been a feature of the old technical education system. The Institute, while continuing to accept a great proportion of its students from the western region, especially in the Schools of Engineering and Applied Science, nevertheless drew on a far wider student population, as was necessary if it was to achieve the standards appropriate to a CAE and indeed continue the tradition of academic success that had been a feature of the diploma school.

There were few intrinsic reasons why the two sections could not function harmoniously under one administration if it were appropriately structured, but there were powerful institutional factors, especially for those TAFE colleges linked with the Education Department, that encouraged a sense of mistrust and injustice within the TAFE sector. These in turn fed on a growing sense of alienation and disjunction between the two sectors which ultimately underpinned moves for separation and autonomy. The two sectors were not rungs on a ladder; only in a very limited number of circumstances were courses at the College exclusive pre-requisites for entry to the Institute. The central problem lay in the administrative relationship between the CAE section and the College established in 1968. As with the secondary school, the Principal of the Institute, (later renamed Director), was appointed by a Council which had clearly defined legal powers and responsibilities only in respect of the CAE section, affiliated with the Victoria Institute of Colleges, but he was also head of the College which continued to be staffed and funded by the Education Department. Under an *ad hoc* arrangement the FIT Council continued to perform its traditional duties in respect of buildings and employment of part-time and "general staff" under Education Department conditions. The position was less anomalous than that of the secondary school, but the College had no legal standing independent of the Institute, nor was it in any sense incorporated into the administrative framework beyond the fact that the Director of FIT was its representative on Council. When, in 1974, the head of the College was elevated to Principal, he found himself in the curious position of being a non-voting adviser to a Council specifically constituted to incorporate representatives of all sectors of the advanced education college but none of the TAFE college. In the event of a direct conflict of interest between the two sections, it was unclear how this should be resolved or by what means the College could present its views to the Council. The Council had certain powers in respect of the College, but there was nothing in its formal composition that endowed it with any necessary authority if, for any reason, the essentially paternalistic relationship with the College broke down.

In the early 1970s, only 100 of the 300 FIT staff were employed in the CAE.[7] Student numbers differed to an even greater extent owing to the large number of apprentices and part-time students. Initially the College was required to make few changes and it had sufficient momentum to carry it forward into the early 1970s relatively unruffled. The appointment of Mills must have been welcomed as one from within the community of educators with which the College staff were familiar, but it was not long before disquiet about the relationship between the two sections found formal expression. Noting that the secondary school Principal had been invited to attend Council meetings as an observer, "a strong request" came from "various members in the trade section", and Mills successfully recommended that the College Vice Principal, Mr Edwards, "be invited to attend Council as an observer and report regularly on the development in that area".[8] This was certainly an important gesture of acknowledgement, but given the operation of a committee system it still denied access to the most crucial policy-recommendation level.

Edwards, who had been appointed in 1972, began to work on an "Educational Specification" for the College[9] and it was painfully clear that the old problems of an Education Department system designed primarily to deliver a relatively uniform primary and secondary education presented special difficulties for the College. Furthermore, the Education Department was restructured in the early 1970s in such a way as to reduce the extent to which Technical Schools Division officers could pursue independent policies.[10] When Edwards received promotion to another school in early 1973, Mills expressed concern that a rapid turnover of vice principals had become inevitable and that this would "seriously inhibit the development" of the College's activities.[11] He suggested that the head of the College should be a Senior Principal Class A and even hinted that the Council might be able to participate in the selection even though this would require a change in the legislation.[12] At this stage it is clear that the FIT Council and administration was keen to take considerable responsibility for the College, rather in the manner of the old council-controlled schools, though time would reveal many disharmonies in those relationships also. The Council attempted to have the Principal of the College made a full member, but the VIC could see no reason why this should be necessary.[13]

The promotion of R. P. Telford, who had succeeded Edwards, from Vice Principal to Principal in 1974 marked the beginning of a gradual move toward autonomy and consolidation of a separate identity for the College. A man with a clear sense of purpose, Telford was committed to developing the College fully in line with the Kangan Report,[14] and he had both the personality and determination to refocus the objectives of the College. Unfortunately, physical resources were rapidly deteriorating and staff shortages at times were acute.[15] The same budgetary restraints that delayed the relocation of the secondary school plagued the College and Telford set to work to prepare graphic documentation of the dire conditions his staff and students were enduring.

Footscray Technical College in 1975 was the senior Education Department institution in the western region offering a wide range of basic vocational (apprenticeship), technician and certificate (Middle Level) courses. In addition, it offered tertiary orientation and other preparatory courses, service courses for industry, and retraining and recurrent education programmes.[16] Enrolment in Preliminary Year or Tertiary Orientation courses and Middle Level courses had been rising for several years and this was only partly offset by the transfer of some apprentice courses to other schools.[17] The loss of the extensive workshops at Ballarat Road, which in the 1950s, had been one of the College's greatest sources of pride, coupled with the increasing demand, meant that accommodation was stretched to breaking point.

In March 1975 Telford submitted to the Education Department an

> urgent plea for immediate assistance to a College in which a dedicated staff, despite the paucity and inadequacy of physical resources, strive to provide excellence of instruction to

persons who are often educationally and socially deprived. Their concern for, and interest in, the students result in a student-staff relationship I have never seen equalled in any other school or college.

In this he was not only supported by the FIT Council but by the Western Regional Council, which was disturbed that the "limitations at Footscray Technical College [had] reduced post-secondary opportunities for people residing in the Western Suburbs" and believed that its "optimum development" ought to be "the first priority for post-secondary education" in the area.[18] Conditions also made the staff restive,[19] and official response to Telford's "Master Plan" was so slow in coming that he sought the help of FIT Council to further pressure the Education Department.[20] There was no doubt of the Council's concern[21] but its power was limited. In the event, the College benefited at least as much as the secondary school from the black bans which forced the Education Department to attend properly to the needs of apprentices through the construction of the Berry Street Annexe.

The trend towards growth in courses unconnected with apprenticeship continued into 1976 when numbers grew overall by approximately 10%.[22] As in the past, the smallness of the Nicholson Street site remained a serious problem but changing patterns of land use made some expansion possible. The Footscray City Council rezoned the area bounded by Nicholson, Buckley and Albert Streets for educational use, and many of the College's newer activities were conducted in old houses. Acquiring the land, however, was expensive and parking became a source of some tension.[23] After much planning and negotiating, Nicholson Street was finally closed to through traffic from Buckley Street in 1981, allowing a full integration of the larger site, but it was quite clear in the mid 1970s that significant growth would require the College to become a multi-campus institution. The trend had begun with the establishment of the Berry Street Annexe, but it was viewed with some consternation by the TAFE Commission because the relationship between the sectors was still unresolved. For some time the Commission continued to favour substantial sharing of resources between the two sectors.[24]

The process of extracting funds from the Education Department was painfully slow, and as with the secondary school, there was a continual overlap of competing educational demands in the region. The 1977 Report of the Tertiary Education Commission further increased the sense of improvement in one sector being traded off against lack of development in another. The Report recommended minimal growth in student numbers and reduced capital-works expenditure for CAEs and universities but increased financial support for the TAFE sector.[25] Even though the greater proportion of TAFE funding actually came from state allocations, and therefore this recommendation had most impact on CAEs and universities, there was no escaping the fact that the three sectors had been placed in direct competition with each other for a shrinking Commonwealth education budget. Essentially, the CAE and TAFE communities were predisposed to co-operation and co-ordination, but in this context the TAFE sector became increasingly restive about what it saw as its dependent, ancillary relationship to advanced education. The issue was nicely encapsulated by the habit of RMIT Technical College staff of referring to their part of the institution as the "Retarded College". The view that the "other section" was getting a better deal spread easily, and almost all colleges in these years were plagued by a sense, in the main unfounded, that the advanced colleges were somehow milking the TAFE sector of some of its resources.[26] The failure to fully integrate the TAFE sector into the governing and administrative arrangements of the CAEs made it extremely difficult for the CAE Councils and administrations to be *seen* to be adequately representing and advancing the TAFE sector in an era when *formal* representation was becoming normal practice. That the Principal of Footscray Technical College had only observer status at Council meetings, when even the students of the Institute had a voting member after 1974, was to make only too clear the inferior and dependent status of the College.

The question of representation and automatic access to information was a nagging sore that eventually poisoned relations to the point where separation was the only possible outcome. Telford had recommended in late 1974 that an advisory committee of FIT Council consisting of the College Principal, three members of FIT Council, three non-members of FIT Council with interest in TAFE, and one full-time staff member be formed,[27] but nothing came of the suggestion. Next he requested that a member of the College staff be appointed to the FIT Staffing Committee, but his suggestion was brushed aside by Mills on the grounds that this Committee was concerned with academic appointments only, though "perhaps a non academic staffing committee could be set up at some time in the future".[28] In 1977, however, when it appeared that FIT was about to offer a course that duplicated a College course, a new note of urgency was injected into the debate.

Early in the year the Report of the Brown Committee investigating the relationship between the VIC and the State College of Victoria revealed only too clearly the climate of the times:

> In the VIC area declining demand for tertiary education in the technologies has been met by diverting energies to the liberal arts, and, in more recent times, to a revival of interest in two year post sixth form diplomas in technologies. This latter activity overlaps in some measure with TAFE courses and is the cause of some disquiet in that quarter.[29]

Mills reported that the Committee believed that a CAE move into teacher education was not the solution but rather that they should develop "lower level technological education".[30] Such a move would put them into direct competition with TAFE colleges, and Telford immediately expressed concern that the Advanced Education section might be tempted to introduce these lower-level courses in the Institute, rather than allow them to be developed in the College, as ought to have been the case in a genuinely integrated institution. His suspicions that this was likely were heightened by what he believed to be the undue haste in which he had been forced to prepare a submission on one such course area, the nature of some of the statements made in the Institute submission and the inadequate representation on it of the College's view.[31]

The area of dispute was a group of courses known as UG3, or associate diplomas, principally in engineering. There was still a body of opinion in the community that the new engineering courses were too theoretical, and that too few middle-level engineers with trade background were coming through the system. The courses were also being expanded to the point where part-time study combined with practical experience had become unrealistic. On the other hand, the Institution of Engineers had served notice that qualifications required for full membership would be further upgraded to *four* years post six completed years of secondary school after 1980. The CAEs were quite willing to move back into two-year courses very similar to the

Certificate of Technology courses offered by the TAFE colleges which, the cynic could not but note, looked likely to be a growth area in funding. The State Council for Technical Education, the Technical Division of the Education Department and the Technical Teachers' Association of Victoria all took a stand supporting the interests of TAFE colleges. They viewed the activity of the VIC in approving these courses in CAEs with grave suspicion and even a touch of paranoia. One member of the State Council for Technical Education remarked that "they [the CAEs] were always trying to pinch our courses".[32] Under the circumstances, it is hardly surprising that tensions rose at places like FIT where the issue was partly simply a battle for control over resources, courses and student numbers, but for the TAFE colleges it was also a fight to maintain the higher-level technological courses that were an essential part of their identity as something more than preparatory and trade schools.

Telford presented FIT Council with a carefully argued proposal for separation in March 1977. He acknowledged that the initial *ad hoc* arrangement had allowed the College a degree of flexibility and autonomy that would not have been possible otherwise. Developments since then however, made the arrangement anachronistic and the time had come for independence. He saw a Council with increasing numbers of representatives from the advanced education section, notably of staff and students, and a greatly increased volume of work as a result of rapid expansion. This, he believed, further weakened the likelihood that the Council would attend properly to the needs of the College which had no voting rights, and therefore, no formal power. It was the virtually unanimous wish of the College staff that separation take place, but Telford was anxious to maintain co-operation and co-ordination and argued that this could best be achieved between two separate and autonomous bodies.[33] Given the strength of the commitment of the FIT administration and the Board of Studies to maintaining the existing arrangements,[34] the natural instinct of the Council was to defer the issue, largely in the hope that the recommendations of the Partridge and Williams Committees would resolve the matter for them.

Things might have rested there if, at the same Council meeting, it had not been revealed that FIT had been given VIC permission to introduce an Associate Diploma (or UG3) in Plant Maintenance in 1978.[35] This galvanised Telford into action, and in April he outlined in detail the threat that the loss of Certificate of Technology courses[36] would mean for the College and the likely impact of this on federal funding.[37] Seriously questioning the demand for the proposed courses and why they could not be conducted at the College rather than the CAE, he brought to the Council one side of an argument exercising the whole technical education community. Mills took an opposing view and put his case in a paper on "The Development of Associate Diploma (UG3) Courses".[38] Telford responded with a long rebuttal presented to FIT Council in May.[39] The issue was indeed a vexed one, but the Tertiary Education Commission had made it clear that funding would not be available for overlapping courses.[40] Furthermore, it was not going to approve *any* associate diplomas in engineering until the Partridge Committee had reported.[41] Ultimately, this particular issue was amicably resolved in ways that revealed the possible virtues of combined activities. The working party set up to determine the relationship between the "Plant Maintenance" course at FIT and the "Maintenance Supervision" course at the College was convinced they did not overlap and that it would be most efficient if they were operated on a joint basis.[42] None of this, however, resolved the larger question of autonomy for the College.

Those who had hoped that the Partridge Report would resolve matters were disappointed. The UG3 issue was left to a proposed Engineering Education Advisory Committee[43] and while, as a general principle, it favoured closer links between CAEs and TAFE colleges rather than separation, it was very conscious that some TAFE divisions were "anxious for separation". The most frequent complaints from TAFE staff were that their interests were not adequately "represented on the common Council,"[44] and split campuses like FIT were acknowledged as presenting special problems. The one clear message from the Report for FIT was that:

> the administrative arrangements of Colleges of Advanced Education which have a TAFE division should be re-organised so as to give the technical college a voice in the governing Council and in the appropriate committees more in proportion to its role within the institution.[45]

A year later the Williams Committee Report reinforced the view that TAFE divisions should "be given a more adequate voice in the management of their institutions".[46] To have done so would have removed the major grievance about paternalistic manage-ment of a large and growing institution, and helped to integrate the College back into the Institute's world, but in the case of former Education Department institutions, it was apparently easier said than done.

Early in 1978 a new factor in Institute/TAFE relations in the region emerged with the proposal to open another TAFE college at Newport. This provided an opportunity for rationalisation of apprentice classes with metal trades going to Newport and Foot-scray College retaining the electrical trades.[47] While some on the FIT Council had doubts about how well they were managing their present responsibilities,[48] Mills agreed to participate in the Newport Technical College organisation.[49] The College com-menced classes the following year under the umbrella of FIT, and the Braybrook Annexe of the Footscray College, which con-ducted classes for crane operators and related activities, was also opened. The administrative arrangements necessitated by this new development finally gave the Colleges improved sta-tus. A formal advisory committee of FIT Council was established to provide a forum in which the special interests of the TAFE sector could be discussed and proposals developed with several members of Council who could be expected to acquire some special expertise in the area. It still, however, failed to address the issue of *formal* representation, automatic right to consulta-tion or control over finances.

1. Quoted in Turner, *op. cit.*, p 43.
2. See R. Milliken, 'Williams Committee Splits Into Impasse', *National Times*, [no date], attachment to Director's Report to FIT Council, 27 February 1979.
3. This was the body which since 1972 had directed the state's former teachers colleges in much the same way as the VIC had controlled the CAEs.
4. Footscray Technical College Report to Council, 27 September 1977.
5. *Ibid.*, 26 February 1974.
6. See above, pp 62–63.
7. D. Mills, *Advertiser*, 3 March 1971.
8. FIT Council Minutes, 25 July 1972.
9. *Ibid.*
10. Turner, *op. cit.* p 35.
11. Director's Report to FIT Council, 22 May 1973.
12. FIT Council Minutes, 22 May 1973.
13. Director's Report to FIT Council, 26 November 1974.
14. Footscray Technical College Report to FIT Council, 24 June 1974.

15. *Ibid.*, 27 February 1973.
16. For details of courses offered see Appendix D.
17. Notably Carpentry and Metal Fabrication. See Director's Report to FIT Council, 26 February 1974.
18. R. P. Telford, Submission prepared in consultation with members of staff and the Council of the FIT at the request of R J Middleton, Assistant Director of Technical Education, 'Current and Future Building Problems Constituting a Crisis Situation', March 1975, FIT Archive.
19. For example, Footscray Technical College Report to FIT Council, 22 April 1975.
20. *Ibid.*, 27 May 1975.
21. FIT Council Papers, Buildings and Equipment Committee, 11 November 1975. Report of Special Meeting, 10 December 1975 to discuss redevelopment of College, FIT Council Minutes, 24 February 1976.
22. Footscray Technical College Report to FIT Council, 23 March 1976.
23. FIT Council Papers, Buildings and Equipment Committee, 11 May 1976.
24. Director's Report to FIT Council, 24 August 1976.
25. *Ibid.*, 27 September 1977.
26. For example, see Murray-Smith & Dare, *op. cit.*, p 424.
27. Footscray Technical College Report to FIT Council, 26 November 1974.
28. FIT Council Minutes, 23 November 1976.
29. Footscray Technical College Report to FIT Council, 24 May 1977.
30. Director's Report to FIT Council, 22 February 1977.
31. Footscray Technical College Report to FIT Council, 22 February 1977.
32. Turner, *op. cit.*, p 53.
33. Footscray Technical College Report to FIT Council, 24 March 1977.
34. FIT, Board of Studies, Minutes, 24 May 1977.
35. FIT Council Minutes, 22 March 1977. UG 3 courses are approved by VIC for FIT's Master Plan. This appears to have occurred "without reference to either the SCTE or the VIC/SCTE Liaison Committee which had been formed specifically to consider such courses". Turner, *op. cit.*, p 55.
36. This is what UG3 courses were called in TAFE colleges.
37. Footscray Technical College Report to FIT Council, 26 April 1977.
38. No copy of this paper has been found.
39. Footscray Technical College Report to FIT Council, 24 May 1977.
40. Director's Report to FIT Council, 22 November 1977.
41. *Ibid.*
42. *Ibid.*, 22 August 1978.
43. For relevant extracts see Footscray Technical College Report to FIT Council, 23 May 1978.

44. Review of the Report of the Post Secondary Education Committee of Enquiry (Partridge), Footscray Technical College Report to FIT Council, 23 May 1978.
45. Director's Report to FIT Council, 28 February 1978.
46. FIT Council Minutes, 25 September 1979.
47. Footscray Technical College Report to FIT Council, 21 March 1978.
48. See, for example the comments of W. Secomb, FIT Council Minutes, 25 July 1978.
49. FIT Council Minutes, 26 September 1978.

CHAPTER FOURTEEN Footscray College of TAFE "goes it alone" 1980–1982

By 1980, with over 1000 full-time students,[1] Footscray Technical College was a mature institution with a clear sense of purpose — "to provide recurrent education and retraining, to dismantle barriers to further education, and to provide a service which is responsive to the needs of special groups".[2] Defining itself as a "Student Centred College", it was also confident enough to make a strong bid to establish itself as the principal heir to the traditions of technical education in Footscray, the special benefits of which were available to present students. The 1980 *Handbook* explained that Footscray's relative isolation had nurtured a "fierce and outstanding community spirit", and recalled the early hope that the technical college would transform Footscray into a "Birmingham of Australia". Much was made of the "very close affinity between the people, the business and commercial sectors and the staff and students of the College, expressed both socially and educationally." In stressing the special qualities of College teachers, the *Handbook* sought to revive the values of the older style of technical education with its strong emphasis on the practical and the personal.

> Many of them only became teachers after years of industrial and commercial experience. Thus they are not ivory-towered, theoretical academics, but practical down-to-earth and approachable men and women dedicated to training college students for the actual work they will face in real life. Many of them are prepared to work long hours for their students and to develop and foster close links with the local and business community. Many have made sacrifices to be at this College

because of the satisfaction they get from teaching the type of students who come here.[3]

Stress was also laid on the achievements of past students who remained advocates of their school and their type of education and the value of attending an institution with a proud past:

> Although times, length of hair, the influx of girl students, students' dress and course content have changed; these underlying factors and traditions still permeate and live on in the present college.[3]

There had been much refurbishment, and more had been approved. Facilities were improving all the time, and a campaign to attract donations for prizes and scholarships was gaining strength.[5] "The way ahead" was

> fairly clear. The future will be exciting, satisfying, productive and demanding of both staff and students as together they strive for greater educational excellence and working conditions. In addition the output of technical colleges, for some time treated as second cousins to tertiary trained students, is being recognised more and more for its intrinsic worth.[6]

In all this, the Footscray Technical College was bidding to co-opt for itself the sense of history and continuity inherent in the history of technical education in the region. By implication, FIT was thus cast in the role of newcomer, with only tenuous links with the aims, aspirations and strengths of the original institution. In the battle between the two institutions that lay ahead, this subtle tussle for 'ownership' of the college's history, traditions and special place in the Footscray community should be appreciated as an undercurrent that explains some of the passion unleashed.

The recommendations of the Partridge Report, which included the establishment of the Victorian Post-Secondary Education Commission (VPSEC) to oversee all tertiary education in the state, and the creation of a separate TAFE Board under it were more than two years in the implementation. For much of that time, therefore, the future of the TAFE sector was still sufficiently ill-defined to allow for continued argument, lobbying and delaying of important decisions. It was not until 1979 that FIT Council squarely confronted the issue of its relationship to the College and the possibility that benevolent paternalism was no longer sufficient. At the April meeting the Council was presented with a series of reports which revealed the difficult terrain through which they had to plot a course. The Director's report outlined a scheme for combining TAFE funds with VIC funds (about \$600 000) to establish a region-wide computing network for all post-secondary education requirements, which seemed to exemplify the benefits of combined operations.[7] A report from the Education Committee, however, spoke of FIT's need to "seize opportunities" opening up in the TAFE sector without diminishing its advanced education role, again revealing the tendency to develop policies within the CAE in isolation from the TAFE section, even when these policies had direct bearing on its role.[8]

In the absence of formal mechanisms for consultation, when Institute people sat down to consider policy, they thought almost exclusively in Institute terms; the ambitions and frustrations of the College were very remote from most people at Ballarat Road. More importantly, the CAE staff had become used to a large measure of autonomy in planning and budgeting. In contrast, the College seemed to be hamstrung all round, answerable to a range of bodies none of which saw TAFE as their primary concern. The education community remained divided on whether there should be a separate TAFE board, who should sit on it if there was, and how the relationship between CAEs and TAFE should be defined.[9] One matter however, remained absolutely clear: close working relations could not occur without a restructuring of the FIT Council to allow equal representation of TAFE interests.[10] However, the Council, faced with a Director who was convinced that a structure would be 'handed down' which would leave FIT in charge of the College, the Principal of the College who was not willing to accept anything less than a separate council, and deteriorating personal relations between the two men, seemed unable to take any decision at all. Meanwhile, simmering discontent in the College approached boiling point.

At the end of 1979 VPSEC recommended that a TAFE board be established, but whether this would be a central body or a series of regional boards remained unclear. In February 1980 the Council considered a paper — "TAFE and Advanced Education at FIT: The Next Stage" by the new Assistant Director, Dr Irwin Herrman. His aim was to refute the proposition of the College

Principal, R. P. Telford,[11]that TAFE was a distinctive education-al sector, which must be given autonomy, or else "be placed in an inferior and educationally unsound position which would be detrimental to [its] function".[12] Theoretically, the arguments for co-operation and amalgamation were sound, but Herrman's paper made no concrete suggestions as to how a new and more nearly equal relationship might be established. It brushed aside too easily an historical relationship of inferiority and the reality of separation at almost all levels. More critically, his paper al-tered the agenda of debate by raising the question of amalgama-tion, where previously the subject had been one of determining degrees of separation and/or representation.

Telford reiterated his argument that the present Council could not manage both sectors and it was left to Hall, Principal of the infant Newport Technical College, to reveal the deep-seated lack of faith in any system that did not incorporate the interests of the colleges into a clearly-defined legal structure. He "spoke highly of the co-operation he had received to date, but had reservations for the future continuation of such co-operation". He agreed with Telford that the current membership of the Council could not successfully manage and control all the developments within TAFE as well as dealing with advanced education matters, and he expressed "concern over the large percentage of time devoted to Advanced Education business at the Council".[13] However many 'rational' argumnts were put forward, TAFE interests were at the mercy of the good faith of the Institute, and that was not satisfactory. As Telford pointed out on another occasion, while "co-operation and co-ordination" had certainly occurred, it was no thanks to any "structure but by responsible people who [were] willing to set out to assist each other".[14] No one could reasonably guarantee the continuance of such arrangements indefinitely. Even the Council was finally forced to admit that "it had been given the responsibility but not the proper authority for TAFE".[15]

At this point senior Institute staff also turned their attention to the issue and discussed Telford and Herrman's papers together with an extract from the "Victorian TAFE Strategy Plan — Organisational Strategy" in March 1980.[16] They came to the con-clusion that "a single post-secondary education institution" would optimise the ultilisation of all resources and eventually provide for the widest range of educational needs".[17] In con-trast, the FIT Professional Staff Association was far more autious. It saw problems for both sides in amalgamation and wanted explicit models of possible future management structures and outlines of proposed changes fully discussed before any FIT staff recommendation was made to Council.[18] The Council, for its part, decided to defer the question of separation for six months and review it in the light of the progress being made in establishing a TAFE Board.

Inside the TAFE sector, staff opinion emerged as a powerful actor. A critical industrial relations issue moved to centre stage as the machinery to put the Partridge Report recommendation for a separate TAFE Board into effect was finally being created. TAFE college staff were deeply concerned about who was to be their employer — the Education Department, an independent board, regional boards or individual councils — and under what terms and conditions. The overwhelming preference was for a central employing authority, and staff mobilised to put that point of view very forcefully. At Footscray, following a meeting of staff from both Colleges, the Interim Staff Committee of Footscray and Newport Technical Colleges sought the opportunity to convey their views to the FIT Council.[19] This was not readily acceded to, and while the FIT Council and administration seem to have been slow to realise it, the issue rapidly developed into a test of the Institute's good faith by which the College staff would judge it as a prospective employer. Little that occurred in the following months did anything to dispel the strong opposition among College staff to any form of amalgamation or regional employing authorities.

The Interim Staff Committee resolutely refused to allow its case to be filtered through the Executive Committee of Council[20] or to participate in a working party until it was assured that it could appear directly before the FIT Council.[21] At the same time several other developments added fuel to the fire of College staff suspicions. Firstly, a report appeared in a local paper in which the Assistant Director was quoted as saying that he hoped the future would see the College "under one administrative body of the Institute".[22] While clearly only the expression of opinion and not a statement of policy, it had the appearance of pre-empting debate and rang predictable alarm bells throughout the Colleges.[23] Matters were further aggravated by the appearance of a report by the FIT Chief Librarian outlining the alleged benefits that would flow to the TAFE library from amalgamation.[24] The response to this report from the College reveals the sense of grievance that had to be allayed if successful amalgamation could be achieved. While conceding that in the early years of poor funding to TAFE close links "may have been beneficial", now that TAFE was a viable, more strongly funded sector they were no longer required. "Voluntary co-operation between equal partners" was

> more desirable and likely to be more effective than forced co-operation in a relationship where one partner is dominant. That any FIT-Footscray Technical College alliance would be dominated by FIT is perhaps exemplified by the fact that despite Mr Bundy's concern for the welfare of Footscray and Newport Technical Colleges, before submitting his statement to Council he neglected to discuss with the librarians of either college the issues it raises.[25]

This increasing tendency to discuss matters of acute importance to the Colleges at Nicholson Street and Newport without the courtesy of consultation was the foundation of a crippling distrust.

Whether it had any basis in fact or not, the view had developed among College staff that the FIT administration was constantly sabotaging any tendency within the Council to support separation. From this flowed the determination to have College staff representatives present their case to the Council in person and their determination finally met with success.[26] At the August meeting the Colleges' Staff Committee was given half an hour to present a case which concluded with the assertion that:

> Given the distinction between the TAFE and Advanced sectors, TAFE Staff are not aware of any rationale or philosophical basis that would support a fully integrated post-secondary institution in the Western Metropolitan Region.
>
> The experience of others, both here and overseas, in the operation of large multi-level institutions suggests to us that the disadvantages far outweigh the advantages.
>
> TAFE Staff at Footscray Technical College firmly believe that the distinctive nature of TAFE necessitates an autonomous TAFE sector in the Western Metropolitan Region. This is seen as crucial to TAFE's effectiveness in the region and to future development.
>
> We believe that a suitable model based on TAFE autonomy

can be developed, embodying the principles of the Partridge and Williams Reports and the TAFE Strategy Plan, that will satisfy the needs of both TAFE and the Advanced sectors and incorporating maximum co-operation and resource sharing.[27]

The following month, the Council agreed that one elected member of staff from the Colleges could attend as an observer until the relationship was resolved.[28]The FIT staff were also acutely aware of the industrial relations issues and had genuine sympathy with the demand for adequate representation of staff views. FIT staff had few objections to a closer relationship but not at the expense of FIT's autonomy which they believed "should still have its own specific Council and terms and conditions should remain unaltered and it should retain full academic responsibility".[29] By implication, this meant the College should have its own Council also.

Early in July 1980 Telford circulated a paper on "Local Governance of TAFE" in which he argued that the Council controlling TAFE should be regional in structure and dedicated to TAFE. He saw a need for twin councils and believed that co-operation would be facilitated rather than hindered by this. The model he proposed was one which placed Footscray Technical College at the apex of a regional system of TAFE education, but it ignored staff preference for a central employing agency.[30] In response to this, the FIT Director, Mills, finally attempted to give some clear leadership to the Council. He set out what he saw as three options, though the first of these — to continue with the present system — was clearly untenable. The second was separation, and the third was a form of restructuring that would "provide for appropriate powers and responsibilities in both sectors with corresponding membership provisions and a desirable committee infrastructure and delegation of authority". He suggested this arrangement had educational and economic advantages, but the bulk of his reasons were strategic and pragmatic. He believed this was the wish of the Williams and Partridge Committees; he reminded the Council that state and Commonwealth authorities were pushing to reduce the number of autonomous institutions in the state and that the TAFE Strategy Plan favoured such a restructure. He also expressed concern about those College staff currently employed by Council. Finally, he said seven other institutions similar to FIT were either currently operating or planning to operate in this manner.[31]

In the course of the discussion which followed Mills and Telford appeared to move very close together, though Telford admitted that he did not know how his staff would react. R. Fordham, Shadow Minister for Education, then took a lead in the debate remarking that he was "'heartened" by Telford's apparent support for option three, and "believed it was a step in the right direction".[32] However Fordham was reluctant to support restructure without hearing the staff position, and he requested that the Director provide more documentation to support his assertions. Ominously, another member expressed his doubt that Telford's conceptual model did in fact coincide with the Director's proposal, a doubt which on careful reading seems well founded.

In October, the Council was scheduled to make a decision. Mills argued that he did not believe that TAFE staff would be given the option of a central employing authority and that since so many developments were still pending it would be foolish of the Council to take any decision which would imply that it did "not wish to share in any further development in the TAFE sector". The Council was quite divided on the matter and finally arrived at a motion which stated that it was "willing to consider" reconstitution to give greater representation to TAFE interests along the lines suggested by the Director.[33] Far from resolving anything, this only served to rouse the College staff to greater heights of indignation. They set out on a campaign to document every situation in which the College might have been disadvantaged by its association with the advanced college and apply every sort of pressure possible.[34] Following a staff meeting on 11 November 1980 at which it was unanimously agreed to oppose the Council resolution,[35] the TAFE staff marched in protest along Nicholson Street to present a petition of 200 signatures to the November Council meeting unsuccessfully seeking its rescission.[36] The Council felt, on the whole, that this was little more than an "enabling motion", but they would have done well to have taken more seriously a question addressed to the Director by Fordham: "What is our motive if we continue to press for integration in view of the obvious opposition from those who will be required to make it work, that is, the TAFE staff?"[37]

The bitterness generated by this decision was only too clear in the public campaign embarked on by the College staff, who, like the secondary teachers a few years before, felt they were fighting for their very existence. "We're trying to get general public support", they declared. "Here we have someone trying to take over the oldest technical college in the whole of the western suburbs". Not only was it old, however, it was especially geared to the needs of the western suburbs:

> The College, formerly, the poor relation of the more affluent and sophisticated institute, has emerged as the pinnacle of access education in the west with annexes and study centres like the Tottenham Tech., Community House, the Braybrook Training Centre, Newport Technical College and Footscray Women's Learning House, flourishing under its wing.[38]

Most members of the Institute were affronted by accusations of elitism and academic distance from students and the needs of the region. If many western suburbs students were poorly equipped for the courses offered at FIT, that was all the more reason to have TAFE colleges to enhance their opportunities. It seems unfortunate that a statement which so perfectly captured the ideal relationship between the two sections —

> FIT is an institute for achievers and the academically inclined, whereas we provide students who would perhaps not otherwise go onto further education with an opportunity to learn skills and adapt themselves to further tertiary education.[39]

— should have been used as a form of accusation by the College against the Institute. It demonstrated only too painfully the communication and credibility gap between the two institutions.

The whole of 1981 was occupied with the continuing tug-of-war for control of the College. Separation of the the TAFE division from the Education Department was scheduled for October, but terms and conditions that would apply to staff remained vague. Mills adopted a strategy of doing nothing in the belief that the tide was flowing in favour of his preference for amalgamation, and relations between him and Telford grew bitter and acrimonious. The administration of Newport College seemed happy enough with this state of affairs, apparently preferring control by FIT to becoming little more than a minor offshoot of Footscray Technical College. Staff opinion appears to have been more divided. Telford and the College staff fought with ever increasing urgency to see that the tide of events were

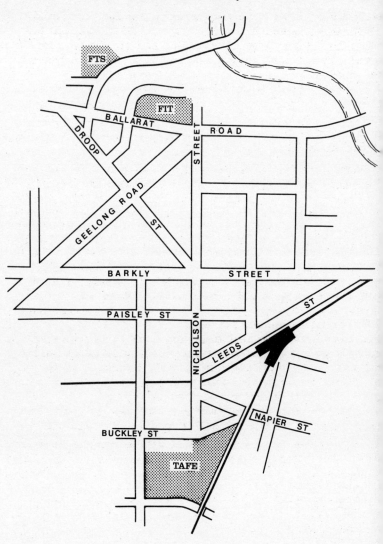

turned in a different direction. The major effect was a continuing decline in the relationship between the two bodies which ensured that, whatever the final outcome, it would remain strained and bitter for some time. One source of deep conflict was reporting procedures in respect of financial management of the affairs of the College and the disagreement as to which section would gain or lose financially as a result of separation. The TAFE section continued to argue the educational benefits of separation, while Mills continued to counter with arguments about administrative convenience, efficiency and the trend of the times.

One of the first tasks of the new TAFE Board was to formalise the administrative arrangements of multi-level institutions. It arrived at a set of principles that pointed out the weakness in the past relationship between institutes and colleges and hence the difficulties in effecting an amalgamation:

> Sectors are able to foster healthy co-operation if they are regarded as having equal capacity to negotiate in the sharing of resources. A situation in which one sector is perceived as having supremacy over the other is not conducive to positive co-operation.[40]

To the extent that the relationship between the two sectors had been healthy in the past, it was in spite of the structural arrangements and it could no longer be deemed "healthy" by any objective assessment. Outside the Institute, the framers of policy were rapidly moving towards the College point of view. The TAFE sector's argument that it was a distinctive form of education and as such required autonomy in any case was rapidly gaining ground, while the staff opposition to localised employment had proved hard to counter. The tide turned against the FIT administration's view and grudgingly, at the last possible moment, it came to accept separation as inevitable.

Sadly, the historical relationship that might have enabled the two sectors to amalgamate had been dissipated, first through benign neglect, then through reluctance to treat sufficiently seriously either the educational philosophy of the TAFE sector or its legitimate claims for closer integration into the government of FIT. The College formally separated on June 30 1982 to become the Footscray College of TAFE, but its new Council ensured a special kind of continuity by including among its foundation members several distinguished 'old boys' who were also members of the FIT Council. If, in the immediate aftermath, relations were strained and bitter, the way was clear in the long run to rebuild the old and natural spirit of co-operation and joint enterprise between two autonomous but complementary institutions. More importantly, the energy that had for so long been diverted into conflict and politicing could be directed to the educational needs of the western suburbs.

1. Footscray Technical College Report to FIT Council, 28 February 1978.
2. *Ibid*, 24 July 1978.
3. *Footscray Technical College Handbook*, 1980, p 5.
4. *Ibid.*, p 6.
5. Footscray Technical College Report to FIT Council, 27 July 1978.
6. *Footscray Technical College Handbook*, 1980, p 7.
7. Director's Report to FIT Council, 24 April 1979.
8. FIT Council Minues, 24 April 1979.
9. Footscray Technical College Report to FIT Council, 24 April 1979.
10. FIT Council Minutes, 22 May 1979.
11. As outlined in a paper entitled, 'Local Administration of TAFE in Victoria', December 1979.
12. Paper presented to Council Meeting, 26 February 1980.
13. FIT Council Minutes, 26 February 1980.
14. R. Telford, 'Local Governance of TAFE', Report to Footscray Technical College/Newport Technical College TAFE Committee, 1 July 1980.
15. FIT Council Minutes, 28 October 1980.
16. FIT Board of Studies, Minutes, 12 March 1980.
17. *Ibid.*, 2 April 1980.
18. J. Horwood, Secretary FITPSA, to FIT Board of Studies, 12 May 1980.
19. J. Bennellick, Secretary TAFE Colleges Interim Staff Committee to K. Burbridge, FIT Registrar, 16 May 1980. Attached to FIT Council Papers, 27 May 1980
20. FIT Council Minutes, 24 June 1980.
21. J. Bennelick to K. Burbridge, 11 July 1980, "Relationship of TAFE and AE 1980".
22. *The Sunshine-Western Suburbs Advocate*, 14 May 1980.
23. FIT Council Minutes, 27 May 1980.
24. This first surfaced at FIT Board of Studies meeting, 11 June 1980, then went on to the Buildings & Equipment Committee of Council.
25. FIT Council Papers, Buildings & Equipment Committee, Report 22 July 1980.
26. J. Bennelick to K. Burbridge, 11 July 1980, *op. cit.*
27. FIT Council Minutes, 26 August 1980.
28. *Ibid.*, 23 September 1980.
29. Recommendation from Fundamental Issues Seminar to Board of Studies, 13 August 1980.
30. 1 July 1980, 'Local Governance of TAFE', *op. cit.*
31. Director's Report to FIT Council, 22 July 1980.
32. FIT Council Minutes, 22 July 1980.
33. *Ibid.*, 28 October 1980.
34. See, for example, Footscray Technical College Report to FIT Council, 13 November 1980.

35. FIT File, Relationship of TAFE and AE, 1980. See also *Footscray Mail*, 12 November 1980.
36. FIT Council Minutes, 25 November 1980.
37. This is from a letter from Fordham to the Director in respect of the October meeting which which was read out at that meeting. It is quoted in Footscray Technical College Report to FIT Council, 13 November 1980.
38. *Footscray Mail*, 26 November 1980.
39. *Western Suburbs Advertiser*, 27 November 1980, p 1.
40. See attachment to FIT Council Minutes, 27 July 1981.

CHAPTER FIFTEEN **"Measured strides towards . . . the light at the end of the tunnel"[1] 1978–1986**

Delivering the Graduation Address in August 1977, H. S. Houston, Chairman of the Advanced Education Council, had painted a most flattering picture of FIT:

> Footscray has a long and enviable record in training professional engineers and scientists. Now with the newer, broader base in Business and Commerce, and the developments in such areas as physics, recreation, tourism and food industry servicing, this Institute stands among the most innovative and adventurous institutions in Australia. In so being the vocational emphasis which provides the fundamental tenet of Advanced Education has been retained; the courses have been sensibly and unextravagantly developed at pregraduate, graduate and post graduate levels and there has been no discernible loss of flexibility or failure to respond to the needs of the community. Furthermore, from the broad representation of industry and government on your many advisory boards, it is evident that strong and positive links with the world of industry and commerce which are expected of the Advanced Education sector, have been firmly established by the Institute. It is also evident that for the expenditures assigned to Footscray, the community is getting good value for its money.[2]

These words captured the essence of FIT's most positive self-image, but they nevertheless masked some continuing weaknesses that assumed greater significance as funds for tertiary education dried up at the end of the 1970s. If the community was getting "good value for its money", there was still a limit to how long FIT could continue to make a virtue of necessity before both quality and reputation were jeopardised by under-funding.

FIT still needed to expand and diversify if it was to achieve long-term viability as a college of advanced education, but the Commonwealth allocation to FIT for the 1978–1980 triennium effectively put the lid on any plans for expansion. The physical education building and the Farnsworth Avenue diversion would be completed, but there were no provisions for the multi-purpose building requested for commencement 1978, the library/union building for 1980, renovation of the secondary-school building or completion of the Boating Complex.[3] As a consequence, quotas were applied to all areas apart from engineering and applied science, and library facilities in particular remained seriously below requirements.[4] Unfortunately, FIT was still seeking money for quite basic resources very late in the 'scramble' for funds to upgrade. The diversion of Farnsworth Avenue and other real-estate costs associated with the development of the Ballarat Road site had absorbed large amounts of capital without significantly expanding the facilities for teaching and learning. FIT had "faced special problems", because "in developing the campus, non-tertiary sections . . . had to be relocated and space limitations . . . meant that old buildings had to be demolished before new construction work could begin". These delays had prevented FIT seeking funds in the earlier period when they had seemed more readily available, and then, just when these problems were behind them, capital funds were cut.[5]

Matters worsened when the VIC adopted a new funding formula based on its assessment of the *minimum* level of support necessary for the *survival* of each institution. This resulted in wide variations in funding per equivalent full-time student, and FIT's allocation was reduced by $60 per unit.[6] FIT protested strongly against this new formula,[7] and began to frame its submissions in terms that highlighted the discrepancies between FIT allocations and those to other CAEs:[8]

Recurrent grants have traditionally been based on student enrolment, explained Mr Mills. However, in recent years medium-sized metropolitan institutions like FIT have been funded at about 12% below the funding level of the large institutions. 'This runs counter to arguments about economy of scale and seems quite unfair'.[9]

This protest had little immediate effect, and in April the Institute learnt that the construction of multi-purpose building K had been deferred indefinitely, even though funds had been found to refurbish the old secondary technical school building.[10] These were dark days for tertiary education. As the Assistant Director complained to the *Age*, not only were institutions of higher learning suffering serious financial constraints, but they had to witness "the unworthy spectacle of leaders of both major parties outdoing each other in vilifying education and thus pandering to the public mood".[11]

There was a quite remarkable quality of optimism within the FIT community that sustained it through this dismal funding period at the turn of the decade. Perhaps partly because FIT had always been far from privileged, even the smallest of advances had more significance in sustaining morale than might have been the case elsewhere. Partly it was the infectious conviction of the leadership that things could not possibly get worse if they could just hang on long enough. Mills' tendency always to err on the side of optimism was coupled with an ability to persist even when it seemed hopeless. His new Deputy Director, Dr Irwin Herrman, was similarly inclined, and capable of marshalling the rhetoric that kept attention focussed on positive developments. Somewhat prophetically in 1980, he suggested that "against a background of increasing demoralisation and retrenchment in advanced education throughout the world", the departure of the secondary school should be understood as more than providing a welcome expansion of space. It was symbolic of FIT's arrival at the end of a "dark tunnel" of thwarted plans and cramped conditions and offered a glimpse into a new decade which would, with the benefit of hindsight, be hailed as "salad days".[12]

The removal of the secondary school was indeed symbolic of the finishing off of certain business that allowed full concentration on the future. This was accompanied by a sharpening of self-definition that made submissions more coherent and persuasive. FIT's submission for the 1982–1984 triennium adopted an expansionary tone arguing a case for growth in student numbers and an increase in allocation per student to compensate for previous under-funding.[13] The target of 3438 equivalent full-time students by 1984 was justified in terms of course mix and geographic position and reflected FIT's continued development "as a multi-discipline college of advanced education possessing a special (perhaps even unique) combination of roles . . . as the only tertiary institution of the Western Region of Melbourne with an expanding population and industrial sector". FIT already possessed "many of the basic resources and much of the infrastructure to allow for growth, despite inadequate past funding and an incomplete building program". It therefore believed that inceased funding "would allow for the emergence of a balanced regional tertiary institution, yet one possessing certain specialised teaching programs unique to and of considerable value to Victoria".[14]

Much of FIT's confidence was based on the fact that it was the only tertiary college in a region that was still very short of educational resources. There were, however, some dangers in overplaying the 'deprived west' theme, in that potential students might choose to go to other colleges if they felt FIT was too lacking in resources. It was rising demand that would best ensure the Institute's claim to a larger proportion of a shrinking budget. When in October 1979, the *Age* ran a series of articles on the "deprived west", FIT was quick to point out that it was principally a "multi-purpose college of advanced education", which offered degree courses for students "across the whole spectrum of aptitudes and interests, from the sciences and technologies through business studies and physical education to the social sciences and humanities". While some of its courses were specially designed for the western suburbs, others were unique in the state and drew "students from the whole metropolitan area to the 'deprived' west".[15]

The underlying challenge for FIT was to find the right balance between specialist programs focussed on regional needs and its more general development as a CAE. Under the circumstances prevailing at the turn of the decade, if it were to rely solely on intake from the western region, it would not obtain sufficient numbers of suitably qualified students to justify its existence as a multi-purpose CAE, and even its role in the engineering and applied science area was doubtful. There was, however, a very strong commitment to serve the region and provide access to courses for disadvantaged students. Many inside FIT assigned it a role in changing the circumstances that created the low participation rate in tertiary education in the region. As the Head of the Department of Humanities, John McLaren, explained in a letter to the *Age*, FIT was part of "a much wider network, extending throughout the western suburbs, of community organisations, information services, support systems and social services", which provided a "basis for social advance in the western suburbs", if they could "be properly co-ordinated and utilised". "The people of the west" were "already helping themselves". All they required was "a recognition by governments of their needs and their efforts, and the provision by governments of public services matched to those needs at the same level as those provided to the rest of the community."[16] FIT could not, however, simply accept all comers, irrespective of their educational background, without additional funds to mount bridging courses. At the same time, there was a strong desire to become a 'centre of excellence', an academically rigorous college attracting students on the basis of its staff and courses alone from across the whole metropolitan area. The students of the western region would not be well served by a second or third-class CAE in any case. The two aims were not incompatible — indeed many saw them as mutually strengthening — but they needed to be held in careful balance.

Once it was established, the Victorian Post-Secondary Education Commission (VPSEC), proved most sympathetic to FIT's funding needs, but believed it was over-optimistic and weaker in a number of areas than it claimed.[17] However good their case, FIT was simply asking for too much at once at a time when higher education seemed to have fallen out of public favour.[18] The prevailing mood in the Commonwealth government was to reduce drastically all services provided out of its Treasury. 1981 was the year of the "Review of Commonwealth Functions", popularly known as the 'Razor Gang', and one of its major recommendations was that several smaller institutions in Victoria should amalgamate with a view to significantly reducing the number of places available for teacher training. As a consequence, the Commonwealth Tertiary Education Commission (CTEC), which, since 1977, had assumed responsibility for all Commonwealth post-secondary education functions,[19] viewed the 1982–1984 triennium as a period of adjustment and consolidation for the advanced education sector. FIT believed it was immune to any effects of this until September 1981,[20] when the publication of Volume Two of the CTEC Report revealed that its cash allocation for each of the three years of the triennium had been reduced by $1 million in order to create a pool of $6 million to help buffer the effects of the amalgamations. If all went as planned, some of this money would be re-allocated, but the effect on FIT was to remove almost entirely the projected increase in funding recommended by VPSEC as compensation for past funding shortfalls.[21] Unfortunately, this announcement was made on the eve of FIT's annual Beanland Lecture which was to be delivered by the Federal Minister for Education, the Honourable Wal Fife. Passions at the Institute boiled over and a small, brief but ugly demonstration proved too much for the Minister, who left without delivering the address.[22] Initially this created some unpleasant publicity,[23] and while the "actions taken by the students . . . may have been excessive, . . . the reasons for their discontent were none the less both real and genuine".[24] In the long run, the incident probably served to highlight the FIT's plight in the larger community and strengthen resolve to overcome the problem.

At the Council meeting immediately following the demonstration it was decided to prepare a pamphlet for wide distribution on the continued under funding.[25] Entitled *What you should know about tertiary education funding in the west*, it carefully outlined the difficulties in the context of a clear statement of FIT's aims. These were employable graduates, regional responsibility and community service. Care was required because the problem of discouraging potential students and unduly antagonising the Commonwealth authorities remained. As if to emphasise this point, Council decided that an alternative brochure should be prepared for distribution to schools,[26] and CTEC did indeed take the view that the brochure was based on statistics that were open to varying interpretations.[27] By the end of 1981, the publicity campaign was rolling well with good coverage in the local press for the "West wants more education" case.[28] Even the *Australian* took up the issue.[29] The campaign received a brief setback when Senator Don Chipp, leader of the Australian Democrats, suggested that "arty crafty" subjects were more suitable to western suburbs students than maths and science,[30] and Fife saw fit to try to defend the charge of unreasonable cut backs in FIT's budget.[31] The response was a series of letters to the appropriate authorities,[32] and a public reply to Fife in the *Age*.[33] One most satisfactory outcome was the decision of Don Chipp to make a major policy statement on education at a public lecture at FIT on 5 March 1982,[34] and to take up FIT's case personally with Fife.[35]

It was, however, the change in the mood of the Australian electorate that most significantly altered the course of FIT's fortunes. The Labor Government that took office in Victoria in March 1982 was predisposed to accept the arguments put forward by FIT and special support in promoting its case in the Commonwealth arena was immediately forthcoming. "I assure you," declared Robert Fordham, Deputy Premier and Minister for Education, "of the total and whole-hearted support of the Victorian Government in endeavouring to get recognition of the need for additional facilities, additional opportunities for the people out here in the west."[36] A few months later, the new Labor Premier of Victoria, John Cain took credit for stopping the planned cut backs, reiterated his government's commitment to the education needs of the western region and hinted that teacher education might at last become a reality for FIT.[37] This was mostly manifest in VPSEC's sympathetic and supportive attitude to FIT's requests for growth in the number of places and an acceleration of the building program.[38] When in March 1983, Labor also won the federal elections, the continued sympathetic treatment of FIT seemed assured, for the initial thrust of the Hawke government's higher education policy was to increase participation rates ·and introduce greater equity across the system.

The thrust of the Hawke government's policies dovetailed with FIT's view that programs ought to be developed to help alleviate the educational deprivation in the western region. Footscray had originally been provided with technical education because some thought the area needed a higher proportion of skilled workers, but it required more than simply *opening* the 'door of opportunity' if skill levels were to match those elsewhere. As McLaren and Treyvaud had pointed out ten years previously, if the colleges were intended to extend educational equality, they had to provide bridging courses for students who were interested in courses for which they lacked prerequisite skills.[39] Initially, this proposition had provided part of the rationale for the development of the TAFE section, but it had rapidly established a distinct, multi-purpose identity of its own, and was not notably successful in providing a bridge to the CAE section.[40] The 'binary system', under which CAEs were the 'poor relations' of universities in funding terms, had not seriously addressed the equity issue even if it had increased the number of tertiary places while the savage financial cutbacks under the Fraser Government had produced a dramatic fall in overall participation. It was not long, however, before the economic and even the social, consequences of this situation aroused profound concern, and the change of government in Canberra had hastened an apparently inevitable policy reversal. The Labor government was convinced that participation and equity could be addressed simultaneously and FIT was perfectly poised to benefit from the new initiatives.

1983 was a year of considerable financial stringency for FIT, but the news for the future was all good. Not only could it admit more students, but the allocation to make up for the chronic under-funding was finally forthcoming.[41] Projected funds for the 1985–1987 triennium allowed for a 35% increase in places over the 1983 level and the introduction of teacher and nurse education programs. A new building to house the School of Business and central administration was approved for 1984.[42] Another general teaching building was approved for commencement later in the triennium.[43] Only the library now remained without the promise of a new building. This expansion was closely tied to the Commonwealth's "participation and equity" strategy. CTEC recommended that about 40% of the projected growth in student numbers should occur in the western suburbs of Melbourne and Sydney,[44] where it believed poor participation rates were a function of limited access and prior educational disadvantage. FIT's extra allocation was part of a $10.7 million Commonwealth government special grant to improve participation for disadvantaged groups under-represented in tertiary education. Its grant of $865 000 was the largest for any university or college in Australia.[45]

The government also made available up to $250 000 in 'tied grants' for the development over a number of years of specific programs to increase participation of disadvantaged groups, such as women, refugees, non-English speaking immigrants and children from non-professional families in higher education.[46] During 1983, FIT had worked on a submission for additional funding for remedial programs,[47] and in March 1984 a working party was established to develop a proposal jointly with Nepean CAE in NSW for "the production of learning material to assist students in developing better skills in the English language, numerical skills and course content".[48] FIT already enrolled above average numbers from some of the target groups, and was "recognised as an institute which has been willing to tackle the area of lower intake standards" with some success. As a consequence, the initial plan was "to strengthen, extend and monitor those existing affirmative action programs which have been developed at FIT over the past few years, in response to a perceived, on-going commitment to to students of the Western Region of Melbourne".[49] The approach thus developed provided the basis for a number of programs to enhance the performance of students suffering various forms of disadvantage that continued throughout the triennium and boosted "the status of FIT as a national leader in the Participation and Equity" area.[50] This in turn enhanced the bargaining power of FIT for continued higher levels of support.

FIT, and the College before it, had always attempted to be *of* its surrounding community, not simply *in* it — sensitive to the special strengths and weaknesses of the region's potential students and the extent to which these were ignored or condescended to by many 'outside'. At most periods, however, the parameters of policy and funding made efforts either to tailor or compensate difficult. The tension between education as a vehicle for social, even economic, change and its role in reinforcing the existing values and reward systems that sustained the *status quo* was ever present. For a period in the 1980s, however, the policy of participation and equity gave national support to FIT's most idealistic interpretation of its role in the community without jeopardising its pursuit of recognition as a quality institution within the higher education sector.

At the same time as it was extending educational opportunities for disadvantaged students, FIT was improving its reputation more generally. Its graduates displayed an excellent record in gaining suitable employment[51] and demand for places rose consistently. This was the result of several factors: a much-improved public relations campaign, closer liaison with local schools, and the expanded course range.[52] In 1977 enrolments rose by 10% and quotas were applied to two graduate diploma courses.[53] In 1979 two students received coveted Post Graduate Research Awards,[54] indicating that the quality base on which to build post-graduate work was developing. The picture from 1978 onwards is of rising demand and rising quality of student intake as measured by cut-off scores in HSC results. Figures presented in the *Staff Bulletin* in March 1982 revealed a trend that was to continue. FIT's popularity had climbed steadily over the previous three years on the basis of student preference registered with the Victorian Universities Admissions Committee. In 1982, FIT was listed as a first preference by 2.9% of students, as compared to 2.2% in 1981. This was the greatest increase for all colleges. First and second preferences increased from 2.3% in 1978 to 3.2% in 1981, and 'all preferences' from 3.2% in 1978 to 4.4% in 1981, double that of the nearest college that experienced an increase.[55] 1983 saw another increase in first preferences, with most course areas sharing the increase in popularity:

> Among the strongest were Accounting, Secretarial Practice, Chemistry, Mathematics and Computing, Australian Cultural Studies, Recreation and Physical Education. Even Engineering which was down on first preferences showed an increase in the 'all preferences' category.[56]

By 1986, FIT was able to report the seventh consecutive increase to a point where it ranked sixth in popularity among metropolitan tertiary institutions.[57]

As of 1981, CAEs in Victoria were empowered to grant degrees in their own right and over the next few years the new degrees of Bachelor of Arts (Australian Cultural Studies, Recreation), Bachelor of Applied Science (Multi-disciplinary) and Bachelor of Business (Food Retailing) were introduced as well as a wide range of new graduate and associate diplomas.[58] Then, in 1984, along with only two other CAEs in Victoria, FIT achieved the ultimate goal of all higher education institutions in Australia — the right to accredit its own courses. This put it on an equal footing with universities,[59] and 1984 seemed to herald the dawn of a new era for FIT. Its academic respectability had been acknowledged, new buildings and better funding were approved, and proposed course directions revealed an enhanced coherence and confidence about its role in the community. The 1985 *Handbook* proudly announced the Institute's new status and placed it firmly in "the vast, culturally rich western region of Melbourne".[60] No longer were community needs to be met merely through limited access to certain facilities, but through courses that were timely and focussed on clearly defined regional needs. In 1985 much planning and agitating — some of it, in the case of teacher training stretching back to the 1950s — came to fruition. There were new degree courses in Multicultural Studies and Primary Education, new diploma courses in Nursing and Primary Teaching, new associate diploma courses in Computing, Fitness Leadership, Labour Studies and Occupational Health and Safety and new graduate diplomas in Exercise Management and Building Project Management.

The degree in Multicultural Studies was a logical development from the Australian Cultural Studies course. It was also a valuable response to the special needs of a region that had for the entire post-war period played host to succeeding waves of immigrants. FIT already offered a range of community languages, and this new course pointed the way in which it could become both a 'Centre of Excellence' and serve specific regional needs. Students would take a major in Intercultural studies and at least one sub major in an accredited community language such as Greek, Italian, Macedonian, Vietnamese[61] or Maltese. The course, designed to produce teachers of social studies, community workers, public servants and language teachers, was available at beginners and advanced language levels.

The introduction of education courses was similarly focussed on the needs and students of the region. The argument that the western region needed its own teacher training facilities had surfaced regularly in the post-war period with little result. Finally in the 1980s a convincing case became possible. Firstly, the western region was not only short of teachers, it needed teachers specially trained to deal with the problems and strengths of the area. Secondly, there were definable characteristics of the region which, it was believed, might best be served by a specially designed program. Thirdly, experience showed that students not only preferred to do their training close to home, but that where they did that training had a pronounced influence on where they ultimately chose to teach.[62] Finally, a high proportion of FIT graduates were, in fact, becoming teachers, but they had to get their qualifications elsewhere, often at some disadvantage to themselves.[63] The principles of participation and equity were easily harnessed to the program with 85% of the intake from the western region. Prospective students had to demonstrate a commitment to working in the area,[64] and it was assumed that at least 45% would come from non English-speaking backgrounds.

The FIT education courses included some innovative features. Several parts of the program were school based, while the multicultural studies component was "significantly community based", sending the students out to be "immersed in the culture of the 'west'". They had to become "actively engaged in local institutions, work places, cultural groups, and various social and political organisations," and, on the basis of this, "develop personal viewpoints about the nature of society in the west and the major features of its culture" and "consider the importance of these features in terms of primary education" in the region.[65] Historically, nurse education had been regional and hospital based, so when the decision was made to move it into some colleges of advanced education, FIT was perfectly poised to establish a nursing department within the Faculty of Applied Science with close links to the Western General Hospital. The new course was specifically geared to the multicultural aspects of nursing and provided a major boost to the proportion of female students studying at FIT.

While these new developments were taking place, the old course areas continued to grow and develop and the Schools were renamed Faculties. The Faculty of Business was flourishing and took the name John Reid Faculty of Business as a result of a generous endowment from Sir John Reid, Chairman of James Hardie Co. The largest of FIT's four faculties in 1985, it offered courses to 1400 students.[66] The Engineering and Applied Science Faculties, like the others, were linked to industry through membership of the Course Advisory Boards which assisted with course design and review. Institute staff in these areas gained an impressive record in the development and application of innovative techniques. The Urban Studies students and staff acquired a prominent place in the local community via their research projects carried out in the region, and several departments began to offer short courses, such as the one for owner/builders of houses, that proved extremely popular. The Physical Education Department began to expand into the paramedical area, catering for the injured worker as well as the high-achieving athlete and community recreational needs. The library achieved national recognition for the development of databases and information networks, even if its book stock was still limited by severe financial constraints and adequate accommodation was still a pipe dream, even in 1986.

Internally, there were also substantial changes in the decade 1976 to 1986, as the principles of 'open government' became more firmly entrenched in policy and practice. Pressure for change from staff was still concentrated on the Board of Studies. Although changes in 1978, particularly the amalgamation of the Policy and Resources Committees, had addressed some of the causes for discontent, the balance of power was still felt to lie with the 'old' departments. The separation of the School of General Studies into two separate Schools of Business and General Studies in 1979 altered this balance but the tensions were bound to increase in a situation of static and even declining resources. A working party to advise on methods of funding allocation within the Institute was established in March 1979 in the hope of devising a "Resource Allocation Model" that would meet the "aspirations and needs of the academic staff to bring a sense of equity and justice of open government to the Institute".[67] One of the initiatives of this working party was to provide an opportunity for the whole Institute to pause and discuss the broad aspects of current practice and future policy that were too easily submerged in the 'busyness' of day to day routines. Progress was not exactly swift, but two days were set aside in June 1980 for the holding of "Fundamental Issues Seminars". These canvassed subjects such as administrative organisation, student numbers, the proportion of graduate to undergraduate students, the balance between teaching, research and community development activities, entrance standards, the relative weighting of job-market factors and broader community needs as well as the criteria for allocation of capital resources.[68]

All this activity helped FIT focus its attention clearly on its role and status. In the short run, the working party managed to demonstrate just how divisive the issue was,[69] and there was much entrenched resistance to a new formula. In the long run, however, substantial reform was achieved. Greater devolution of decision making to individual faculties, combined with the establishment of a Planning Office, led to more sophisticated management of the Institute's resources, and the last vestiges of highly centralised and authoritarian administrative practices finally gave way. A new spirit of openness was taking hold. No longer was the Board of Studies to be a secretive, non-representative body, but rather membership of it was to be regarded as conferring certain rights, one of which was "access to information". At the same time it also conferred the responsibility to share such information with other members of staff.[70]

At the student level, a tiny campus like FIT did not usually generate headline news. Students were susceptible to the same trends and issues as those in similar institutions, but the dominance of subjects requiring 'practical' work, and therefore a large number of class-contact hours, reduced the time for students to spend together out of class. Even with the 'humanising' of the the campus, through the introduction of arts courses, physical education, nursing and teaching, the applied emphasis of these courses and anxiety about employment prospects that was a feature of the 1970s tended to militate against the relaxed student life that breeds sophisticated student politics. Perhaps this was just as well, for till the old secondary school building was in part refurbished to house the student union and various student services in the early 1980s, there were very few places for students to group together comfortably. Even more importantly, a number of student rights were incorporated in the initial constitution of FIT without any student battles to achieve them, while the style of the Beanland era had been very authoritarian in its dealing with the SRC. As a consequence, despite the long existence of an SRC, there was only a weak tradition of forthright and responsible student participation in the affairs of the institution, and it was not until Mills arrived that the separate interests and rights of students were taken even vaguely seriously. Radicalism barely ruffled the campus for much of the 1970s, though student publications gave predictable doses of offence to the administration. Students were not notably interested in student politics, to the regular lament of members of the SRC and other groups of activists. Even social activities were difficult to organise at various times, and in the early years it even proved difficult to find enough students to sit on the Institute bodies that allowed for student representation.

Many would still shudder to think that the ability to organise a demonstration was a sign of maturity in a student body, but the broader purposes of tertiary education imply the development of individuals who can think critically about their work and take positions. In lamenting a demonstration opportunity that was lost in 1971 when the Governor-General opened building D, the Editor of *Seed* argued that in order to make it clear that FIT was something more than a

> centre for students to be trained in a certain field and then be used as skilled labour by the industrial and commercial interests who run the Institute and make sure they receive their quota of freshly trained engineers and accountants . . . the SRC should have at least organized a demonstration . . . The demo. didn't have to be large and rowdy, but just large

enough and well enough organized to show all our autocratic rulers who run the Institute that all is not milk and honey at the Institute.[71]

Notwithstanding the protests that Council would have made, this was a point of view that needed airing, and communications between Council and students were seriously in need of improvement at this stage. By the end of the decade, students could be found to engage in predictable demonstrations, albeit on a small scale, such as the protest against the opening of the Hoadley Sports Complex by the Duke of Edinburgh in 1981.

Of even greater significance than this rather sensational form of student activity, however, was the increase in the number of students actively and constructively engaged in general student affairs and in representing student interests on decision-making bodies within FIT. The redefinition of the relationship between the student body and administration and staff that was implicit in FIT's development into a fully autonomous tertiary institution was very slow, partly because the issues appeared so much less urgent than a number of the other relationships, but gradually more formal arrangements were put in place. Several developments in the late 1970s were symptomatic of greater student sophistication. The first of these was the gradual revival of the SRC, which had lapsed in the mid-1970s after the introduction of the student group Forum and the Student Association, into little more that a political club under the control of the Union Board which was effectively dominated by staff members. In 1984, after some agitation, it was reconstituted as a properly independent and representative body[72] of the sort that a mature tertiary college required if the voice of students was to be heard in a coherent and organised way. This new SRC took a much more critical interest in the affairs of FIT in a climate that was increasingly supportive of constructive participation and access to information. The SRC usually provided the student representative on Council, and further improvement in the lines of communication between student bodies and Council was achieved with the formation of a Council/Union Liaison Committee in 1979. Changes also took place within the Union Board itself, and by 1986 students had succeeded in altering its composition so that student members outnumbered staff members by two to one.

At the Council level, the increasing volume and complexity of work had required a restructuring of the committee system[73] and a much more careful consideration of its composition and involvement with the institution as a whole. Efforts to link the members of Council more generally into the life of the Institute had been largely successful and the requirement that Council members attach themselves to a Course Advisory Board was no longer felt necessary in 1985.[74] Council proceedings were made more accessible under pressure from both staff and students, and the Cain government's 'Freedom of Information' legislation made even clearer the responsibility to make their proceedings and records accessible to all with a legitimate interest. One of the major ways of implementing the spirit of these new expectations was to allow a greater number of groups either direct representation or at least observer status. FIT moved quickly to grant observer status to the Professional and General Staff Associations, the SRC and the Union Board.[75] This was later expanded to include representatives of the regional municipal councils.

The granting of full autonomy in 1984 required further alterations to the Constitution, but the pressure of business delayed serious consideration of this for some time. On the question of membership, however, steps to achieve representation from a broader cross-section of the community had to be taken immediately, for the new state Labor government had very strong views on the composition of such bodies.[76] This led to the establishment of a "Tertiary Register" and advertising in the local press for interested people to put themselves forward.[77] The Council had, in any case ceased to be simply a group of men with industrial expertise largely recruited from the Rotary or 'old boy' network, but there was a need for members with skills related to newer course areas and, for women members. New members who came onto Council in the 1980s included Mrs Joan Kirner, Labor member for Melbourne West Province in the Legislative Council; Ian McKechnie, Manager of Engineering Training with Telecom; David Penman, Anglican Bishop of the western region; Len Coysh, Executive Director of the Australian Federation of Airline Pilots; Sister Mary Kehoe, Director of the Institute of Catholic Education, Mercy Campus; Edna McGrath, Director of Nursing, Western General Hospital; Eric Charles, Victorian Manager, James Hardie Co.; Susan Fordham, secondary teacher and local resident; and Sadie Stevens, Head of the

Junior Division of Penleigh and Essendon Grammar. The Council also benefited from the quality and commitment of the elected representatives who were instrumental in strengthening the links between those who attended daily to the tasks and routines of higher education and the external members.

By 1986, building K was nearing completion and building G under way. FIT had reached a confident maturity as student numbers began to edge toward the 5000 mark and the itegration of teaching and community service seemed to have reached a nice balance. The partnership between the Physical Education Department and the community was expressed through the Boating Complex on the banks of the Maribyrnong River, the maintenance of the public playing fields and tennis courts, and public access to the facilities in the Hoadley building itself. The library was open for public use and the Footscray Foundation sought to develop the arts in the region. All the faculties offered an available resource of expertise. Principally, of course, FIT served the community by seeking to "provide a first rate and rigorous education"[78] that produced employable graduates. It also sought to behave as a concerned and committed citizen trying to balance the needs of the community, as expressed at local level, with wider 'national' imperatives as these were defined through Commonwealth and state education policy. By the 1980s, relevance and accountability had become central features of education policy, and it was a mould into which FIT seemed ready to fit comfortably.

Much had changed since the foundation of the School. The simple vocational model, which was largely the product of a class-based assumption that the working class needed training and industry needed skilled operatives, had lost ground. So too had the tendency to equate 'technical' with a simple-minded notion of 'practical'. The new emphasis was encapsulated in the word 'applied'. Courses still had a quite specific occupational focus — 'practical work' was important — but theoretical study and academic rigour were also essential elements. The era when science and technology had stood apart — one pursuing understanding of the world, the other seeking to control and order it — had passed. Technology had come to seem a natural extension of science. The separation between technology and the humanities had been even wider, but the uses of technology had profound social consequences, and the social and economic world provided a host of problems to which the understanding gained in the study of the arts and social sciences could be 'applied'. In any case, the boundaries between all these were blurring.

The technical schools and colleges of advanced education had let in general studies only very reluctantly. It *might* have been possible to 'liberalise' technical education by teaching engineering and chemistry in ways that did not neglect the civic, social, human and cultural dimensions necessary to a total education — an education valued for its intrinsic merit rather than simply for the uses to which it could be put. In the post-war period, lip service was paid to the notion that students needed education for 'life as well as a living', but the humanities subjects remained 'add ons', often scorned or tamed into 'useful' units such as 'report writing'. The CAEs, therefore, were 'liberalised' — exposed to the influences of the liberal arts — by the introduction of separate courses, then departments, and eventually whole faculties. With these courses came a much expanded definition of 'vocational' and 'applied' that allowed for 'community needs', as well as industry needs, in ways that had not been possible earlier. With them also came a questioning and an urgency that had rarely ruffled the engineering classrooms. FIT in the 1980s was producing graduates able to apply themselves to the social and cultural, as well and the economic and industrial, development of the region.

The foundation Principal, Arch Hoadley, would have been well pleased with these particular developments and the enormous expansion of the School he pioneered. The separation of Footscray Technical School into three distinctive institutions catering for more segmented educational demands, was a clear expression of the change and development in the provision of educational services in the area. Footscray, and the expanding western suburbs as a whole were, at last, gaining opportunities which had long been taken for granted in other parts of the metropolitan area. There were a range of secondary schools and TAFE colleges. FIT offered a necessary cap to this system, providing courses with a special focus on the region as well as many courses found in colleges elsewhere in the state. Special needs were being met, but opportunities were not limited by these alone.

Footscray in the 1980s, of course, was no more the 'Birmingham of the South' than it had ever been. The technical school had not altered the industrial destiny of the area. The economic forces that shaped the western suburbs of Melbourne were scarcely amenable to such minor details, but the School had played a critical role in the destiny of individuals. Education has played a central part in determining the life chances of Australians, those who succeeded achieved an almost certain elevation of social status. The School undoubtedly made a major contribution to raising the skill level in the community. The best of its early graduates, especially those with diplomas, did not so much apply themselves to advancing Footscray's particular economic dreams, but rather entered the large state enterprises extending the power, energy, transport and communication resources of Victoria. The institution's history mirrors the shifts and changes of educational philosophy and policy over 70 years, but with increasing autonomy came an enhanced ability to define and serve local needs while conforming to national objectives. Its greatest value to the region in the future lies in maintaining that ability.

In some ways, Footscray had changed less than the schools that served it. The western suburbs had spread far out over the dry, windswept Werribee Plain, well beyond Footscray, Yarraville and Sunshine. The newest suburbs were less obviously working class and more purely residential. They did not mix factories and dwellings the way the old industrial suburbs had done, but the older areas remained essentially industrial. Footscray and Sunshine alone still accounted for 46% of manufacturing establishments in the region in 1981.[79] These covered a diverse range of industries dominated by fabricated metal products (17.9% of establishments), machinery and equipment (13.8%), wood products and furniture (12.4%), chemicals, petroleum and coal products (9.8%) and food and beverages (8.0%).[80] More people continued to be employed in manufacturing than in any other sector of the workforce, but the proportion was declining. The economic downturn of the 1970s reduced employment in manufacturing by 10% between 1976 and 1981 alone.[81] To some extent this decline and the similarly significant reduction in employment in the retail and wholesale sector has been made up by an increase in areas such as community services, but unemployment remains more serious than in other parts of Melbourne. It is obvious that FIT and the Footscray College of TAFE have a critical role to play in softening the transition to a scaled-down manufacturing sector in the region, as well as offering appropriate courses to the large numbers of children growing up in the outlying areas.

The industrial history of Footscray followed lines clearly discernible in 1916, but the discontinuity in population structure is marked. The inner western suburbs became a major receiving area for immigrants from many countries and many made their permanent homes there. Of the 1981 population, 33% had been born overseas, compared with 27% for Melbourne as a whole, with the major proportion coming from the United Kingdom, Italy, Yugoslavia and Malta. The region also included a fast-growing Vietnamese population, and recent arrivals constituted 10% of the total overseas born population.[82] Here again, the opportunities for FIT and the TAFE College to address the very specific needs of a multicultural community are finding concrete expression in special courses or special programs designed to enhance success rates in more traditional course areas.

The year 1986 was, finally, a time of great loss for FIT, marked by the untimely death of the foundation Director, Doug Mills, just as it became possible to pause and take pride in his achievements. Mills came at a time when FIT desperately needed leadership. He took up the challenge and revealed himself capable of cultivating a new type of institution quite unlike anything he had experienced. He had the quality of vision necessary to transform an engineering school into a multi-purpose college of advanced education, when it would have been so much easier to have stayed with a much simpler definition of 'technical'. Within the Institute, he sought consensus, but nevertheless took decisions firmly and was widely respected by his peers throughout the education community. He committed little to paper, and was not especially involved in policy development. Rather, he was an administrator who understood the mechanisms by which policy could best be implemented. His energy, affability and, above all, his fierce and unswerving commitment to FIT, earned him affection and respect, even if it sometimes created conflicts that were difficult to resolve. Among his great strengths were an irrepressible optimism that enabled him to lead effectively through periods when gloom and pessimism might well have prevailed, an easy informality that made for open communication at most levels, and an ability to harness rather than stifle the various talents of those around him. An energetic 'builder' in his private time, he took special pride in the handsome new buildings gracing the Ballarat Road site and the naming of building K in his honour was a fitting memorial.

Sad as the loss was, the times had changed and FIT had grown to a size where one person would be unlikely even to want to dominate it in the way Hoadley, Beanland and Mills had effectively done. The process of selecting a successor was undertaken by the Council in consultation with the whole staff, revealing that a true partnership between these two was developing soundly. The choice of the Assistant Director, Dr Irwin Herrman, an experienced and successful administrator with a political science background, demonstrated emphatically that the old assumption that only an engineer could run a technical institution had finally died.

1. I. M. Herrman. "Statement by Assistant Director at Policy and Resources Committee Meeting", *op cit.*, p 5.
2. 10 August 1977; Copy of speech attached to FIT Council Minutes, 25 October 1977.
3. Director's Report to FIT Council, 23 August 1977.
4. *Ibid.*, 28 February 1978.
5. *Staff Bulletin*, 14 June 1979.
6. FIT Council Minutes, 22 August 1978.
7. *Ibid.*
8. *Ibid.*, 22 May 1979.
9. *Staff Bulletin*, 14 June 1979.
10. FIT Council Minutes, 24 April 1979.
11. *Age*, 5 February 1980, p 10.
12. I. M. Herrman, 'Statement by Assistant Director at Policy and Resources Committee Meeting', *op. cit.*, p 4.
13. "Submission to VPSEC from the Council, FIT, for special grant of $600,000 to remedy past deficiencies in funding and for an increase of 12.5% in the level of funding for the Institute for the 1982–1984 triennium", FIT Council Minutes, 25 September 1979.
14. D. R. Mills to G. J. Allen, Chairman VPSEC, 28 September 1979.
15. J. McLaren to *Age*, 22 October 1979, p 10. Also *Footscray Mail*, 24 October 1979.
16. J. McLaren, *Footscray Mail*, 24 October 1979.
17. Director's Report to FIT Council, 27 November 1979.
18. FIT Council Papers, Buildings and Equipment Committee Report, 10 February 1981; Director's Report to FIT Council, 22 April 1980 & 27 May 1980.
19. This new body incorporated the Universities Commission, the Committee on Advanced Education and the TAFE Commission.

20. See, for example, "Razor Cuts won't alter bright FIT future — Acting Director", *Staff Bulletin*, 14 May 1981.
21. *Staff Bulletins*, 1 & 29 October 1981, FIT Council Minutes, 27 October 1981.
22. *Staff Bulletin*, 1 October 1981.
23. *Ibid.*, 15 October 1981.
24. *Ibid.*, 4 March 1982.
25. FIT Council Minutes, 27 October 1981.
26. *Ibid.*, 24 November 1982.
27. H. S. Houston to G. Longbottom, 10 February 1982. Attachment to *ibid*.
28. *Melton Bacchus Marsh Mail*, 20 January 1982, p 14; *Footscray Mail*, 8 December 1981, 19 January 1982; *Keilor Messenger*, 8 December 1981; *Sunshine Advocate*, 27 January 1982; *Western Times*, 3 March 1982.
29. 20 January 1982.
30. *Footscray Mail*, 2 February 1982. This statement was made in the context of opinion that it was no good educating students for jobs that were disappearing.
31. Letter to the Editor, *Age*, 20 February 1982.
32. Attachments to FIT Council Papers, 23 March 1982.
33. M. Carey President, FIT Professional Staff Association, 1 March 1982.
34. *Staff Bulletin*, 4 March 1982; *Footscray Advertiser*, 25 February 1982.
35. *Ibid.*, 13 May 1982; I. Herrman to Don Chipp, 19 April 1982, thanking him for his efforts. Attachment to FIT Council Papers, 27 April 1982. *Footscray Advertiser*, 20 May 1982.
36. *Staff Bulletin*, 24 June 1982.
37. *Ibid.*, 25 November 1982.
38. *Ibid.*, 17 February 1983.
39. E. R. Treyvaud & J. McLaren, *Equal but Cheaper The Development of Australian Colleges of Education*, MUP, Melbourne, 1976, p 78.
40. I. Herrman, "Present at the Creation", Address to the AGM of TAFE College Councils Association, 16 September 1985, p 8.
41. The proposal from VPSEC was for twice the average per full-time student. Director's Report to FIT Council, 25 October 1983.
42. This alone would allow enrolments in business studies and applied science courses to grow by 500 full-time places. *Staff Bulletin*, 27 October 1983.
43. *Ibid.*, 24 November 1983.
44. *Ibid.*, 24 May 1984.
45. *Ibid.*, 2 February 1984.
46. I. Herrman, "Present at the Creation", *op. cit.*, p 6.
47. FIT Board of Studies Minutes, 14 September 1983 & 12 March 1980.
48. *Staff Bulletin*, 29 March 1984.
49. *Ibid.*, 11 October 1984.
50. I. M. Herrman, 'Curriculum Vitae', p 5, FIT Archive.

51. For example, 96% of FIT's 1978 graduates were employed or pursuing further study, *Footscray Mail*, 29 August 1979. 95% of 1979 graduates employed, Staff Bulletin, 21 August 1980.

52. *Staff Bulletin*, 18 March 1982.

53. FIT Council Minutes, 22 February 1977.

54. Only about twenty of these were awarded to CAEs each year, *ibid.*, 27 February 1979.

55. *Staff Bulletin*, 18 March 1982. Note also *Footscray Advertiser*, 28 February 1980.

56. *Staff Bulletin*, 9 December 1982.

57. *Ibid.*, 17 July 1986.

58. Graduate Diplomas: Industrial Relations, Vacuum Technology, Accounting, Business Science, Hospitality and Tourism, Urban Planning, Commercial Data Processing, Exercise for Rehabilitation, Plant Engineering; Associate Diplomas: Digital Electronics and Computing.

59. *Staff Bulletin*, 2 February 1984 & FIT Council Minutes.

60. FIT *Handbook*, 1985.

61. FIT was the first tertiary institution outside Indo-China to offer Vietnamese.

62. *Staff Bulletin*, 12 May 1983.

63. 9.5% of FIT graduates undertook teacher training compared with 2.3% from Ballarat, 1.0% from RMIT, 0.5% from PIT and 3.2% form CIT, *Staff Bulletin*, 3 March 1983.

64. *Community and Real Estate News*, 17 September 1985; *Staff Bulletin*, 14 February 1985.

65. FIT *Handbook*, 1987 pp 405–406.

66. *Staff Bulletin*, 24 October 1985.

67. Board of Studies Minutes, 12 March 1980.

68. *Staff Bulletin*, 29 May and 26 June 1980.

69. FIT Board of Studies Minutes, 10 December 1980.

70. I. M. Herrman, 'Statement by Assistant Director at Policy and Resources Committee Meeting', *op. cit.*, p 4.

71. *Seed*, Vol. 3, No 11, p 2.

72. Report Council/Union Liaison Committee, FIT Council Papers, 6 May 1982.

73. FIT Council Minutes, 22 February 1977.

74. *Ibid.*, 28 May 1985.

75. FIT Council Papers, Executive Committee Minutes, 2 August 1983. See also *Staff Bulletin*, 29 September 1983.

76. FIT Council Minutes, 23 August 1983.

77. *Staff Bulletin*, 25 October 1984. FIT Council Minutes, 27 November 1984.

78. I. M. Herrman, *Staff Bulletin*, 24 October 1985.

79. K. G. Wilson, *Manufacturing Industry in the Western Metropolitan Region of Melbourne, Vol. II An Introductory Analysis of Firm Data*, Melbourne Western Region Commission, March 1985, p 49.

80. *Ibid.*, p 26.

81. K. Weiss, "Western Region Social Profile", Western Suburbs Regional Centre, Department of Community Services, April 1984, p 31.

82. *Ibid.*, pp 22–25.

Appendices

A. COUNCIL MEMBERS 1915–1986

(in chronological order of appointment)

A J Pearce
: 1915–1919,
President 1916
Secretary Engine Drivers' and Engineers' Union
First Labor member Footscray City Council.

H M Box
: 1915–1963
Medical Doctor
Member Mechanics Institute
Vice president 1916–1917, 1933–43
President 1918
1919 presented inaugural scholarship grant of £200
i.e. £10 per annum.

J H Hooper
: 1915–1922
J H Hooper & Co Drapery Store
Vice president 1916
President 1917
1921 provided £200 to found scholarship for commercial classes.

E Johnstone
: 1915–1925
Assistant Manager Michaelis Hallenstein in 1916,
later opened his own tannery in North Melbourne
Executive member Mechanics Institute
Secretary 1915–June 1916
Treasurer 1916–1918.

J A Carmody	1915–1949 Footscray City Electrical Engineer Secretary 1921–22.
J L Dearie	1915–1916 Briefly a Labor member of Footscray City Council.
W H Fielding	1915–1916 Worked for Harbour Trust before starting business as a wood dealer & provision merchant Member Yarraville PLC, MLC, Melbourne West Province Footscray City Councillor.
J R Johnston	1915–1920 Manager Tyne Foundry, South Melbourne Footscray City Councillor.
J Lemmon MLA	1915–1916 Labor MLA for Williamstown.
J Millar	1915–1916.
P R Richardson	1915–1919 D Richardson Gears Pty Ltd Treasurer 1918.
F E Shillabeer	1915–1918 Building Contractor Mayor Footscray 1902 & 1916.
E W Trend	1915–1932 Works Manager Mt Lyell Co. Graduate Ballarat School of Mines President 1919–1932 Vice president TSAV 1927–1928 President TSAV 1928–1929 Technical Schools representative on Melbourne University Council 1928–1932.
C Walker	1915–1918 'Independent' Footscray.
D Bayley	1916–1922 General Manager, Colonial Ammunition Works Vice president 1921.
J Jamieson	1916–1922 *Footscray Advertiser* Proprietor Treasurer 1919–1922.
S G Garnsworthy	1916–1919 Australian Glass Manufacturers.

E S Hallenstein

1916–1939
One of the Proprietors of Michaelis Hallenstein Tannery.

T F M Smith

1916–1920
1920 donated scholarship £10 per annum
Made annual donation to the library
Bequeathed £300 as endowment for scholarships and prizes 1934.

R Ferguson

1917–1943
Assistant Chief Mechanical Engineer, Railways (Newport Workshops)
Vice president 1922–37.

R G Parsons

1918–1974
General Manager, Colonial Gas Association
Vice president 1922–1932
President 1932–43, 1951–1955
Member Committee TSAV 1932–53
President TSAV 1935–36, 1936–37
Member University of Melbourne Council
Member Council for Public Instruction
Appointed Swinburne Technical School Council 1935, (President 1954–72).

H E Richardson

1919–1937
Chairman Directors Richardson Gears
Treasurer 1922–31.

A E Hughes

1920–1948
Engineer in Chief Colonial Sugar Refinery.

Dr A J Leach

1920–1924
District Inspector of Schools.

L B Lloyd

1920–1930
Member Footscray City Council
1923 LB & M Lloyd and their uncle donated £600 at 5% p.a. for the 'LBM' scholarship but wished to remain anonymous.

C A Hoadley

1921–1922
During the period he was General Manager, Richardson Gears Ltd. and not principal of the school.

W H Cuming

1921–1929
Proprietor Cuming Smith & Co.

W A McKinna	1921–1954. Amalgamated Engineers Society President 1944–45 Treasurer 1932–43, 1946–54.
I H Boas	1923–1939 Chemical Engineer, Michaelis Hallenstein 1928 appointed to head Forest Products division of CSIR.
J A Stephens	1923–1926 Footscray City Councillor.
E R Davey MA	1924–1939 District Inspector of Schools.
E A Mollard JP	1925–1930, 1964–1984 FTS Student Director of Industrial Service Engineers and Associated companies. Chairman and Managing Director of Jamec Tools Pty Ltd Member of Victorian Council of Australian Institute of Exports Vice president 1967–1968 President 1970–1976.
D O'Toole	1927–1936 Footscray City Councillor.
J T Gray M.C.E.	1929–1955 Represented Williamstown City Council.
N Taylor	1929–1945 Imperial Chemical Ltd Vice president 1938–1944.
N K S Brodribb O.B.E. F.I.C.	1930–1938 Chemical Engineer in charge of Munitions Dept, Maribyrnong.
J Cuming	1933–1938 Commonwealth Fertilizer Ltd.
A V Hansen	1937–1939 Footscray City Councillor.
F Ayre M.I.Gas. E.	1938–1945 General Manager Parkinson Stove Co.
G O'K Simcock	1938–1954 Australian Consolidated Industries, Glass manufacturing Treasurer 1944–45 Vice president 1947–1950.

M M O'Loughlin   1938–1951
AMIE (Aust)   Munitions Dept
Vice president 1945–1946
President 1947–1950.

A R Ashton   1939–1948
B.Sc Dip.Ed.   District Inspector.

W W de Steiger   1940–1947
Distribution Engineer of Electrical Engineering
Branch, Victorian Railways.

J R Wilson   1940–1948
Power Station Superintendent, Newport
Vice president 1944–1945
President 1946.

J Edgerton   1945–1953
General Manager Melbourne (Lion) Iron & Steel
Mills
Vice president 1947–1951.

J Wood B.Sc   1945–1946
Chief Engineer ICIANZ.

A E Shepherd MLA   1947–1952
Attended Bendigo School of Mines.
Labor MLA for Sunshine — later MLA for Footscray
Footscray City Councillor.

H C Richardson   1948–1957
Vice president 1950–1956.

A Blomfield   1949–1955
CSR.

J Haddow   1949–1952
B.A.Dip.Ed.   District Inspector of Schools.

R Rankin   1950–1986
AMIE (Aust)   Student FTS
Engineer Victorian Railways
Treasurer 1955–1976.

E J W Herbert   1951–1966
General Manager Ordnance Factories
Vice president 1953–1955
TSAV Committee 1952–1962
President 1956–1958.

E C T Mathewson   1951–1957
District Inspector.

W J Cuming BME   1953–1986
                      Works Manager Commonwealth Fertilizer &
                      Chemicals Ltd Yarraville, then Technical Manager
                      ICIANZ
                      Vice president 1959–1964
                      President 1965–1969
                      Foundation member of Board of Studies of VIC.

J W D Ebeling   1954–1964
                      Joint Managing Director C E Ebeling & Sons Pty
                      Ltd
                      Vice president 1962–1964.

R F Vian   1955–1964
                      Area Manager ACI Subsidiaries Spotswood
                      Deputy Chairman Lower Yarra Crossing Authority
                      Vice president 1956–1958
                      President 1959–1961.

A R Hallenstein   1957–1959
                      Director Michaelis Hallenstein Pty Ltd
                      Son of former Council member
                      Vice president 1958–59.

R Chapman   1957–1962
B.A.Dip.Ed.   District Inspector.

J A Smithson   1957–1977
                      General Manager, Olympic Tyre & Rubber Co.
                      Vice president 1960–1961
                      President 1962–1964.

A N Barlow   1957–1961
                      Engineer, Victorian Railways
                      Footscray City Councillor.

G R Schintler   1959–1976
J.P. O.B.E.   MLA for Yarraville.

I T Perry   1961–1966
                      Senior Examiner of Airmen, Civil Aviation Dept.
                      Footscray City Councillor.

W A Tippett   1962–?
MASME,AMIE   Managing Director Harland Engineering (Aust)
                      Pty Ltd
                      Vice president 1965–67.

J B Prichtor   1962–1963
                      District Inspector.

N E Gilbert   1963–1965
                      Factory manager James Hardie Pty Ltd.

J H Hood	1964–1971 Works Manager Australian Glass Manufacturers Co Pty Ltd and then technical officer ACI Vice president 1965.

J H Breardon
B.A.B.Ed.
1964–1977
District Inspector.

P S Parkin
1965–1967
General Manager Petroleum Refineries Altona.

Dr E Barraclough
1965–1968
Deputy Managing Director of Monsanto Chemicals
Vice president 1966.

T A Roberts
1967–1976
Manager Commonwealth Government Marine Engine Works
FTS Diplomas
Vice president 1970–76.

P Perry
B.Sc. B.E.(Sydney)
1967–1974
Works Manager Union Carbide
Vice president 1968–74.

W H Roberts
Master M.E. Dip M.E.
1967–1969
Secretary for Fuel and Power, Victorian Government.

S Rust
1967–1970
Area Manager ACI Ltd.

J F Bristow
1968–
Army Design Establishment
Footscray City Councillor (ALP).

D R Mills B.E.E.
1968–1970
Inspector Technical Schools
VIC Representative.

R W Boschen
B.Sc Dip.Ed TPTC
1968–1970
First Staff representative.

A G Murray
B.Sc Dip.M.E.
Dip E.E. Dip Appl Sc
TTTC
1968–1978
Vice Principal/Assistant Director
Board of Studies Representative.

M D McCluskey
1969–1969
VIC Representative.

G D Thompson
1969–1986
FTS student.
Formerly Acting principal RMIT and head of Moulding department.

R Armitage B.A.B.Sc Dip.Ed.	1970– Education Department Representative Vice president 1985–1986.
A Ferguson	1970– VIC Representative University of Melbourne (Electronics).
G J Lowe	1970–1973, July 1979– Staff Representative.
H B Tribe	June 1970– Director Monsanto Aust. and Business Director Resin & Moulding Compounds Director Australian Fluorine Chemicals Pty Ltd & Revinex Australia Ltd. (Both associate companies of Monsanto) Vice president 1975–76 President 1977–79 FTS student.
W P Beevers	1970–1982 Grazier, Managing Director of several companies Director of Prism Paints Pty Ltd then Palm Motel Pty Ltd Vice president 1977–81.
G Longbottom	1971– Marketing Manager Michaelis Bayley later with Madehurst Pty Ltd Vice president Oct 1976–79 President 1980–84.
W de Campo	1973–1974 SEC Assistant General Manager (Administration) FTS student.
D English	1974–1976 Staff Representative.
L Perry	Student Observer 1974.
R C Fordham	1974–1982 MLA Footscray (ALP).
A J Galea	Student Observer 1975.
F Dennis	1975–1977 General Manager Melbourne Hilton President Catering Institute of Australia.
I Malloy	Student Observer 1976.

P Green	1976– Staff Representative.
J Rankine	Staff Observer 1976–1977.
I Secomb	1976–1983 Principal Arthur Secomb and Co.
G Thoms	1976–1978 Obstetrician, Western General Hospital.
D Worland	1977–1978 Staff Representative.
D Blake	Student Representative 1977.
F Trimboli	1977– Real Estate Agent, Footscray.
A Wallace	1977–1980.
J Betson	1977– Board of Inspectors, Secondary Division.
N Hartmann	1978– General Manufacturing manager and a Director, Dunlop Olympic Tyres Vice president 1982–85.
J McIntosh	1978– Executive ICIANZ Former president Western Industries Association Waite Consulting Management Group FTS Student Vice president 1980–84 President 1985–1986.
S Ruffini	Student Representative 1978.
Dr I Herrman	1979–81, Assistant Director Board of Studies Representative.
G Brown	Student Representative 1979.
T Tsoudalakis	Student Representative 1980.
G George	1981–1982 Staff Representative.
G Sandy	1981–1984 Staff Representative.
A Baer	Student Representative 1981.
W Van Lint	1982–1983 Staff Representative.

I Hilton	1982–1984 Board of Studies Representative.
Miss A Boyd	Student Representative 1982.
J Barton	1982–1983, March 1984– Academic Staff Representative.
Joan Kirner	1982–1985 MLC Melbourne West Province (ALP).
Miss D Manallack	Student Representative 1983.
J Horwood	1983– Academic Staff Representative.
I McKechnie	1983– Manager Engineering Training Telecom.
D Penman	1983–1985 Anglican Bishop Western Region 1982–1984 Elected Anglican Archbishop of Melbourne 1984.
R Vinen	1983– Academic Staff Representative.
B Wise	1984– Board of Studies Representative.
D Cowie	Student Representative 1984.
L Coysh	1985– Executive Director Australian Federation of Airline Pilots.
Sr Mary Kehoe	1985– Director, Institute of Catholic Education, Mercy Campus.
Edna McGrath	1985– Director of Nursing, Western General Hospital.
P Nazum	Student Representative 1985.
E Charles	1985– James Hardie.
S Fordham	1985–
J Yiannis	Student Representative 1985.
R Batrouney	1986– Arthur Secomb & Co Solicitors.
G Ryan	Student Representative 1986.
Mrs S Stevens	1986– Head, Junior Division, Penleigh & Essendon Grammar School.

B. DURATION OF COURSES OFFERED IN VICTORIAN TECHNICAL SCHOOLS

1919–1946

	1919	1926	1939	1946
YEAR 8				DIPLOMA
YEAR 7	DIPLOMA		DIPLOMA *	DIPLOMA
YEAR 6	DIPLOMA	DIPLOMA	DIPLOMA	DIPLOMA
YEAR 5	DIPLOMA	DIPLOMA	DIPLOMA	I.T.C.
YEAR 4	DIPLOMA	DIPLOMA		I.T.C.
YEAR 3	DIPLOMA	INTERMEDIATE TECH. CERT.	INTERMEDIATE TECH. CERT.	J.T.C.
YEAR 2	JUNIOR TECHNICAL CERTIFICATE	JUNIOR TECHNICAL CERTIFICATE	JUNIOR TECHNICAL CERTIFICATE	J.T.C.
YEAR 1	JUNIOR TECHNICAL CERTIFICATE	JUNIOR TECHNICAL CERTIFICATE	JUNIOR TECHNICAL CERTIFICATE	J.T.C.
GRADE 6				

*Fourth year of part-time study added to the diploma course in 1939.

Year two was equivalent to grade eight in a higher elementary school or high school and Merit Certificate could be taken out at a technical school instead of or in addition to the technical certificate until 1947 when it was abolished.

Until 1944 high school courses leading to university entrance were of five years duration.

C. POST PRIMARY TECHNICAL EDUCATION
1950s

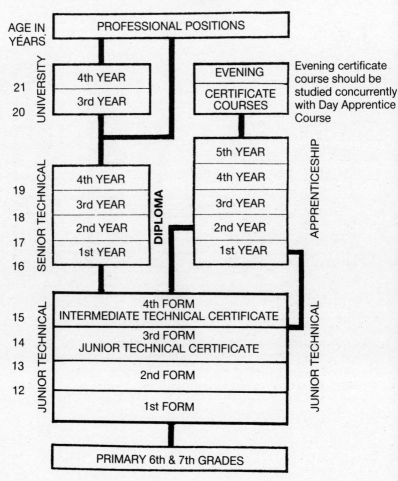

AGE IN YEARS

PROFESSIONAL POSITIONS

UNIVERSITY

21 — 4th YEAR
20 — 3rd YEAR

EVENING CERTIFICATE COURSES

Evening certificate course should be studied concurrently with Day Apprentice Course

SENIOR TECHNICAL

19 — 4th YEAR
18 — 3rd YEAR
17 — 2nd YEAR
16 — 1st YEAR

DIPLOMA

APPRENTICESHIP

5th YEAR
4th YEAR
3rd YEAR
2nd YEAR
1st YEAR

JUNIOR TECHNICAL

15 — 4th FORM INTERMEDIATE TECHNICAL CERTIFICATE
14 — 3rd FORM JUNIOR TECHNICAL CERTIFICATE
13 — 2nd FORM
12 — 1st FORM

JUNIOR TECHNICAL

PRIMARY 6th & 7th GRADES

D. COURSES IN TECHNICAL SCHOOLS 1961

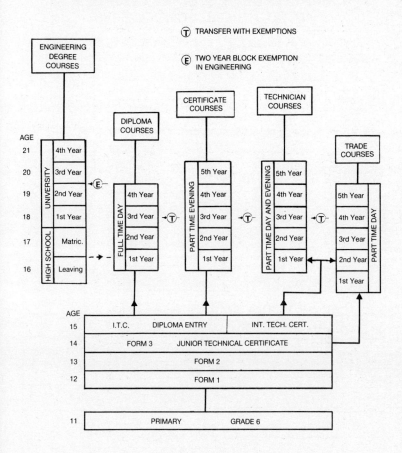

E. BUSINESS STUDIES COURSES
IN TECHNICAL SCHOOLS 1967

Courses are available Full Time and Part Time. Part Time
Students will normally take twice the time indicated on chart.

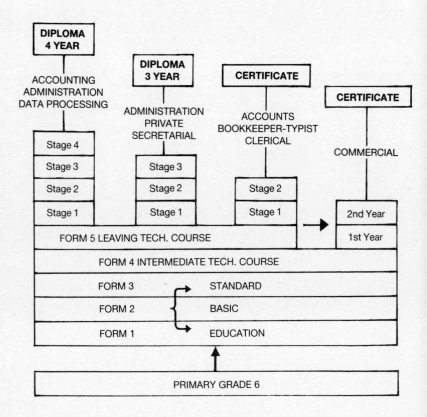

F. ENGINEERING COURSES IN TECHNICAL SCHOOLS 1965

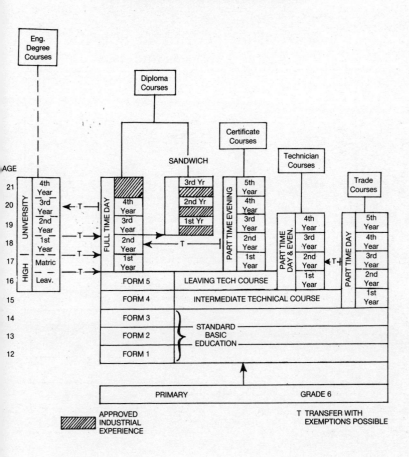

G. STUDENT ENROLMENTS

FOOTSCRAY TECHNICAL SCHOOL
Student Enrolments 1916–1968

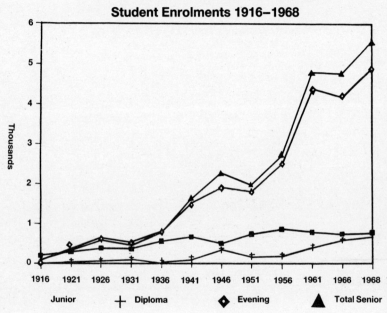

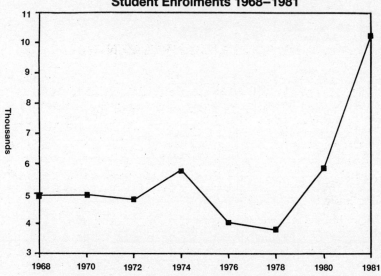

FOOTSCRAY COLLEGE OF T.A.F.E.
Student Enrolments 1968–1981

FOOTSCRAY INSTITUTE OF TECHNOLOGY
Student Enrolments 1968–1988

H. RELATIONSHIP BETWEEN FIT AND GOVERNMENT AGENCIES 1970–1983

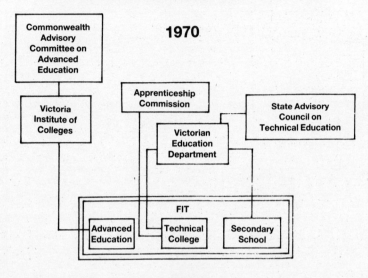

1970

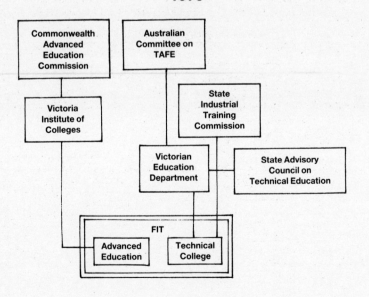

1975

1978

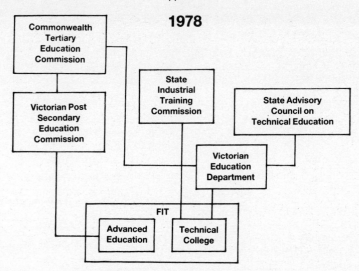

1981

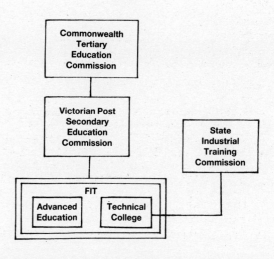

I. SCHOLARSHIP HOLDERS, 1943

Front Row: A. S. Stevenson, J. M. Walker, D. Duncan, L. B. Matthews, A. E. Phillips, B. R. Beech, K. J. Minett, A. J. Clifton, J. A. Le Roy, K. M. McDougall, D. Biggs, L. G. Wood, J. E. Petersen, G. J. Eddie, K. G. Powell, I. Foreman, R. A. McBean, R. J. Cordy, W. J. Gilbert, S. G. Titter.

Second Row: H. J. Williams, D. W. Letcher, J. H. Law, I. C. Feddersen, M. G. Flockhart, R. Cook, N. Deane, M. Cooper, L. A. Irwin, W. de Campo, F. L. Phillip, J. R. Wilson (Headmaster), C. A. Hoadley (Principal), H. D. Hymamson, D. C. Gaff, E. G. Rankin, L. J. Skinner, G. S. Richards, G. B. Alexander, A. Downie, R. A. Musgrove, D. W. Jones, R. S. Chapman, T. J. McGregor.

Third Row: D. R. Murdoch, K. J. Blacker, N. G. Maher, I. H. Cook, G. G. Lake, J. W. Orr, A. G. Skeggs, A. D. Oxley, E. J. Barker, G. S. Fountain, A. W. Bridson, M. H. Williams, J. Pitt, D. A. Studley, F. A. Mitchell, K. I. Castell, J. A. Ellis, W. J. Callen, R. Sandrs, R. M. Glenn, R. D. Loose.

Fourth Row: J. A. Hodson, A. C. Love, H. Ball, A. W. Fulton, J. F. Rodoni, R. R. Gathercole, R. D. Billington, N. J. McNeill, R. C. Wallace, W. McDowell, K. J. Simons, F. T. Clark, E. D. Johnson, I. H. Ashe, B. L. Powell, R. G. Sibley, R. T. Ducret, S. T. Wookey, W. T. Weybury, G. L. Copeland.

Back Row: W. G. Matton, R. W. Cox, W. J. Fatchen, J. C. Welsford, I. H. Redman, J. C. Johnson, S. Watt, J. E. Williams, C. S. Halik, D. R. Birchall, S. A. Pashallis, R. G. Cameron, G. T. Rees, M. Carless, R. P. Dunn, J. K. Chamier

(see Plate X)

J. COURSES AVAILABLE AT FOOTSCRAY TECHNICAL COLLEGE 1975

Basic vocational (apprenticeship) Courses

Boat building, Cabinet making, Electrical Fitting, Electrical Mechanics, Fitting and Machining, Metal Fabrication, Plumbing, Sheetmetal.

Technician

"Post trade" Toolmaking, Numerical Control of Machine Tools, Industrial Electronics, Armature Winding, Electric Motor Control and Circuitry, Oxy-acetylene and Electric Arc Welding, Furniture Design, Pipeline Design; "Technician Courses" in electrical, mechanical, Production, and Metal Fabrication.

Certificate (Middle Level) courses

Business Studies Certificates — Accounting, Data Processing, Office Procedures, Personnel, Production, Secretarial, Supply, Work Study, Supervision; Certificates of Technology — 9 Engineering, 3 Detail Drafting, 5 Design Drafting, 4 Applied Science, 1 Library Studies.

Tertiary orientation and other preparatory courses

Tertiary Orientation, HSC, and Technician Orientation

Service courses for industry

These were short courses designed to meet the needs of particular employers.

Select Bibliography

FIT Archive

All files pertaining to FIT after 1968 and the Council Minutes 1916 to 1986 are held in the FIT Central Registry. The FIT *Staff Newsletter* and Newsclipping Files are held in the FIT Information Office. All other material is held in a special collection in the FIT Library.

J Aberdeen, Principal's Reports, 1947–1950.
W J Bassett, Annual Reports, 1967–1969; Principal's Reports, 1967–1969.
Bates, Smart & McCutchcon, FIT Development Campus Plan, November 1971.
C H Beanland, Principal's Reports, 1951–1967; Report to Inspectors, 1951–1967.
Association of Principals of Victorian Technical Schools, *A Survey of Curricula in Junior and Senior Technical Schools*, October 1941.
Blue and Gold, FTS School Magazine, 1941–1967.
Brown and Red, FTS School Magazine, 1919.
'Council for Public Education, Report to Parliament', June 1943.
FIT, Annual Reports 'Focus on FIT', 1983–1986.
FTS, FTC and FIT, Council Minutes, 1915–1986.
FIT, *Education Specification*, March 1970.
FTS & FTC Files, 1951–1968.
FIT, *Handbooks* and Course Guides, 1972–1987.
FTS, FTC and FIT, Minutes of Board of Studies, 1926–1982.
FTS Mothers' Association, Minute Books, July 1926–June 1951.
FIT, News Clipping Books.
FIT, *Staff Bulletin*, 1978–1986.
FTS, FTC, *Prospectus*, 1924–68.
FTS, Student Record Book, 1916–1932.
FIT Professional Staff Association Bulletin, *Fits*, 1971–1973.

FTS/FTC SRC, *The Integral*, No 2, November 1946.
     The Swot, 1948.
     SRC Herald, Vol. 2, No.2, July 1963.
     Minute Books, May 1946–October 1955.
FIT SRC, *Seed*, 1968–1986 (incomplete).
C A Hoadley, Annual Reports, 1916–1946.
Minister of Public Instruction/Education, Reports to Parliament, 1938–1965.
R G Parsons, 'Presidential Address to 21st Annual Conference of Technical Schools Association of Victoria at Gordon Institute of Technology, October 1938.
M J C Radcliffe & B R Smith, 'Footscray Technical College: the Furtive Years 1916–1929', MS, 1976.
Victorian Education Department, Inspectors' Reports, 1936–1967.
Victorian Education Department, booklets on Technical Education, 1961, 1964.

Manuscripts

Donald Clark Papers in possession of Stephen Murray-Smith.
Footscray City Council Records, 1919–1975.
Footscray Historical Society Records.
J McLaren Diaries, 1976–77.
F Tate 'Record of a Camping Holiday Christmas 1918', Typed MS, University of Melbourne Archives.
Technical Schools Association of Victoria, Records 1921–1940. Held at the Offices of ACPPIV Koonung Heights Primary School.
Victorian Education Department, Files relating to Footscray Technical School:

    a) Ministry of Education Records pertaining to staff and buildings. These files are incomplete, in poor condition and have not been stored in such a way that easy retrieval of any particular file is possible.

    b) Public Records Office VA 714 Education Department, VPRS 5675, 10298, 10275; VA 571, Victorian Institute of Colleges, VPRS 3298, 2272, 3301; VA 2310 Victorian Council of Public Education.

Victorian Teachers' Union, Minutes of Technical Men's Branch, 1924–1930. Held by Technical Teachers Union of Victoria.

Unpublished theses and papers

B Bessant, 'Education and Politics in the development of the Education Systems of New South Wales and Victoria 1900–1940, with particular reference to Post Primary Education.' Ph.D., Monash University, 1971.
E Dale, 'Policy Development in the Victoria Institute of Colleges: A Case Study of the Development of Policy for College Degrees in

Humanities 1965–1973', M.Ed., University of Melbourne, 1983.

A J Dare, 'The Movement to Establish a Higher Technical Institute in Victoria 1940–1963', M.Ed., University of Melbourne, 1976.

S L Davies, 'Establishing the Martin Committee; A Case Study of the Setting Up of the Committee and Its Preliminary Discussions', M.Ed., University of Melbourne, 1981.

O Ford, 'The Early Local Origins of the Footscray Institute of Technology 1856–1916', B.Ed., University of Melbourne, 1976.

G R Holmes, 'The Role of School Governing Bodies with Special Consideration of the Role of School Councils in Victoria and School Boards in the Australian Capital Territory. A Comparative Study', M.Ed., University of Melbourne, 1981.

C Hooper, 'Footscray Girls' High School', Victorian Ministry of Education, History of Education Unit.

D M Hudson, 'Post Primary Teachers Organisations in Victoria 1905–1950', M.A., University of Melbourne, 1971.

J Ingleby, 'Participation: Action Research and the Politics of Change in Working Class Schools. A View from the Inside', M.A., FIT, 1985.

R N Ling, 'Colleges for Working Men. A Comparative Analysis of the Foundation of the Technical Colleges of Sydney and Melbourne and of their Autonomy in their Early Years', M.Ed., University of Melbourne, 1975.

J R Lublin, 'Case Study of a Victorian Metropolitan CAE: To determine in 1974 the extent of its Functional Confluence with the Criteria of Differentiation.' M.Ed., La Trobe University, 1977.

R Mathews, 'Conflicting Demands Affecting the Development of Secondary Education in Victoria 1910–1970' M.Ed., University of Melbourne, 1971.

S Murray-Smith, 'A History of Technical Education in Australia with special reference to the period Before 1914', Vol. II, Ph.D., University of Melbourne, 1966.

F J Olsen, 'Technical Education and Industry. A Study of the Relationship Between Technical Education and Industry, with particular reference to Newcastle, NSW', M.Ed., University of Melbourne, 1944.

G A Reid, 'The Origins and Early History of State Secondary School Teachers in Victoria 1872–1926', M.Ed., University of Melbourne, 1968.

D I Robson, 'The Development of Junior Technical Education in Victoria 1868–1966', M.Ed., University of Melbourne, 1967.

B Simm, 'Bendigo School of Mines', Victorian Ministry of Education, History of Education Unit.

A Turner, 'Independent Working Class Education in Australia 1917–1929, with an Introductory Account of the United Kingdom Background', M.Ed., University of Melbourne, 1981.

R P Wakeham, 'Vocational Education and Apprenticeship. A Study of Vocational Education in the Twentieth Century in England, Australia and the United States with Special Reference to the role of Apprenticeship Training and with Recommendations for the Modification of that Training', M.Ed., University of Melbourne, 1978.

K Weiss, 'Western Region Social Profile', Western Suburbs Regional Centre, Victorian Department of Community Services, April 1984.

R H Whitely, 'Donald Clark, the First Chief Inspector of Technical Schools', M.Ed., University of Melbourne, 1980.

Books and Articles

D S Anderson, 'The Prospects for Student Power in Australia', *Australian University*, Vol. 6, No. 3, 1968, pp 207–221.

W G Armytage, *A Social History of Engineering*, Faber & Faber, London, 1961.

E Ashby, *Technology and the Academics. An Essay on Universities and the Scientific Revolution*, Macmillan, London, 1958.

J O Anchen, *Frank Tate and His Work for Education*, ACER, Melbourne, 1956.

A M Badcock, 'The Vocational Fallacy in State Secondary Education in Victoria 1900–1925', E L French (ed.), *Melbourne Studies in Education*, 1965, pp 187–221.

C H Beanland, *A Lifetime in Technical Education*, Footscray College of TAFE, 1987.

I K F Birch, & D Smart, *The Commonwealth Government and Education 1964–1976: Political Initiatives and Developments*, Melbourne, 1977.

L J Blake (ed.), *Vision and Realisation A Centenary History of State Education in Victoria*, 3 Volumes, Victorian Government Printer, Melbourne, 1973.

E Byrne, 'Social Class and Educational Disadvantage — The Conceptual Muddle of Education Policy', *Melbourne Studies in Education*, 1985, pp 117–136.

D Clark, *Reminiscences of Technical Education in Victoria*, Working Men's College, Melbourne 1923. 'The Training of the Craftsman and the Operative' Paper delivered to Technical Schools Association Conference, 1922.

D Clark, *Some notes on the Development of Technical Instruction in Victoria*, Working Men's College, Melbourne, 1929.

L Connell, *Carnegie A History of Carnegie College and School of Physical Education 1933–1976*, Leeds, 1983.

A H Corbett, *The Institution of Engineers Australia: A History of the First Fifty Years 1919–1969*, Angus & Robertson, Sydney, 1973.

S F Cotgrove, *Technical Education and Social Change*, Allen & Unwin, London, 1958.

J Cuming, *An Autobiography*, privately printed, Melbourne, 1916.

J Davidson, 'Francis Ormond, Patron' in S Macintyre (ed.), *Ormond College Centenary Essays*. MUP, Melbourne, 1984.

W Dick, *A Bunch of Ratbags*, Penguin, Melbourne, 1965.

C H Dobinson, *Technical Education for Adolescents Some Thoughts on Present Problems*, London, 1951.

J Docherty, 'The Technical Division' in L J Blake *Vision and Realisation A Centenary History of State Education in Victoria*, Vol. 1, Victorian Government Printer, Melbourne, 1973.

G Dow (ed.), *Parent, Pupil, School Victoria's Education System*, Cassell, Melbourne, 1966.

E P Eltham, 'The Teaching of Engineering in Technical Schools', Paper delivered to Technical Teachers Association Conference, 1922.

G S Emmerson, *Engineering Education: A Social History*, Crane, Rusack & Co. New York, 1973.

F T Fargher, *The First Twenty Five Years Being a Short History of the Association of Principals of Victorian Technical Institutions 1939–1966*, Melbourne School of Printing & Graphic Arts, Melbourne, 1969.

Whither Advanced Education?, Papers delivered at the Federation of Staff Associations of Australian Colleges of Advanced Education Conference, La Trobe University, May 1974.

Footscray Advertiser and Footscray City Council, *Footscray's First 100 Years, The Story of a Great Australian City*, Footscray, 1959.

Footscray Rotary Club, *Forty Years of Active Service 1937–1977 The History of the Rotary Club of Footscray*, Footscray, 1977.

G Harman and D Smart (eds), *Federal Intervention in Australian Education Past, Present and Future*, Georgian House, Melbourne, 1982.

G Harman & C Selby Smith (eds), *Australian Higher Education Problems of a Developing System*, Sydney, 1972.

B Hames, *Swinburne 75 Years of Distinction*, Swinburne College Press, 1982.

B C Horne & B Wise, *Learning and Teaching in the CAE's 1969*, ACER, Melbourne, 1970.

W D Kennedy, *The Story of Gilwell in Victoria*, Australian Boy Scouts Association, Melbourne, 1963.

J Lack, '"Worst Smelbourne": Melbourne's Noxious Trades', in G Davidson et al., *The Outcasts of Melbourne*, Allen & Unwin, Sydney, 1985. "Melbourne and its Urban Sprawl" — A Critical Commentary'. *Melbourne Historical Journal*, 1971, pp 48–53.

B E Lloyd, *The Education of Professional Engineers in Australia*, Association of Professional Engineers Australia, Melbourne, 1968.

Living Museum of the West, *Harvester Diary*, Footscray 1987. *Lifeblood of Footscray Working Lives at the Angliss Meatworks*, Footscray 1985.

P M Martin, 'Some Reflections on the Australian Higher Education System Part I Colleges of Advanced Education', *Forum of Education*, Vol., 44, No. 1, 1986, pp 3–16.

D Mawson, *The Home of the Blizzard Being the Account of the Australasian Antarctic Expedition 1911–1914*, Abridged Popular edition, Hodder & Staughton, London, 1930.

D P Mellor, *The Role of Science and Industry*, Vol. 5 of Series 4 (Civil),

Australia in the War 1939–1945, Australian Government Printer, Canberra, 1958.

H Michel (ed.), *Footscray's First Fifty Years*, Footscray Advertiser, Footscray, 1909.

C E Moorhouse, 'Technical and Technological Education in Australia', *The Australian Journal of Education*, Vol. 4, No. 3. November 1960, pp 175–190.

S Murray-Smith, 'Technical Education: The lines of Development', in C Sanders (ed.), *Technical Education for Development*, University of Western Australia Press, Perth, 1966, pp 1–28.

S Murray-Smith, 'Technical Education in Australia: An Historical Sketch', in E L Wheelwright (ed.), *Higher Education in Australia*, Cheshire, Melbourne, 1965.

'Technical Education in Australia 1788–1914: A Select Bibliography', in *Melbourne Studies in Education*, 1967, pp 210–246.

S Murray-Smith & A J Dare, *The Tech A Centenary History of the Royal Melbourne Institute of Technology*, Hyland House, Melbourne, 1987.

C O'Donnell, 'The Relationship between Social Class, Labour Market Segmentation and Educational Credentials', *Melbourne Studies in Education*, 1985, pp 137–162.

J R Peart, 'E P Eltham: First Chairman of the Apprenticeship Commission of Victoria', *The Educational Magazine*, May 1966, pp 165–167.

A J Peters, 'The Changing Idea of Technical Education', *British Journal of Educational Studies*, Vol. 9, No. 2, May 1963, pp 142–166.

S S Richardson, 'A Role and Purpose for Colleges of Advanced Education', in G Harman & C Selby Smith, *Australian Higher Education*, Sydney, 1972, p 1–14.

D L Robbins, *Opportunity's Open Door Suffolk University 1906–1981*, Suffolk University, Suffolk 1982.

T Roper, *The Myth of Equality*, NUAUS, Melbourne 1970.

C Sanders (ed.), *Technical Education for Development*, University of Western Australia Press, Perth, 1966.

D Smart, 'The Pattern of Post War Federal Intervention in Education', in G Harman & D Smart (eds), *Federal Intervention in Australian Education*, Georgian House, Melbourne 1982, pp 15–34.

A Spaull, *Australian Education in the Second World War*, University of Queensland Press, St Lucia, 1982.

E Sweetman, *A History of State Education in Victoria*, Victorian Education Department, Melbourne, 1922.

H Schoenheimer, *Good Australian Schools and Their Communities*, TTAV, Melbourne, 1973.

R J W Selleck, *Frank Tate: A Biography*, MUP, Melbourne, 1982.

SEC, *Three Decades The Story of the State Electricity Commission of Victoria from its inception to December 1948*, Hutchinson, Melbourne, 1949.

M Theobold, *Ruyton Remembers 1878–1978*, Hawthorn Press, Melbourne, 1979.

T Thomas, 'Footscray Tech's Object Lessons', *Business Review Weekly*, 8 March 1985, pp 80–85.

R C Traill, *Development and Perspectives of the Victoria Institute of Colleges*, VICSAC Publication, No. 72, June 1972.

E R Treyvaud & J McLaren, *Equal but Cheaper The Development of Australian Colleges of Advanced Education*, MUP, Melbourne, 1976.

A Turner, *State Councils for Technical Education in Victoria 1961–1980*, Victorian Education Department, Melbourne, 1984.

A F Tylee, 'Technical and Technological Education in Victoria', in E L Wheelwright (ed.), *Higher Education in Australia*, Cheshire, Melbourne, 1965.

Victorian Education Department, *Technical Education in Victoria 1868–1934*, Melbourne, 1934.

J H Weiss, *The Making of Technological Man The Social Origins of French Engineering Education*, MIT Press, Boston, 1982.

E L Wheelwright (ed.), *Higher Education in Australia*, Cheshire, Melbourne, 1965.

H S Williams, 'Technical Education', in *The Australian Journal of Education*, Vol. 10, No. 3, October 1966, pp 305–318.

H S Williams, 'The Technical Colleges', in *Tertiary Education in Australia*, AIPS, Sydney, 1965, pp 66–95.

K G Wilson, *Manufacturing Industry in the Western Region of Melbourne Vol II An Introductory Analysis of Firm Data*, Melbourne Western Region Commission, March 1985.

Newspapers and Periodicals

Argus 1927, 1929, 1934.

Education Gazette and Teachers' Aid, 1916–1948.

The Educational Magazine, 1960–1977, especially Vol. 20, No. 9, Special Issue on technical education.

Footscray Advertiser, 1910–1986.

Footscray Mail, 1971–1974.

SEC News, March 1986, No. 312.

TTAV Associate News, 1974–1976.

Victorian Scout, March 1947.

VTU, Teachers' Journal, 1921–1961.

Tapes and Videos

B Larin, 'Footscray College of TAFE A Brief History of its role in the development of the Western Region of Melbourne', Video, 28 mins, 1985.

Monash University, Faculty of Education, Oral History Archives, Tapes, J L Griffiths, B McIlroy, O C Phillips, H E Brittain, J Harriott, J R Peart, H O Anchen, J M Allen.

Footscray College of TAFE, Interviews on Tape:
Gladys Hope, Hubert Harris, Leo Grant (A Rosenthal), Daryl Evans (S Mitchell), Erin Moran (L Aleksovska), Bill Jamieson (F Ganino), Jack Faulkner (A Henczel), Eric Wilde (J Sesta), Eric Allen (J Portelli), Alan Morey (J Scuderi), Sophie Eflikou (H Fam), Des Walters (L Wainwright), Ian Faulkner (A Smith).

Index